Boston

Kim Grant

D0684029

LONELY PLANET PUBLICATIONS
Melbourne • Oakland • London • Paris

Boston
2nd edition – June 2003
First published – August 2000

Published by
Lonely Planet Publications Pty Ltd ABN 36 005 607 983
90 Maribyrnong St, Footscray, Victoria 3011, Australia

Lonely Planet offices
Australia Locked Bag 1, Footscray, Victoria 3011
USA 150 Linden St, Oakland, CA 94607
UK 10a Spring Place, London NW5 3BH
France 1 rue du Dahomey, 75011 Paris

Photographs
Many of the images in this guide are available for licensing from
Lonely Planet Images.
W www.lonelyplanetimages.com

Front cover photograph
Baseball players waiting to bat (Todd A Gipstein/Corbis)

ISBN 1 74059 106 2

Contents – Text

Contents – Maps

AMERICA'S WALKING CITY

EXCURSIONS

COLOR MAP SECTION   171

3

The Author

Kim Grant grew up near Boston and began taking the commuter train into the city on weekends as soon as she could board trains alone. After graduating from Mt Holyoke College in 1984 and traveling around Europe for two years on $10 a day, she 'settled' in Boston's North End and was determined to make a living traveling, writing and photographing.

Almost 20 years later, s he finds herself the author or coauthor of Lonely Planet's *New England*, *Miami* and *Florida*, as well as *Cape Cod, Martha's Vineyard & Nantucket: An Explorer's Guide*, *Best Places to Stay in Hawaii* (someone's gotta do it) and *Best Places to Stay in New England*. Represented by Lonely Planet Images, Kim's photography (W www.kimgrant.com) is also published under the Bindu Press imprint. She credits her creative intuition to the regular practice of t'ai chi chih, which she also teaches. Kim lives with her partner in a c. 1900 Victorian in Dorchester, Boston's largest, oldest and most diverse neighborhood. But you might find her tooling around the US in a VW camper van.

FROM THE AUTHOR

Thanks, thanks and more thanks to Lisa Otero, whose support knows no bounds. Although I have made Boston my home since 1986, I would have found it impossible to write a book like this without the help of many fearless friends, chief among them Julia Regan. After Julia and I researched one of her favorite neighborhoods under the pressure of a deadline, she declared, 'I thought this would be fun. I was wrong. Since you're my friend, do me a favor: get a new job.'

Thanks to Colby Smith for unbridled enthusiasm and diligence. Thanks to Bob Taylor, my 7th-grade history teacher, whose knowledge and passion about post-Blackstone Boston are legendary. Thanks to Wendy Zazik, Tierney Bianconi and Julie Patiño for their personal picks. With friends like these, who needs paid assistants? Thanks to the Greater Boston Convention & Visitors Bureau for many leads. Thanks to the fine columnists and reporters at the *Boston Globe*, who provide daily accompaniment to my morning espresso. And, oh, did I thank Lisa?

At Lonely Planet the stylin' Michele Posner earns serious kudos for making the hard decisions about this book's place in the world. With my last day on this project coinciding with her last day as LP commissioning editor, it's easy to reflect on what a pleasure she's been to work with. Good luck, Michele! And huge thanks to Aussie Danielle North, who cares about much more than crossing t's and dotting i's. She's a credit to her profession!

This Book

This 2nd edition of *Boston* was updated by Boston native Kim Grant, who also wrote the 1st edition.

FROM THE PUBLISHER
This edition of *Boston* was produced in Lonely Planet's Melbourne office. Danielle North coordinated the editing, with invaluable assistance from Liz Filleul, Kyla Gillzan, Tom Smallman and Gabbi Wilson. Herman So coordinated the mapping. Barbara Benson drew the climate charts. The book was designed and laid out by Jacqui Saunders. Katie Cason produced the color wraps. Thanks to Pepi Bluck for assistance with design, and to Lonely Planet Images for the photographs. Simon Bracken designed the cover. Many thanks to Ann Seward for her help with the index.

Commissioning editors Michele Posner and Valerie Sinzdak and project manager Bridget Blair streamlined the whole process.

Special thanks to Lachlan Ross of production services and Piotr Czajkowski and Simon Tillema of the GIS unit for assisting at crucial times.

Grateful acknowledgment is made to Massachusetts Bay Transportation Authority for permission to reproduce the MBTA Subway Map ©2001.

Thanks

Many thanks to the travelers who used the last edition of *Boston* and wrote to us with helpful hints, useful advice and interesting anecdotes:

Jon J Anderson, Hilmir Asgeirsson, Antje Becker, Edwin Breukelman, Marianne Busch, John Ciappetta, John Connolly, Jenny Cooper, David E Evans, Marion Evans, Mary Beth Floyd, Liz Ging, Geraint Jones, Gottfried Kaiser, Dave Kennerley,i Susan Lavender, Dermot Luddy, Natasha McCready, Stephanie Minns, Kate Needham, Martin Spacek, Kevin Spillane, Frederick Stewart, Eric Thomsen, Cas van der Avoort, Mike Watkins, Julie Webb, Doug Welch, Andrew Young

Foreword

ABOUT LONELY PLANET GUIDEBOOKS

The story begins with a classic travel adventure: Tony and Maureen Wheeler's 1972 journey across Europe and Asia to Australia. There was no useful information about the overland trail then, so Tony and Maureen published the first Lonely Planet guidebook to meet a growing need.

From a kitchen table, Lonely Planet has grown to become the largest independent travel publisher in the world, with offices in Melbourne (Australia), Oakland (USA), London (UK) and Paris (France).

Today Lonely Planet guidebooks cover the globe. There is an ever-growing list of books and information in a variety of media. Some things haven't changed. The main aim is still to make it possible for adventurous travellers to get out there – to explore and better understand the world.

At Lonely Planet we believe travellers can make a positive contribution to the countries they visit – if they respect their host communities and spend their money wisely. Since 1986 a percentage of the income from each book has been donated to aid projects and human rights campaigns, and, more recently, to wildlife conservation.

Although inclusion in a guidebook usually implies a recommendation we cannot list every good place. Exclusion does not necessarily imply criticism. In fact there are a number of reasons why we might exclude a place – sometimes it is simply inappropriate to encourage an influx of travellers.

UPDATES & READER FEEDBACK

Things change – prices go up, schedules change, good places go bad and bad places go bankrupt. Nothing stays the same. So, if you find things better or worse, recently opened or long-since closed, please tell us and help make the next edition even more accurate and useful.

Lonely Planet thoroughly updates each guidebook as often as possible – usually every two years, although for some destinations the gap can be longer. Between editions, up-to-date information is available in our free, monthly email bulletin *Comet* (W www.lonelyplanet.com/newsletters). You can also check out the *Thorn Tree* bulletin board and *Postcards* section of our website, which carry unverified, but fascinating, reports from travellers.

Tell us about it! We genuinely value your feedback. A well-travelled team at Lonely Planet reads and acknowledges every email and letter we receive and ensures that every morsel of information finds its way to the relevant authors, editors and cartographers.

Everyone who writes to us will find their name listed in the next edition of the appropriate guidebook. The very best contributions will be rewarded with a free guidebook.

We may edit, reproduce and incorporate your comments in Lonely Planet products such as guidebooks, websites and digital products, so let us know if you don't want your comments reproduced or your name acknowledged.

How to contact Lonely Planet:
Online: e talk2us@lonelyplanet.com.au, W www.lonelyplanet.com
Australia: Locked Bag 1, Footscray, Victoria 3011
UK: 10a Spring Place, London NW5 3BH
USA: 150 Linden St, Oakland, CA 94607

Introduction

It's hard to pinpoint the lure of Boston, and that's exactly what attracts visitors, retains college graduates and draws back the temporarily sidetracked. Boston is more than the sum of her historic buildings, cultural attractions, academic institutions and fine restaurants. She is spirited, lovely, historic and a jumble of contemporary paradoxes. Perhaps most importantly, she's manageable.

Boston is an amalgam of vibrant neighborhoods, from working-class Charlestown to elegant Beacon Hill, from the hip South End to the Italian North End. Despite the ethnic diversity of its residents old and new, Boston doesn't seem to change. In a curious way, something deeply embedded in the city's character eventually converts newcomers into Bostonians as if by osmosis.

Boston's magnetism comes in part from its long history as a prosperous port and regional center of commerce. Calling this quaint and charming city the 'hub of the universe' and the 'Athens of America' might seem a bit of braggadocio now, but these weren't empty boasts in the 19th century. The city's glory is retained and radiated by its grand architecture, its significant population of literati, artists and educators, and its world-renowned academic and cultural institutions. Regardless of the inevitable changes, Boston's soul somehow remains both grand and familiar.

Bostonians aren't trendsetters. They see themselves as civilized and their city as mature. They're in it for the long haul, which helps explain the city's conservative character. Contrary to their reputation, however, Bostonians are not crusty, musty or genteel, but down-to-earth folks who value loyalty. Of course, extreme loyalty seems to define Boston's parochial and provincial political system.

Boston's stellar universities and colleges attract students from all over the world. From September through May, the city over-flows with their exuberance. This renewable source of cultural energy supports numerous sporting events, foreign cinema, theater, art galleries, literary cafés, hip bars, musical performances, shopping and nightlife.

Despite impetuous drivers and insane traffic, Boston is one of the easiest cities to explore on foot. You can walk everywhere. And at this leisurely pace, it's easier to register the city's pulse. Thanks to low-rise buildings that allow the city to retain a human scale and an urban core that is home to people of all classes, Boston has a thriving street life. Its brick sidewalks and sidewalk cafés have more in common with London or Paris than with Chicago or Los Angeles.

The Atlantic Ocean, Boston Harbor and Charles River vary the cityscape and provide a sense of openness. Urban planning, including the long Emerald Necklace of parks, gardens and verdant thoroughfares, brings a bit of the country right into the city. Nonetheless, Boston is the hub of New England, and part of its lure is that it serves as a great jumping-off point for nearby mountains and beaches. Just 30 minutes outside of town, you'll find yourself among cornfields, gardens, beautiful colonial towns, scenic rivers and country roads ideal for cycling.

Even if you have a sense of historical Boston, she may surprise you. The country's founding fathers – many of whom walked these same streets – would expect nothing less. Just when you've written off residents as dour and preoccupied, someone will probably offer you assistance. Just when you've decided Boston is full of stuffed shirts and bow ties, you'll encounter a band of pierced, orange-haired, skateboarding teens. Just when you've equated Boston to a tightly wound parent, the curfew will be lifted and she'll spin like a top. Then again, the bars still close at 2am, and the T shuts down well before that. The Grand Dame can let her hair down only so far.

Facts about Boston

HISTORY
17th-Century Origins

Prior to AD 1600 there were plenty of Native American tribes throughout New England but none on the centrally located Shawmut Peninsula (the original extents of Boston proper). This 800-acre hilly peninsula was connected to the mainland by a narrow causeway or 'neck.' To the east was an excellent harbor; to the west a great back bay, an estuary of the Charles River; to the north was another smaller peninsula, known today as Charlestown.

In 1614, English explorer Captain John Smith toured the New England coastline for King James I. Though the coast had many natural ports, Boston was blessed with the best geography. Captain Smith's reports were so glowing that, in 1620, an English separatist group (the Pilgrims) came over and built the first permanent English settlement in New England at Plymouth Harbor, some 50 miles south of Boston.

In 1624, 27-year-old Reverend William Blackstone (or Blaxton), an ordained minister from the Church of England and a Cambridge University graduate, became the first European to settle on the Shawmut Peninsula, near present-day Spruce and Beacon Sts.

In England, King Charles I decreed that all Englishmen follow the dictates of his Anglican Church. But the self-proclaimed Puritans had a dream: to settle far enough away that they would be able to worship freely. Thanks to influential friends, they managed to get King Charles to charter the Massachusetts Bay Colony in New England in 1629.

In March 1630, Elder John Winthrop, a deeply religious member of the landed English gentry, penned his vision of their Puritan mission: 'We shall establish a city upon a hill – a Beacon Light for all mankind.' Is it any wonder modern day Bostonians cannot imagine a city to rival theirs?

After Winthrop's flagship *Arbella* landed in Salem, an advance party was sent to claim the peninsula just north of Shawmut and build settlements on the south side of Bunker Hill. Almost immediately, though, the community faced illness and lack of food and water. Their neighbor, Blackstone, invited the new settlers over to his side of the river to show them sources of springwater, pasture for animals and a fine, deep harbor for ships. Winthrop liked what he saw, and on September 7 they named it Boston after a town in Lincolnshire, England. The center of Puritan culture and life in the New World was established. And in October, Winthrop, now governor, wrote home to his wife, 'We are here in paradise' – a boast you might hear on the streets today.

Reading, Writing & Religion

The Three Rs were very important to the intellectual and theocratic Puritan leaders. They established the Boston Public Latin School in 1635 (today it remains an elite public high school) and Harvard College in 1636. In 1647, they passed the first public school law, ensuring that communities of 50 or more households would hire teachers, their wages to be paid by the public. A mere five years later, Boston had a public library, and by 1704 produced the 13 original colonies' first newspaper. It's no wonder that educational excellence remains central to the city.

Puritan churches were organized as independent congregations. At annual town meetings, citizens would decide by a show of hands which projects to undertake and how to fund them. In other words, local self-government was born in Boston. But in spite of these democratic leanings, Puritans were not tolerant. People who disagreed with the leaders were expelled. Those who dared return, as did Quaker Mary Dyer, were hanged.

For the colonists, material success and property acquisition became more and more important. Bostonians were successful with cod fishing, coastal trading, shipbuilding and the production of rum from molasses. By 1692, a large segment of the 7000-strong population had built fine homes and climbed the social ladder. Boston was the wealthiest town in the American colonies.

In the early 18th century, as England warred with France, the colonies operated with greater independence. But in 1760 there was a major setback – a terrible fire around Dock Square leveled 300 buildings. Ships, docks and stores were destroyed; more than 1000 people were made homeless. In the hard times that followed, unemployment was high and taxes were raised to pay for reconstruction.

Cradle of Liberty

Late-18th-century Boston is often called the 'cradle of American liberty.' Certainly, Boston took center stage as a hotbed of revolutionary ideas and the breeding ground for protests against England's authority. Patriot leaders, incensed by King George III's efforts to control the colonists' freewheeling economies and political liberties, began asserting their independence.

As far back as 1753, King George III and the British Parliament instituted a program (the Townshend Acts) to raise money in America, reduce colonial self-government and assert more royal authority. Americans reacted strongly against the taxes, and Boston's leaders, well informed and politically mature, often led the way.

Britain needed cash to retire her debts and to station a standing army of 10,000 troops in America. In 1765, the British Parliament passed the Stamp Act, requiring colonists to buy special stamps to execute a will, sell a house, get an inn license or buy a newspaper. Bostonians, led by Samuel Adams, objected violently. 'Sons of Liberty,' self-avowed supporters of American liberty and rights, attacked officials and supporters of the new act. Parliament repealed the act one year later, realizing it was more trouble than it was worth. Boston rejoiced.

In 1767, British customs agents triggered more problems with arbitrary, antagonizing searches. If they seized a ship for violations, the ship and its cargo were sold and the proceeds divided between the British treasury, the governor of the colony and the customs officers. Agents took particular aim at John Hancock, probably Boston's richest merchant. When they seized his ship, *Liberty*, fellow merchants united in his defense and the British Parliament had to send regiments to protect their officials.

In 1769, Charles Townshend (of the Townshend Acts fame and now the British treasurer) was back proposing more taxes. As the chief American city, Boston always drew London's attention and as such, tax collectors would be quartered in Boston. The next year, protest escalated and erupted in what soon became known as the Boston Massacre (see the boxed text 'Boston Massacre' in the Things to See & Do chapter).

Tempest in a Teapot

More trouble came in 1773. The British Parliament passed the Tea Act, granting a monopoly to the huge and financially troubled British East India Company. American patriots objected strongly and colonial coastal merchants refused tea shipments. In 1774 the royal governor refused to allow three tea ships to return full to London and the Sons of Liberty refused to allow the tea to be offloaded and taxed. When the owner of the *Dartmouth* was denied a pass to leave port on December 16, Sam Adams rose at a special town meeting and said, 'This meeting can do nothing more to save the country!' This signaled more than 100 patriot supporters, disguised as Indians, to board the tea ships and dump the tea overboard. Paul Revere and others later carried the news to other colonies.

When all of England read about the destruction of tea, Parliament passed four bills to punish Boston, 'the center of rebellious commotion in America, the ring leader in every riot.' It closed Boston's port to all trade until England was compensated for the ruined tea. And it dictated that British troops would be housed in private homes in Boston. General Thomas Gage was sent to rule Boston by martial law.

Up and down the coast, colonists talked about this 'horrid attack upon the town of Boston.' Sam Adams sent letters to every colony, making the case for Boston and Massachusetts Bay against the British. Anger bubbled higher. Minutemen, local citizens who would defend their rights against British tyranny with military force at a minute's notice, began training on town commons.

Shot Heard Round the World

General Gage was sent over with 4000 British troops and a fleet of warships. In the spring of 1775, when Gage learned that minutemen were storing military supplies in nearby Concord, he sent 700 troops to destroy the stockpile. At dawn on April 19, 1775, these British forces killed eight of the 70 minutemen they confronted. Later that morning in Concord, the British were attacked at North Bridge. This so-called shot heard round the world was the opening volley of the War for Independence. At the day's end, far more British lives had been lost than American.

These events, commemorated today as Patriots' Day, united the 13 colonies. Revere, Hancock, and Sam and John Adams (younger cousin of Sam) went off to lobby for a unified declaration of independence. George Washington was chosen to command the newly formed American army. In early 1776, Washington seized Dorchester Heights, and his army installed cannons facing Boston. British general William Howe was trapped. After much looting (especially of Hancock's ships), the British sailed out of Boston Harbor on March 17, 1776 (celebrated today as Evacuation Day). Boston was liberated.

Rebuilding & Federalism

When a federal Constitution was submitted to the states for approval in 1787, Boston supported it but western Massachusetts farmers did not. A standoff ensued until Sam Adams and John Hancock suggested it be approved with a provision: the first Congress would write amendments, a Bill of Rights. Boston celebrated and promptly elected Hancock, followed by Sam Adams, to serve as governor.

Ocean trade slowly regained its importance. Commerce with the West Indies, South America and China brought prosperity to Boston. By 1810 the town had a population of about 30,000, up from 6000 during the war.

Brahmins Are Born & the City Incorporates

When commerce and shipping suffered during the War of 1812, Boston's maritime merchants looked for new investments. The burgeoning industrial revolution – in particular, cotton thread and textile manufacturing – brought great fortunes to dozens of Boston Yankees. And the upper classes, the Yankee blue-blooded merchant-manufacturers, began to dominate Boston's spiritual, social and political life.

Though typically conservative and traditionalist, freedom-loving Bostonians began to accept a new liberal Unitarian religion and possessed a sense of social responsibility. As an untitled aristocratic class (later called Brahmins, in reference to the highest caste in the Hindu social system in India), they considered it their birthright 'to keep Boston a model of excellence...a latter day concept of a city upon a hill.'

On January 7, 1822, the city of Boston was incorporated and its 43,000 citizens proceeded to elect Brahmins as the city's first two mayors.

Reform Movements & Abolitionism

Between the 1830s and the 1840s there were many reform movements in Boston: Mayor Quincy started a welfare reform movement; a temperance society attacked alcoholism; Horace Mann led educational reform; and Dorothea Dix encouraged a movement to improve conditions in mental hospitals and prisons.

Boston became a breeding ground for writers and publishers, arts and letters, intellectual clubs and magazines, medicine and technology. Beacon Hill was the nexus for this cultural growth and development.

It was a radical reform movement, however, that gripped conservative Boston for 30 years. The Abolition Movement, which advocated nothing short of the eradication of slavery in the US, was born in Boston. Newspaper writer and editor William Lloyd Garrison, operating out of a small office on Washington St, began publishing a monthly paper called the *Liberator* in 1831. Garrison was an agitator, and a force to be reckoned with by 1835. In October, when Garrison was attending an anti-slavery meeting, a mob broke in and dragged him to Boston Common to be hanged. He was rescued but told to leave Boston.

As the years went by, more and more Brahmin leaders joined the anti-slavery movement. John Brown, the militant abolitionist who led the fight to rid Kansas of slaveholders and help free slaves in Virginia, came to Boston for money, weapons and supplies for his activities.

When the Civil War broke out in 1861, President Lincoln called for volunteers. Massachusetts called up four regiments, two of which were among the first units to defend the capital. Once Lincoln issued the Emancipation Proclamation in 1863, the 54th Massachusetts Regiment became the first African-American regiment raised in any state. The 54th saw action in South Carolina under Brahmin general Robert Gould Shaw's leadership (see also Beacon Hill in the Things to See & Do chapter).

Expansion & Immigration
After the war, Boston became wealthier and grew in size. Bays and estuaries were filled in the Back Bay and the South End. Adjacent towns were annexed. For many, the city was growing too fast and had attracted too many immigrants.

In the 1840s great waves of Irish fled domestic crisis and the devastating potato famine. Not only poor, but also in poor health, these Irish immigrants were not welcomed or easily accepted into the city's economic and social framework. In stores across the city, signs went up: 'Wanted: workers. Irish need not apply.' Religious bigotry intensified. Popularly referred to as the 'Catholic Menace,' this generation faced a very difficult assimilation into American culture and society. But as the Irish grew in strength and numbers, determined to succeed, they built cohesive neighborhood communities, which in turn formed the bases for political power.

Most recently, Vietnamese, Koreans and Brazilians have been making their mark on the city, too, settling and establishing themselves in the city's older neighborhoods as earlier generations did.

Cultural Institutions Flourish
The Museum of Fine Arts was established in 1870, the Boston Symphony Orchestra in 1881. Also in 1881, Frederick Law Olmsted created the 'Emerald Necklace,' a string of ponds and parks stretching from the Public Garden to Franklin Park. The Boston Public Library was enlarged in 1895.

Mayors Move the City
In 1913, and then on and off through the 1920s, '30s and '40s, James Michael Curley was elected mayor. Curley rejected ward politics and Boston Brahmins, carving out his own style of leadership. He was vibrant, energetic and boastful; he spoke directly to neighborhood residents. And the people responded to his cult of personality, electing him time and time again. Curley handed out favors and jobs all year long, enlarging the city hospital, and building beaches and bathhouses, playgrounds, stadiums, recreation facilities and a tunnel to East Boston. While ignoring the center of the city, he raised taxes and mired the city with enormous debt.

By the 1940s corruption was taken for granted as a part of public life in Boston. Although under indictment for mail fraud in 1945, Curley ran for office again and won. He was convicted and served time in a federal penitentiary. By 1949, the center of Boston was seedy and rundown; businesses and people were moving out.

By contrast, the next mayor, John Hynes, was mild-mannered and soft-spoken, an efficient administrator. In the next 10 years he transformed and modernized the city, paving the way for the honest and nonpartisan John Collins (elected in 1967) to move the city further forward. He secured billions of federal dollars to transform and modernize the waterfront, Quincy Market, City Hall and Government Center.

Around this time, a group of business leaders banded together and began discussing local issues in a room adjacent to a basement vault in the Boston Safe Deposit

Boston Firsts

1634	Boston Common is the first public park.
1635	Boston Public Latin School, the first public secondary school, is founded.
1716	Boston Harbor gets the first lighthouse.
1795	Paul Revere organizes the first labor union.
1800	Bostonians are first given the nickname 'bean eaters,' since baked beans, made from a recipe of beans richly mixed with sugar, molasses and salt pork, was a staple Sunday meal in colonial and Federalist Boston. Baked beans were prepared on Saturday night because on Sunday, a day of rest, no cooking was to be done.
1806	The first church built by free blacks opens on Joy St, Beacon Hill.
1831	The first abolitionist newspaper, the *Liberator*, is published.
1836	Elizabeth Peabody opens the first kindergarten.
1845	Elias Howe invents the sewing machine.
1861	Oliver Wendell Holmes, a 19th-century 'Proper Bostonian' doctor and poet, coins the term 'Brahmin' in his novel *Elsie Venner*. He wrote that a Bostonian 'comes of the Brahmin caste of New England, this is the harmless, inoffensive untitled aristocracy.'
1875	Lois Prang prints the first American Christmas card.
1876	Alexander Graham Bell demonstrates the first telephone.
1880	Frances Perkins, born in Boston, becomes the first woman to serve in an American president's cabinet. As Secretary of Labor under Franklin D Roosevelt, she served 12 years and helped create a minimum federal wage, child labor laws, the Social Security Act and the Fair Labor Standards Act.
1893	Arthur Shurtleff lights a candle in the window of his parents' home, beginning the tradition of Christmas lights.
1897	The first American subway system opens.
1910	Dr John Collins Bossidy of Holy Cross College refines a 1905 Harvard alumni dinner toast: 'And this is good old Boston, the home of the ocean and the cod, where the Lowells talk only to Cabots and the Cabots talk only to God.'
1924	Mutual funds are invented by Massachusetts Investors Trust.

& Trust Co. This group of men, known unofficially as 'the Vault,' developed a vision for a 'New Boston.' They also had the clout, influence and power to implement it. Boston was a city on the rebound, and the Vault would play an important role in it – bailing out the city financially and supporting leading cultural institutions.

Mayor Kevin White faced the problems of conflicting neighborhood needs throughout the city, for a while promoting Boston as a truly 'livable' city. But in the mid-1970s, racism exploded. Court-ordered school busing caused racial conflicts and polarized the city for years (see the boxed text 'School Busing & Segregation' later in this chapter).

In the 1980s the Vault helped push Boston toward the ranks of a world-class city, a destination, a hub of culture, learning and economic growth. But in 1997 the Vault ceased to operate because the corporate leadership in Boston had dropped to an unsustainable level. In today's world economy, Boston is a satellite, not a hub.

The New Millennium

For all its ties to the past, Boston has always looked forward. With the country's largest public works project (see the boxed text 'The Big Dig' in the Getting Around chapter), and with the largest redevelopment project since the filling of Back Bay underway in the new South Boston Waterfront district, Boston is definitely not resting on the past. In fact, she's betting her future on quality-of-life issues and on sustained preeminence in the technology and financial services sectors. It's a safe bet.

Despite a weak national and state economy, Boston is in the midst of a renaissance, thanks to the near-completion of the Big Dig. (Perhaps that's one reason why the Democratic National Convention chose Boston to host its 2004 quadrennial shindig.) Affluent emptynesters, encouraged by a low crime rate, are moving back in droves. Still, young professionals with high salaries are the only ones who can reasonably afford housing in the city since the demise of rent control in the mid-1990s.

By now everyone in the developed world knows that terrorists boarded planes at Logan International Airport in Boston on the morning of September 11, 2001. Although the planes hit the World Trade Center, the Pentagon and rural Pennsylvania, they 'hit' Bostonians hard in another way. How could this have happened from our city? Truth is, it could have happened from any airport; Boston was just close to the intended targets. As a consequence, Logan International Airport has complied with new FAA regulations faster than other airports and is keenly aware that it had better not happen on its watch again.

Despite the chip Boston has on its shoulder in regard to New York City, it's solidly poised to be one of the most livable cities in the country. Can New York say that?

GEOGRAPHY
Boston is 48.4 sq miles, smaller even than tiny San Francisco. Its topography is determined by the Charles River, which empties into Boston Harbor and separates the twin cities of Boston and Cambridge. With the exception of Beacon Hill, the city is compact and flat, not surprising since much sits atop landfill.

GOVERNMENT & POLITICS
Careers have been made observing Boston politics. Whether you're a serious scholar, an investigative reporter or a comedian in need of a juicy repertoire, there is plenty of fodder. Boston has probably had more than its share of colorful characters and patronage-

Milestones in Medicine

Boston has always been a prominent center for medical education, treatment and research.

1781	America's first medical school is established at Harvard.
1846	General anesthesia is first used during an operation at Mass General Hospital (MGH).
1866	The surgical treatment for appendicitis is implemented at MGH.
1929	The iron lung, a machine used to save polio patients, is first used at Peter Bent Brigham Hospital (PBBH).
1954	The world's first successful kidney transplant takes place at PBBH.
1967	Open-heart surgery is first performed at Boston Children's Hospital.
1987	A gene responsible for one form of Alzheimer's disease is discovered at MGH. In 1995, research teams went on to discover the second and third genes, too.

wielding leaders. It's also had fine ones with vision.

The city government consists of a mayor, who is elected to a four-year term, and a city council of 13 members, each of whom is elected to two-year terms. Councilors meet at City Hall at noon on Wednesday. Meetings are open to the public, but the dissected minutiae can be equally excruciating and fascinating.

Voters are heavily Democratic and Independent, but citywide elections are generally nonpartisan. Despite the fact that politics is a blood sport, voter turnout is low. (Wards in South Boston and Dorchester are the most active.)

Nowhere in the US is politics more provincial and ethnicity-driven than in Boston. The late Thomas P 'Tip' O'Neill, respected Speaker of the House of Representatives, coined the phrase 'All politics is local.' If the mayor can keep the garbage picked up, the streets cleared quickly after a snowstorm and the parks green, he's 'in like Flynn' (the long-serving Irish-Catholic

School Busing & Segregation

In 1972 federal judge W Arthur Garrity Jr found that the Boston public school system was deliberately segregated and that black youngsters had indefensibly inferior educations. Garrity did what no elected officials had the backbone to do: upend the underpinnings of systemic discrimination in Boston. He ordered that students be bused to other neighborhoods to create racial balance in schools. Beginning in September 1974, about 15,000 African-American students were bused into white neighborhoods daily, pitting the most adversarial communities of South Boston and Roxbury against each other.

Storms of protest exploded in South Boston, East Boston and Charlestown. There were strikes, boycotts and violence in the streets. But there was no turning back: public institutions could not benefit one constituency to the exclusion of another. It took years for tempers to cool, but by about 1983, bitter racial tensions had calmed considerably.

When Ray Flynn took office in 1984 in a racially divided city, the new 'people's mayor' declared harmony his priority. The following year, Judge Garrity returned control of the Boston schools to the elected city School Committee. By this time, the school population – after suburban 'white flight' and an influx of Latino and Asian students – comprised almost 75% students of color. But by this time, too, thanks to Garrity's courage and some forward-looking political leaders, the city knew it had to face its demons.

mayor Ray Flynn, that is). The popular mayor Tom Menino, Boston's first Italian-American mayor, has made micromanaging a priority (the streets are visibly cleaner).

ECONOMY

Mutual funds, an enormously popular investment tool for individual retirement plans, originated in Massachusetts. The largest company, by far, is Fidelity Investments, a privately held company controlled by Ned Johnson and his daughter Abigail. Massachusetts Financial Services (MFS) and Putnam Investments are also based in Boston.

Boston has long been considered the premier university center in the USA. Many graduates, having enjoyed the city in their youth, choose to stay in the area, helping fuel local booming commerce in computer research, Internet and software development, and computer and telecom hardware and manufacturing.

For technology, it all began back in 1865 when the Massachusetts Institute of Technology (MIT) opened its doors in Back Bay. By 1928, MIT researchers developed the first computer. Wang Computers, Digital Computers, Prime and Data General all began in the Boston area. The region still attracts a disproportionate amount of what little high-tech venture capital is left.

Cambridge, particularly Central and Kendall Squares, has become a mecca for the genome industry, which is intent on developing new drugs and therapies based on the mapping of 100,000 human genes. Small biotech companies, pharmaceutical giants and academic bastions, such as the Whitehead Institute/MIT Center for Genome Research, constantly vie for advantages and collaborations.

Gillette, the razor powerhouse, is based in South Boston.

POPULATION & PEOPLE

At the end of WWII, nearly 800,000 people lived in Boston, the majority of whom were Irish. Urban renewal and suburban flight reduced those numbers, but the core of the city was never abandoned like it was in some cities. Today, Boston is home to about 590,000, making it the 20th-largest US city. Boston, along with DC and San Francisco, are the only US cities that have more jobs than residents.

More than 3 million souls inhabit Greater Boston, and the breakdown goes like this: 54% are Caucasian (or white); 25% are African American; 14% are Latino; 7% are Asian; and less than 1% trace their ancestry to Native American peoples. The largest ethnic group is Irish. In the 21st century,

Boston is also attracting immigrants from Brazil, Haiti and Southeast Asia.

Boston is home to large numbers of Christian Protestants and Roman Catholics and smaller numbers of Jews, Muslims, Hindus and Buddhists. A few religious traditions began in Boston, among them Transcendentalism and Christian Science (founded in 1866 by Mary Baker Eddy), which now has churches in 70 countries throughout the world.

ARTS
Boston is synonymous, in many minds, with culture. The place isn't known as the 'Athens of America' for naught. Although high culture is mainly what comes to mind, what with Boston's great universities and rich literary, philosophical and political traditions, rest assured that Boston is home to a number of decidedly lowbrow artistic pursuits, too. See the Entertainment chapter.

Literature
The city's traditional reverence for the written word was brought by the Puritans and nurtured over the centuries by the area's great universities and literary societies.

Phillis Wheatley (1753–84), an African-American poet who began writing poetry at the age of 14, was encouraged to get an education by her slave master.

Ralph Waldo Emerson (1803–82) and Henry David Thoreau (1817–62) wrote compelling essays about their beliefs and attempts to live in accordance with the mystical unity of all creation (Transcendentalism). Thoreau's writings, notably *Walden, or Life in the Woods* (1854), which advocated a life of simplicity and living in harmony with nature, and *Civil Disobedience* (1849), a treatise well before its time, qualified him as America's first hippie.

Concordian Nathaniel Hawthorne (1804–64) was America's first great short-story writer and author of *The Scarlet Letter* (1850) and *The House of the Seven Gables* (1851). Neighbor Louisa May Alcott's (1832–88) largely autobiographical novel *Little Women* (1868) is a classic, beloved by generations of young women. Cambridge resident Henry Wadsworth Longfellow's

> ### How to Survive Boston
> Some cautions are in order:
>
> • Don't call Boston 'Beantown.'
> • Don't wear a NY Yankees cap in the vicinity of Fenway Park.
> • Don't park in a tow zone – you'll actually be towed.
> • Don't jaywalk or ignore traffic signals.
> • Don't expect to get an authoritative answer if you ask for directions.
> • Don't swim in the Charles River.
> • Don't wear orange in Southie on St Patrick's Day.
> • Don't call the North End 'Little Italy.'
> • Don't wear your Harvard sweatshirt until you get home

(1807–82) poems 'Song of Hiawatha' and 'Paul Revere's Ride' are memorized by school children as cherished (mythical) accounts of American lore.

In 1903, Harvard graduate and sociologist Dr WEB Du Bois (1868–1963) wrote his seminal tract *The Souls of Black Folk*, in which he sought to influence the way blacks dealt with segregation, urging pride in African heritage.

Henry James' *Bostonians* (1886) and John P Marquand's *Late George Apley* (1937) are piercing novels of Boston parlor society.

The Last Puritan (1935), by George Santayana (1863–1952), explores what it might be like for someone with 17th-century Puritan ideals to attend Harvard in the 20th century.

Robert McCloskey's *Make Way for Ducklings* (1941), a classic children's book, describes the story of a mother duck and her ducklings lost in Back Bay.

Johnny Tremain (1943), by Esther Forbes, describes the Revolutionary War as seen by a fictional boy.

Edwin O'Connor's *The Last Hurrah* (1955), a fictional work based on Mayor Curley's antics, is just as fun as Jack Beatty's

Film & Television

Boston, with its diverse architecture, scenic coastline and college campuses, is a hot film location.

The original *Thomas Crown Affair* (1968), starring Steve McQueen and Faye Dunaway, depicts the city as the perfect place to stage the perfect crime. Speaking of which, director William Friedkin of *The Brink's Job* (1978) insisted on authentic North End locations and hired local ex-cons to play toughs.

Love Story (1970), with Ryan O'Neal and Ali MacGraw as Harvard and Radcliffe undergraduates, told us that 'love means never having to say you're sorry.' *The Paper Chase* (1973) stars John Houseman as the classically stern, Socratic Harvard law professor.

The Bostonians (1984) stars Vanessa Redgrave and Christopher Reeve in a period piece based on the Henry James novel of Boston politics and manners c. 1876.

History guided two more films: *Glory* (1989), starring Denzel Washington and Matthew Broderick, tells the true story of the first Civil War black volunteer infantry unit. *Amistad* (1997), with an all-star cast directed by Stephen Spielberg, tells the true story of an 1839 mutiny aboard a slave ship and the ensuing legal battle to vindicate and free the mutineers.

Good Will Hunting (1997) put Southie on the Hollywood map and started the careers of Cambridge boys Matt Damon and Ben Affleck (who wrote the screenplay and starred along with Robin Williams).

The art-house hit *Next Stop Wonderland* (1997), a heartwarming independent film about a young woman's dating travails, refers to the final outbound stop on the T Blue Line.

As for small-screen TV set in Boston, look for creator David Kelley's *The Practice*, a legal drama, and *Boston Public*, about teachers. And if you're desperate, look for reruns of *Cheers* (where 'everybody knows your name'), *Ally McBeal* (a wacky legal show), *Spenser for Hire* (a detective who walked the streets) and *St Elsewhere* (*the* medical drama before *ER*).

The Rascal King (1992), a biographical account of Curley's flamboyance.

The Friends of Eddie Coyle (1972), by George Higgins, narrates life in one of Boston's less heralded neighborhoods; it provides a crash course in the Boston dialect.

David Foster Wallace's *Infinite Jest* (1996), a 1000-page philosophical and satirical tome that takes place all over Boston, has intricate descriptions of Comm Ave, Back Bay and Boston Common.

The former governor William Weld penned a sometimes witty political mystery *Mackerel by Moonlight* (1998).

Michael Patrick McDonough's *All Souls: A Family Story from Southie* (2000) chronicles a life of gangs and drugs in a storied neighborhood.

A book of short stories by Joe Hayes, *This Thing Called Courage: South Boston Stories* (2002), chronicles coming out in a deeply Catholic community where boys are boys and they're expected to like girls.

The Curse of the Bambino (2000), by *Boston Globe* sportswriter Dan Shaughnessy, marvelously describes the plight of the Boston Red Sox.

Music

Lots and lots of internationally known alternative groups (the Lemonheads, Morphine, the Mighty Mighty Bosstones and the Pixies, for example) and rock bands (Aerosmith, Boston, and the Cars, for example) got their start in Boston clubs. So did Aimee Mann, Juliana Hatfield and New Kids on the Block. For the latest, check out Ⓦ www.bostonbands.com or the band guide under Ⓦ www.bostonphoenix.com.

Boston is also home to a thriving folk tradition. Tracy Chapman sang in Harvard Square while a student at Tufts University. Patty Larkin got her start here as well. Club Passim is the most venerated folk venue.

Jazz thrives (but not like in New York City), inspired in part by the influential presence of Berklee College of Music, but the blues scene is a bit less developed. Cambridge has a few respected venues that attract well-known performers like GE Smith, Cesar

Boston English

The Boston dialect is famous for broad-vowel English. 'Pahk the cah in Hahvahd Yahd' (translation: Park the car in Harvard Yard) is the common illustration of the peculiar 'r.' During JFK's presidency, his speech was satirized for its disappearing r's ('chowdah' for chowder) and for r's that mysteriously replaced 'a' at the end of words ('Cuber' for Cuba). Then there is the adverb 'wicked' (pronounced 'wikkid' and meaning 'very') and the adjective 'bizarre' (pronounced 'bzah'). All together now: 'The weathah heah is wikkid bzah.'

Bostonians are also known for abbreviating names. Massachusetts Avenue becomes 'Mass Ave'; Commonwealth Avenue is always 'Comm Ave'; Harvard Business School becomes 'the B-School'; Cape Cod is 'the Cape'; the subway system is always 'the T.'

Some place names just don't follow standard American English usage and pronunciation:

- It's **Boston Common**, not 'commons.'
- **Copley** is 'kop-lee,' not 'kope-lee.'
- **Faneuil**: Nobody agrees on pronunciation but it's most common to say 'fannel' or 'fan-yul.'
- The **Public Garden** is singular, not plural, and never called the Boston Garden.
- **Tremont** St is pronounced 'treh-mont,' not 'tree-mont.'
- **Worcester** is an hour west of Boston but to save grave embarrassment, it's 'wooster.' (Locals say 'woostuh.')

Bostonians have also reinvented food and place names. Some tips:

- **Tonic** is a carbonated soft drink or soda pop.
- **Grinders** are hot or cold meat sandwiches, known elsewhere as submarine sandwiches or 'subs.'
- A **frappe** is a milkshake (blended ice cream and milk drink).
- **Jimmies** are tiny, waxy chocolate bits sprinkled on ice cream treats.
- **Southie** is South Boston, the neighborhood.
- **Boston cream pie** bears no relation to pie; it's yellow cake with a custard filling, covered in chocolate icing.

Rosas, Duke Robillard, Big Jack Johnson and Abbey Lincoln. There are also plenty of smaller clubs where you'll find talented acts.

Classical music has a long-celebrated tradition in Boston. The Boston Symphony Orchestra, founded in 1881, is finely woven into the cultural fabric of the city. The city's favorite 'pop' icon, the Boston Pops, plays popular classics, rousing marches and Broadway show tunes in Symphony Hall throughout the spring and fall.

Theater

Boston's strong Puritan roots have always exercised a stranglehold over her desire to become a world-class city, and this clash is most apparent in the city's stunted theater tradition. It was not until the mid-1800s that Boston even attempted to host performances like those routinely staged in Europe or New York.

In 1860, Edwin Booth was Boston's featured thespian. (His career was derailed when his brother, John Wilkes Booth, assassinated President Lincoln in 1865.) Throughout the late 1800s, various societies formed and clamored for censorship and decorum. Vaudeville and burlesque, said to have originated in Boston, merely served to keep the censors working overtime.

Boston's high-handed morality made it the butt of many jokes, as savvy marketing moguls designated their productions 'banned in Boston' and were therefore guaranteed a full house elsewhere. In 1929, Eugene O'Neill's *Strange Interlude* was banned and moved to nearby Quincy, where it was enthusiastically received. Boston loosened up a bit in the 1940s and '50s and became a tryout venue for Broadway-bound shows like Tennessee Williams' *A Streetcar Named Desire*, and the musical extravaganza *Oklahoma!*

In 1965 the American Civil Liberties Union (ACLU), stalwart guardian of free expression, took the city to court, finally exposing the tacit censorship agreement that existed between City Hall and theater managers. Still, the Puritans' posthumous reach was not entirely severed. The musical *Hair* was closed prematurely in 1970, allegedly because it depicted the desecration of the American flag.

Censorship is no longer a problem in Boston, but its legacy casts a long shadow. Unfortunately, the city is thus seen as a less than desirable venue for interesting alternative or cutting edge theatrical productions, whether homegrown or from afar.

Painting

John Singleton Copley (1738–1815) is considered the first great American portrait painter. Many of his best-known works, though painted after he relocated to London in 1774, are at the Museum of Fine Arts. Winslow Homer (1836–1910), famous for realistic Maine coast scenes, began as a popular press illustrator before dedicating himself to painting. By the 20th century, Boston supported world-class artists such as John Singer Sargent (1856–1925), who painted telling portraits of Boston's upper class, and Childe Hassam (1859–1935), who used Boston Common landscapes for his impressionist works. After Hassam, Boston lost pace with the rest of the Western world. Today, Newbury St galleries specialize in fairly conservative fare. For more cutting edge work, look for notices of artists' open studios.

Facts for the Visitor

WHEN TO GO

Boston draws crowds year-round, but there's a lull in November and from January through March. Spring is ephemeral. Blink, and the leaves have turned from buds to full-blown shadow puppets. If you time your visit right – late April to early June – you'll long remember Back Bay magnolias and the early roars of Red Sox Nation. June through August, though at times steamy, is high tourist season. September and October are predictably pleasant, with clear blue skies, cool mornings and evenings, and warm afternoons. Though there isn't much foliage in the city, New England leaf peepers fly in and out of Logan (so rooms are still expensive and hard to obtain). November always has a few warm days known as 'Indian summer.' The city puts on festive finery between Thanksgiving and New Year's Day. January and February winds and temps are harsh, but snowfall accumulation is measured in inches rather than feet and rooms are less expensive. A freak April Fools' snowstorm, burying poor little daffodils, isn't impossible.

The city is situated on the cusp of competing weather patterns: air masses from the Great Lakes and Canada collide with moderate Gulf Stream currents. Thus, the old saying 'if you don't like the weather, wait a minute' is only a slight exaggeration. Dress in layers and be ready for anything. Perhaps surprisingly, Boston is windier than Chicago and gets more rain than Seattle.

The short-range forecast is broadcast on the top column of the John Hancock building: steady blue, clear views; flashing blue, clouds are due; steady red, rain ahead; flashing red, snow instead. In summer, lights flash red to indicate a canceled Red Sox game.

WHAT TO BRING

Bostonians aren't particularly fashion-conscious. If someone looks really cool, or is wearing only black, chances are they're a foreign student. Often in the spring and fall, you need a jacket in the morning and

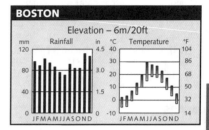

BOSTON

Elevation – 6m/20ft

evening, but only a T-shirt by day. Bring the warmest coat, scarf and gloves you own for wintertime visits.

ORIENTATION

For a city of its stature, Boston is quite small. The sights of principal interest to travelers are contained within a 1- by 3-mile area. The compact neighborhoods are quite distinct, abut one another and are best explored on foot.

Brahmin Beacon Hill, its brick streets lit by gas lanterns and lined with patrician townhouses, is one of the loveliest areas. Downtown boasts many important colonial Freedom Trail sites. The aromas and accents of the North End rival those of any Little Italy in America. The rejuvenated waterfront renews Boston's historic maritime ties. Back Bay, created as a mid-19th-century landfill project, is more orderly, with streets laid out east to west in alphabetical order. The gentrified South End is thick with restaurants, artsy shops and Victorian brownstones. Kenmore Square is home to a vibrant nightclub scene and lots of students, while the Fenway includes a 4-mile-long grassy byway that leads to two important museums and an arboretum.

The Charles River, with a popular grassy esplanade along both banks, separates Boston from Cambridge, home to Harvard University and the Massachusetts Institute of Technology (MIT). Cambridge's 'other' squares (besides Harvard) are often more vibrant and happening than their famous relative.

Expressways

Two highways skirt the Charles River: Storrow Dr runs along the Boston side and Memorial Dr (more scenic) runs along the Cambridge side. There are exits off Storrow Dr for Kenmore Square, Back Bay and Government Center.

Both Storrow Dr and Memorial Dr are accessible from the Mass Pike (I-90) and I-93. A turnpike extension connects the Mass Pike, via the Ted Williams Tunnel, to the airport.

MAPS

Lonely Planet's *Boston City Map* features detailed downtown and metropolitan maps in a full-color, easy-to-use format. Plastic-coated for extra durability, the map includes public transport routes and an index of all streets and sights.

Although you'll be hard-pressed to beat this guide's maps, the Arrow map of Boston is excellent. Also look for the smaller, laminated Streetwise maps of the city, useful for longer stays. **Professor Pathfinder** (☎ 800-933-6277; W www.hedbergmaps.com) produces a detailed map of Harvard Square, the university and other parts of Cambridge.

If you plan on bicycling beyond the banks of the Charles River, get hold of the fantastic *Boston's Bike Map*, produced by **Rubel BikeMaps** (☎ 617-776-6567; W www.bikemaps.com; PO Box 401035, Cambridge, MA 02140). It costs $5 and is available from the Globe Corner Bookstore (see the boxed text 'Booklover's Paradise' in the Shopping chapter) or directly from Rubel. Rubel also produces 50 little laminated 'Pocket Rides' (usually sold in packs of five for $9) for trips within Greater Boston and from commuter train stations in the area. The maps are worth every penny.

TOURIST OFFICES

Prior to your visit, contact the **Greater Boston Convention & Visitors Bureau** (GBCVB; Map 6, #38; ☎ 617-536-4100, 800-888-5515; W www.bostonusa.com; 2 Copley Place, Suite 105, Boston, MA 02116). For statewide information, contact the **Massachusetts Office of Travel & Tourism** (MOTT; Map 6; ☎ 617-973-8500, 800-447-6277, 800-227-6277 for

Bird's-Eye View

The 50th-floor **Prudential Center Skywalk** (Map 5; ☎ 617-859-0648; 800 Boylston St) offers a spectacular 360-degree view of metro Boston and Cambridge. It's open 10am to 10pm daily, and the last tickets are sold 30 minutes prior to closing. Tickets are $7 adults, $4 seniors and children age two to 10.

recorded events; W www.massvacation.com; Transportation Building, 10 Park Plaza, Suite 4510, Boston, MA 02116; open 9am-5pm Mon-Fri).

For subway and bus maps, head to the GBCVB's **Boston Common Visitors Information Center** (Map 2, #36; ☎ 617-536-4100; cnr Tremont & West Sts; open 8:30am-5pm Mon-Sat, 9am-5pm Sun), which has public rest rooms. The GBCVB also maintains a Back Bay **booth** (Map 5; Center Court, Prudential Center mall, 800 Boylston St; open 9am-5pm daily).

The **National Park Service Visitors Center** (NPS; Map 4, #6; ☎ 617-242-5642; W www.nps.gov/bost/; 15 State St; open 9am-5pm daily in winter, 9am-6pm daily in summer) has historical literature and free walking tours.

The Harvard Square **Visitors Information Booth** (Map 8, #38; ☎ 617-441-2884, 800-862-5678; open 9am-5pm daily) has information on local events and self-guided walking tours.

TRAVEL AGENCIES

STA Travel has several area offices that can satisfy just about every travel-related need. At press time, **Council Travel** and STA merged and they were contemplating moving several locations. Telephone numbers will remain the same.

Offices include those in Back Bay (Map 5, #26; ☎ 617-266-1926, 800-226-8624; W www.statravel.org; 273 Newbury St; open 10am-6pm Mon-Sat); on Harvard Square (Map 8, #64; ☎ 617-497-1497; 12 Eliot St, 2nd floor; open 10am-6pm Mon-Fri); and on the MIT campus at Stratton Student Center (Map 9, #60; ☎ 617-225-2555; 84 Mass Ave; open 9:30am-5:30pm Mon-Fri).

DOCUMENTS
Passports & Visas
To enter the US, Canadians must have proof of citizenship, such as a citizenship card with photo ID or a passport. Visitors from other countries must have a valid passport, and many visitors are required to have a US visa.

However, there is a reciprocal visa-waiver program in which citizens of certain countries may enter the USA for stays of 90 days or less with a passport but without first obtaining a US visa. At the time of research these countries were Andorra, Argentina, Australia, Austria, Belgium, Brunei, Denmark, Finland, France, Germany, Iceland, Ireland, Italy, Japan, Liechtenstein, Luxembourg, Monaco, the Netherlands, New Zealand, Norway, San Marino, Slovenia, Spain, Sweden, Switzerland and the UK. Under this program you must have a round-trip ticket that is nonrefundable in the USA, and you will not be allowed to extend your stay beyond 90 days.

Other travelers will need to obtain a visa (usually by mail) from a US consulate or embassy. Your passport should be valid for at least six months longer than your intended stay, and you'll need to submit a recent photo 1½ inches square (37mm x 37mm) with the application.

The most common visa is a Non-Immigrant Visitor's Visa, B1 for business purposes, B2 for tourism or visiting friends and relatives. A visitor's visa is good for one or five years with multiple entries, and it specifically prohibits the visitor from taking paid employment in the USA. The length of time you'll be allowed to stay in the US is ultimately determined by US immigration authorities at the port of entry. If you're coming to work or study, the company or institution that you're going to should make the arrangements. Allow six months in advance for processing the application.

If you want to stay in the USA longer than the date stamped on your passport, go to the local office of the **Immigration & Naturalization Service** (INS; ☎ 800-375-5283); for locations, look in the local White Pages telephone directory under 'US Government – Justice Department') *before* the stamped date to apply for an extension.

HIV & Entering the USA
Everyone entering the USA who isn't a US citizen is subject to the authority of the Immigration & Naturalization Service (INS). The INS can keep people from entering or staying in the USA by excluding or deporting them. Though being HIV-positive is not grounds for deportation, it is 'grounds for exclusion,' and the INS can invoke it to refuse admission. It's rare but it can happen.

Visitors should know and assert their rights. It's best to discuss them and your options with a trained immigration advocate before applying for a visa. For legal immigration information and referrals, contact the **National Immigration Project of the National Lawyers Guild** (☎ 617-227-9727, fax 617-227-5495; 14 Beacon St, Suite 602, Boston, MA 02108).

Bring along income verification documents and a character witness.

Travel Insurance
A travel insurance policy to cover medical expenses, luggage theft or loss, ticket loss, and cancellations or delays in your travel arrangements is a good idea. At the very least, you want coverage for the worst case scenario. Coverage depends on your insurance and type of ticket, so ask both your insurer and your ticket-issuing agency to explain the finer points. STA Travel offers travel insurance options at reasonable prices.

Copies
All important documents (passport data page and visa page, credit cards, travel insurance policy, air, bus and train tickets, driver's license etc) should be photocopied before you leave home. Leave one copy with someone at home and keep another with you, separate from the originals.

US EMBASSIES & CONSULATES
US diplomatic offices abroad include those in:

Australia (☎ 02-6270-5000) 21 Moonah Place, Yarralumla ACT 2600
Sydney: (☎ 02-9373-9200) Level 59, MLC

Centre, 19–29 Martin Place, Sydney NSW 2000
  Melbourne: (☎ 03-9526-5900) 553 St Kilda
  Rd, Melbourne, Victoria 3000
Canada (☎ 613-238-5335) 100 Wellington St,
  Ottawa, Ontario K1P 5T1
  Vancouver: (☎ 604-685-4311) 1095 W
  Pender St, Vancouver BC V6E 2M6
  Montreal: (☎ 514-398-9695) 1155 rue
  St-Alexandre, Montreal, Quebec
France (☎ 01-42-96-12-02) 2 rue Saint Florentin,
  75001 Paris
Germany (☎ 228-33-91) Deichmanns Aue 29,
  53170 Bonn
Ireland (☎ 1-668-8777) 42 Elgin Rd, Ballsbridge,
  Dublin
Israel (☎ 3-519-7575) 71 Hayarkon St, Tel Aviv
Japan (☎ 3-224-5000) 1-10-5 Akasaka Chome,
  Minato-ku, Tokyo
New Zealand (☎ 4-722-068) 29 Fitzherbert
  Terrace, Thorndon, Wellington
UK (☎ 020-499-9000) 24 Grosvenor St,
  London W1
  Edinburgh: (☎ 0131-556-8315) 3 Regent
  Terrace, Edinburgh EH7 5BW
  Belfast: (☎ 028-328-239) Queens House, 14
  Queen St, Belfast BT1 6EQ

CONSULATES IN BOSTON

Most foreign embassies in the US are in Washington, DC, but a lot of countries, including the following, have consular offices in Boston. If your country's embassy or consulate is not listed below, call ☎ 617-555-1212 in Boston, or ☎ 202-555-1212 in Washington, DC, or look in the Yellow Pages telephone directory under 'Consulates.'

Canada (☎ 617-262-3760) 3 Copley Place, Suite
  400, Boston, MA 02116
France (☎ 617-542-7374) 31 St James Ave,
  Suite 750, Boston, MA 02116
Germany (☎ 617-536-4414) 3 Copley Place,
  Suite 500, Boston, MA 02116
Ireland (☎ 617-267-9330) 535 Boylston St,
  Boston, MA 02116
UK (☎ 617-248-9555) 600 Atlantic Ave, 25th
  floor, Boston, MA 02210

CUSTOMS

US customs allows each person over the age of 21 to bring 1L of liquor and 200 cigarettes duty-free into the USA. US citizens are allowed to import, duty-free, $400 worth of gifts from abroad, and non-US citizens are allowed to bring in $100 worth. Should you be carrying more than $10,000 in US and foreign cash, traveler's checks, money orders or the like, you need to declare the excess amount. There is no legal restriction on the amount that may be imported, but undeclared sums in excess of $10,000 may be subject to confiscation.

MONEY
Currency

US dollars are the only currency accepted in Boston. The US dollar ($) is divided into 100 cents (¢). Coins come in denominations of 1¢ (penny), 5¢ (nickel), 10¢ (dime), 25¢ (quarter), and the seldom seen 50¢ (half dollar) and $1. Hoard quarters, the coins most commonly used in vending machines and parking meters. Bills, all the same size and color, come in $1, $2, $5, $10, $20, $50 and $100 denominations.

Exchange Rates

At press time, exchange rates were:

country	unit		dollars
Australia	A$1	=	US$0.56
Canada	C$1	=	US$0.63
euro zone	€1	=	US$1.05
Hong Kong	HK$10	=	US$1.28
Japan	¥100	=	US$0.84
New Zealand	NZ$1	=	US$0.52
UK	UK£1	=	US$1.60

Exchanging Money

To exchange currency, call **Fleet Boston** *(☎ 877-353-3839)* for the nearest location, or head to its **International Personal Banking Office** *(☎ 617-556-6050; 1414 Mass Ave)* in Harvard Square. Visit **w** www.xe.com for currency exchange converters.

Cash & Traveler's Checks Traveler's checks, which can be replaced if lost or stolen, are as good as cash in the US – but only if they are in US dollars. Keep a record of the check numbers separate from the checks themselves. Buy checks in denominations of $100, with one packet of $20, so that at the end of your stay you aren't left with too many dollars.

ATMs Found at banks and in shopping areas, ATMs are convenient for obtaining cash from a bank account back home. They're open 24 hours a day. There are various ATM networks, and most banks are affiliated with several. Exchange, Star, Plus and Cirrus are the predominant networks. For a nominal service charge, you can withdraw cash from an ATM using a credit card or a charge card. Credit cards usually result in higher fees on top of interest, which mounts until you pay it back. Using bank cards linked to your personal checking account is usually far cheaper. Check with your bank or credit card company for particulars.

Credit & Debit Cards Major credit cards are accepted at hotels, restaurants, gas stations, shops and car-rental agencies. In fact, you'll find it hard to perform certain transactions, such as renting cars or purchasing concert tickets, without one. Visa and Master Card are the most widely accepted.

Places that accept Visa and MasterCard are likely to accept debit cards, which deduct payments directly from the user's checking account and charge a minimal transaction fee. Confirm that your debit card will be accepted in other states or countries.

Contact your bank if you lose your ATM card; contact your credit card company immediately if your cards get lost or stolen. Following are toll-free numbers for the main credit card companies:

American Express	☎ 800-528-4800
Diners Club	☎ 800-234-6377
Discover	☎ 800-347-2683
MasterCard	☎ 800-826-2181
Visa	☎ 800-336-8472

Security
Be cautious – but not paranoid – about carrying money. If your hotel or hostel has a safe, keep your valuables in it. Don't display large amounts of cash in public. Use a money belt under your clothes for excess currency when you're on the move. The back pocket of your pants is a prime target for pickpockets, as are handbags and the outside pockets of day packs and fanny packs (bum bags).

Costs
The cost of living in Boston is among the highest in the nation. With advance planning you can secure a hostel bed, but if that's not your bag, expect to spend at least $100 nightly (probably more like $150). There are plenty of places to spend more.

Food can be very reasonable. The occasional splurge at a first-rate restaurant will cost anywhere between $25 and $50 depending on where you are, but good restaurant meals can be found for $10 – or even half that for some lunch specials.

Tipping
Tipping is expected in restaurants and better hotels, and by taxi drivers and baggage carriers. Tip 15% even if service is less than stellar, 20% if service *is* stellar. In bars the unspoken minimum is $1 for one or two beers; otherwise, it's 15%. For cabbies the minimum on a $6 fare is $1; from there it's 10%. Hairdressers get 15%. Baggage carriers get $1 per bag. Valet parking warrants $2, paid on receipt of your car.

Taxes
There is no national sales tax (such as VAT), but there are state and local taxes. In Boston, lodging sales tax is 12.75%, unless it's a three-room B&B, in which case it's nil. There is no tax on clothing, unless it's a pricey luxury item. Otherwise, restaurant meals, drinks, car rentals and most other purchases are taxed at 5%. Prices in this book don't include taxes.

POST & COMMUNICATIONS
Post
Boston's **main post office** (Map 4, #71; ☎ 800-275-8777; 25 Dorchester Ave; open 24 hr daily) is just one block southeast of South Station. Mail can be sent to you here marked c/o General Delivery, Boston, MA 02205, USA.

Post offices are generally open from 8am to 5pm weekdays and 9am to 3pm on Saturday, but it all depends on the branch. Neighborhood branches are indicated on each map, and you can find the phone numbers in the 'Government Listings' section of the White Pages.

At press time, rates for 1st-class mail within the USA were 37¢ for letters up to 1oz (23¢ for each additional ounce) and 23¢ for postcards.

International airmail rates (except to Canada and Mexico) are 80¢ for a 1oz letter, and 70¢ for a postcard. Letters to Canada and Mexico are 60¢ for a 1oz letter, and 50¢ for a postcard. Aerograms are 70¢.

Telephone

The separate Boston Area Yellow Pages and White Pages, which include Brookline, Cambridge and Somerville, are comprehensive directories.

All USA phone numbers consist of a three-digit area code followed by a seven-digit local number. Boston's area code is ☎ 617. In the Excursions chapter, listings have area codes of ☎ 508, ☎ 781 or ☎ 978. Even if you are calling locally in Boston, you must dial ☎ 617 + the local seven-digit number. If you are calling long distance, dial ☎ 1 + area code + seven-digit number.

Local calls from pay phones are usually 50¢; hotels' access charges are often astronomical. Toll-free phone numbers begin with ☎ 800, ☎ 888, ☎ 866 or ☎ 877. Numbers beginning with ☎ 900 usually incur high fees.

For local directory assistance, dial ☎ 411. Outside your area code, dial ☎ 1 + three-digit area code of the place you want to call + 555-1212. For directory assistance regarding toll-free numbers, dial ☎ 1-800-555-1212. Dial ☎ 0 for the operator.

Cell phones may be rented through the Boston-based company **National Cell Phone Rentals** (☎ 617-262-5712; **w** www.cell phonerentals.net; 326 A St, Suite 5B, Fort Point Channel).

International Calls

Calling from abroad, the international country code for the USA is ☎ 1. For direct international calls from Boston, dial ☎ 011 + country code + area code + number. You may need to wait as long as 45 seconds for the ringing to start. International rates depend on the time of day and the destination. Call the **operator** (☎ 0) for rates.

ekno Communication Service

Lonely Planet's ekno global communication service provides low-cost international calls – for local calls, you're usually better off with a local phonecard. The ekno service also offers free messaging services, email, travel information and an online travel vault, where you can securely store all your important documents. You can join online at **w** www .ekno.lonelyplanet.com, where you will find the local-access numbers for the 24-hour customer-service center. Once you have joined, check the ekno website for the latest access numbers for each country and for updates on new features.

Fax & Telegram

Fax machines are common and easy to find in the USA at shipping companies such as Mail Boxes Etc, photocopy stores and hotel business service centers, but be prepared to pay high prices (over $1 a page). Telegrams can be sent through **Western Union** (☎ 800-325-6000).

Email & Internet Access

Most hotels that cater to business travelers make Internet and email access easy. Or you may head to a public library to log on (but not receive email). For a worldwide list of cybercafés, browse **w** www.traveltales.com or **w** www.netcafeguide.com. Copy centers, such as Kinko's, often charge high hourly rates for computer usage. At press time, there was only one cybercafé left in Boston: **Designs for Living** (Map 7, #55; ☎ 617-536-6150; 52 Queensberry St).

DIGITAL RESOURCES

The World Wide Web is a rich resource for travelers and there's no better place to start your explorations than the **Lonely Planet** website (**w** www.lonelyplanet.com). Here you'll find succinct summaries on traveling to most places on earth, postcards from other travelers and the Thorn Tree bulletin board, where you can ask questions before you go or dispense advice when you get back. You can also find updates to many popular guidebooks, and the subwwway section links you to the most useful travel resources elsewhere on the Web.

BOOKS

Boston does not have a shortage of truly exceptional general- and special-interest bookstores. See the boxed text 'Booklover's Paradise' in the Shopping chapter.

Guidebooks

Lonely Planet's *New England* covers the spectacular, diverse region surrounding Boston, while *Boston Condensed* is an alternative for shorter trips. Susan Wilson's *Boston Sites & Insights* provides historical anecdotes on 50 major landmarks. Architecture buffs will appreciate the *AIA Guide to Boston*, by Susan and Michael Southworth. *Blue Laws, Brahmins & Breakdown Lanes*, by Karen Cord Taylor, is an opinionated A–Z guide about this quirky city.

History & Politics

J Anthony Lukas' *On Common Ground: A Turbulent Decade in the Lives of Three American Families* is the definitive account of the 1970s busing trauma. Jack Beatty's *Rascal King: The Life and Times of James Michael Curley, 1874–1958* follows the trajectory of the state's most 'colorful' politician.

Furthering the architecture discussions are Jane Holtz Kay's *Lost Boston*, and *Cityscapes of Boston*, by Peter Vanderwarker and Robert Campbell. *Boston: A Topographical History*, by Walter Muir Whitehill, is a fascinating and lively history of Boston from the 1600s to the 1960s. Alex Krieger and David Cobb's *Mapping Boston* is a wonderful book that chronicles Boston's development and history through maps, photos and essays.

NEWSPAPERS & MAGAZINES

Copley Square News *(Map 5, #56; cnr Boylston & Dartmouth Sts)*, an outdoor kiosk, has been selling hundreds of magazines and many foreign-language periodicals since the 1930s.

Out of Town News *(Map 8, #36; ☎ 617-354-7777; Harvard Square; open 6am-10pm)*, a National Historic Landmark, sells papers from virtually every major US city, as well as from cities around the world.

Boston has two major dailies: the highly regarded *Boston Globe* (**w** www.boston.com), owned by the *New York Times*, and the plucky

---

Volts & Ounces

Time GMT/UTC minus five hours
Daylight Saving Time Set clocks forward one hour on first Sunday in April and back one hour on last Sunday in October
Electricity 110V, two flat pins, sometimes with a third round pin
Weights Ounces, pounds and tons
Measures Distance in feet, yards and miles; gasoline in US gallons (about 20% less than the imperial gallon)

---

tabloid *Boston Herald* (**w** www.bostonherald.com). The *Globe* publishes a useful Thursday 'Calendar' section and a daily feature 'Go!', while the *Herald* has a Friday 'Scene' section. *Boston Magazine* (**w** www.bostonmagazine.com) is the city's glossy monthly. The venerable *Atlantic Monthly*, eclectic, esoteric and cerebral, is published in Boston.

The sassy, biweekly *Improper Bostonian* is available free from sidewalk dispenser boxes. The excellent weekly *Boston Phoenix* (**w** www.bostonphoenix.com) is an alternative paper focusing on arts and entertainment.

TELEVISION & RADIO

There are no television surprises in Boston. WGBH (channel two), the public television affiliate, pays more attention to national and world affairs (it produces the award-winning *Nova* and *Frontline* programs) than it does to local programming.

Boston is blessed with two public radio stations – WGBH (89.7 FM) and WBUR (90.9 FM) – broadcasting news, classical music and radio shows. If you want to hear what Bostonians are thinking, try the David Brudnoy show weeknights on WBZ (1030 AM). For sports talk radio all the time, tune into 850 AM.

PHOTOGRAPHY & VIDEO

For equipment and film purchases, head to **Bromfield Camera** *(Map 4, #33; ☎ 617-426-5230; 10 Bromfield St)*, **SBI** *(Map 8, #69; ☎ 617-576-0969; 57 JFK St, Harvard Square)*, **Ferranti-Dege** *(Map 8, #46; ☎ 617-499-2750;*

1300 Mass Ave, Harvard Square), or **Calumet** *(Map 9;* ☎ *617-576-2600; 65 Bent St, Kendall Square area).*

For quality same-day processing, **Color Tek** *(Map 4, #62;* ☎ *617-345-9080; South Station Concourse • Map 5, #31;* ☎ *617-267-6503; 251 Newbury St)* is the best choice.

Overseas visitors thinking about purchasing videos here need to know that the USA uses a video standard not compatible with that of some other countries.

LAUNDRY

There are self-service, coin-operated laundry facilities in most neighborhoods. Service is reasonable – about $1.50 to wash and $1 to dry. Look under 'Laundries – Self-Service' or 'Cleaners' in the Yellow Pages.

TOILETS

Public toilets are so difficult to find in Boston that a website sprang up to expose them: ⓦ www.boston-online.com/restrooms.html. The humorous interactive site also rates their cleanliness.

HEALTH

For most foreign visitors, no immunizations are required for entry, though cholera and yellow fever vaccinations may be required of travelers from areas with a history of those diseases. There are no unexpected health dangers, excellent medical attention is readily available and the only real health concern is that a collision with the medical system can cause severe injuries to your financial state.

Medical Attention

In a city world-renowned for health care, **Massachusetts General Hospital** *(MGH; Map 3;* ☎ *617-726-2000; 55 Fruit St)* is one of the city's biggest and best. The staff can often refer you to smaller clinics and crisis hotlines. In real emergencies call ☎ 911 for an ambulance. But be aware that emergency room (ER) charges in the USA are incredibly expensive. It's a very good idea to have health insurance while traveling; many travel insurance policies include medical coverage. See Travel Insurance earlier in this chapter.

CVS *(Map 10, #22;* ☎ *617-876-5519; Porter Square shopping mall, Mass Ave, Cambridge)* is the area's only 24-hour pharmacy.

WOMEN TRAVELERS

Although women often experience less harassment in Boston than in other major American cities, it's not a bad idea to travel with a little extra awareness of your surroundings.

If you are the victim of a crime, call the **police** *(*☎ *911)* or the **rape crisis hotline** *(*☎ *617-492-7273).*

The **National Organization for Women** *(NOW;* ☎ *617-232-4764;* ⓦ *www.boston now.org; 214 Harvard Ave, Brighton)* is a good resource, while **Planned Parenthood** *(*☎ *617-616-1600, 617-616-1616 hotline;* ⓦ *www .plannedparenthood.org; 1055 Comm Ave)* offers medical advice and counseling.

GAY & LESBIAN TRAVELERS

Gay men have spiffed up the South End, lesbians the outlying neighborhood of Jamaica Plain. Incidents of gay-bashing are reported with consistency in the Fenway area, just south of the community gardens.

The **Fenway Community Health Center** *(Map 7;* ☎ *617-267-0900; 7 Haviland St)*, the **AIDS Action Hotline** *(*☎ *800-235-2331)* and the **Bisexual Resource Center** *(Map 6;* ☎ *617-424-9595;* ⓦ *www.biresource.org; 29 Stanhope St)* do good work. Check the Yellow Pages under 'Social & Human Services' for community resources.

Pick up the weekly *Bay Windows* and monthly *Sojourner* at **We Think the World of You** *(Map 6, #63;* ☎ *617-267-3010; 540 Tremont St)*, Boston's gay bookstore.

DISABLED TRAVELERS

Boston attempts to be wheelchair accessible (with curb cuts, ramps on public buildings, special T van service), but it falls short for such a so-called world-class city.

These organizations specialize in the needs of disabled travelers:

Access-Able Travel Source *(*☎ 303-232-2979; ⓦ www.access-able.com) PO Box 1796, Wheat Ridge, CO 80034

Society for Accessible Travel and Hospitality
(SATH; ☎ 212-447-7284; W www.sath.org)
347 Fifth Ave, Suite 610, New York, NY 10016
Twin Peaks Press (☎ 360-694-2462) PO Box 129,
Vancouver, WA 98666. Publishes directories and
access guides

SENIOR TRAVELERS

Boston is a popular destination for retirees.
Though the age when the benefits begin
varies, travelers from 50 years and up can
expect to receive cut rates and benefits at
hotels and museums.

Some national advocacy groups include:

American Association of Retired Persons
(AARP; ☎ 800-424-3410; W www.aarp.org)
601 E St NW, Washington, DC 20049
Elderhostel (☎ 877-426-8056; W www.elder
hostel.org) 11 Ave de Lafayette, Boston, MA
02111. Offering academic learning adventures
Grand Circle Travel (☎ 617-350-7500, 800-59/-
3644; W www.gct.com) 347 Congress St,
Boston, MA 02210

BOSTON FOR CHILDREN

Boston is one giant living history museum,
the setting for many educational and lively
field trips. The Museum of Science on the
Charles River near Kendall Square is serious
hands-on fun and the waterfront Children's
Museum is first rate. Nearby, children enjoy
the reenactment of dumping bales of tea into
the harbor at the Tea Party Ship before heading over to the New England Aquarium. In
the Public Garden, the *Make Way for Ducklings* statues are a perennial hit with small
ones, but the swan boats are a bit slow for
kids raised on computer games. The Franklin
Park Zoo is a prime afternoon's outing.

Simply getting around the city on the
subway is the least expensive and possibly
most adventurous thing to do in Boston.

Kidding Around Boston, by Helen Byers,
is good. If you haven't traveled with children, you might find some encouragement
in Lonely Planet's *Travel with Children*.

SAFETY CONCERNS

The crime rates in Boston have dropped in
recent years, but that doesn't mean you
should be lax with regard to pickpockets,

muggers and carjackers. And while Boston
doesn't have quite the same problem with
scams, gangs, drugs, and prostitution that
other US cities have, that doesn't mean you
won't see it. This book does not cover areas
frequented by gangs.

A few specifics, though: avoid the Fenway
after dark. There are still one or two X-rated
businesses whose leases have not expired
around lower Washington St in Chinatown.

In general, always lock cars and put valuables out of sight. Be aware of your surroundings and who may be watching you.
Avoid walking on dimly lit streets at night,
particularly when alone. Walk purposefully.
Use ATM machines in well-trafficked areas
only. Lock valuables in your suitcase or in
a hotel safe.

EMERGENCIES

Dial ☎ 911 for police, ambulance and fire
emergencies; this is a free call from any
phone. Services in Boston include the **Good
Samaritans** (☎ 617-247-0220) for suicide prevention, the **rape crisis center** (☎ 617-492-
7273) and the **Bay Cove Substance Abuse
Treatment Center** (☎ 617-371-3030).

Traveler's Aid Society (Map 4, #64; ☎ 617-
542-7286, 617-737-2880; 17 East St; open
9am-4:30pm Mon-Fri), just off Atlantic Ave,
across from South Station, is a nonprofit
agency that helps stranded travelers in des-
pair. From stolen wallets to practical information to transportation assistance to 'bedless
in Boston,' Traveler's Aid is there to help. At
the airport there's the **Logan Airport
'Terminal E' Traveler's Aid** (☎ 617-567-5385;
open noon-9pm daily).

BUSINESS HOURS & PUBLIC
HOLIDAYS

Businesses are generally open 9am to 5pm
weekdays. Most shops stay open longer and
through the weekends, and many big super-
markets are open 24 hours. Banks are generally open 8am to 4pm weekdays; some are
open for a few hours on Saturday morning.

National public holidays are celebrated
throughout the USA. Banks, schools and government offices (including post offices) are
closed and transportation and other services

are on a Sunday schedule. Holidays falling on a weekend are usually observed the following Monday.

New Year's Day January 1
Martin Luther King Jr's Birthday January – 3rd Monday
Presidents' Day February – 3rd Monday
Memorial Day May – last Monday
Independence Day July 4
Labor Day September – 1st Monday
Columbus Day October – 2nd Monday
Veterans Day November 11
Thanksgiving Day November – 4th Thursday
Christmas Day December 25

SPECIAL EVENTS

These are just the highlights, a few events and festivals it may be worth planning your trip around. Call the **GBCVB** (☎ 617-536-4100, 800-888-5515; ☒ www.bostonusa.com) for details on the following:

January & February

Chinese New Year (Late January or early February) The first day is celebrated with a colorful parade, firecrackers, fireworks and lots of food.

March

St Patrick's Day (March 17) Ireland's patron saint is honored by all those who feel the Irish in their blood and by those who want to feel Irish beer in their blood. Everyone wears green (or you might get pinched). The large and vocal South Boston Irish community hosts a parade on West Broadway St, but since the mid-1990s, it's been marred by the decision to exclude gay and lesbian Irish groups from marching. Officially, the day off is for celebrating Evacuation Day, the day the British pulled out of Boston Harbor in 1775.

April

Patriots' Day (3rd Monday) Paul Revere's historic ride from the North End to Lexington and battles in Concord and Lexington are reenacted. See Shot Heard Round the World in the Facts about Boston chapter.

Boston Marathon (3rd Monday) Later in the morning, thousands of runners compete in a 26.2-mile run (☒ www.bostonmarathon.org) that has been an annual event for more than a century. The race finishes on Boylston St in front of the Boston Public Library.

May

Lilac Sunday (3rd Sunday) Arnold Arboretum celebrates the arrival of spring, when more than 400 varieties of fragrant lilacs are in bloom. It is the only day of the year that visitors can picnic on the grass at the venerable arboretum.

Magnolia trees (Mother Nature decides the date) Trees bloom all along Newbury St and Comm Ave.

June

Bunker Hill Day (June 17) A parade and battle reenactment at Charlestown's Bunker Hill Monument.

Gay Pride (Mid-month) Tens of thousands of participants and spectators line the parade route, which culminates in a big party on Boston Common.

Harborfest (Late June) During this weeklong maritime celebration, you can sample dozens of chowders at the Chowderfest on City Hall Plaza.

July

Independence Day (July 4) The Boston Pops gives a free evening performance of Tchaikovsky's *1812 Overture*, complete with brass cannon and synchronized fireworks for a half million people. It's broadcast nationally.

July & August

Italian festivals (Weekends throughout the summer) North End patron saints are honored with food and music.

September

Boston Film Festival (Two weeks mid-month) Indies are screened at venues citywide.

October

Head of the Charles Regatta (3rd weekend) The world's largest rowing event draws more than 3000 collegiate rowers, while cheering fans line the banks of the river, lounging on blankets and drinking beer (technically illegal).

Halloween (October 31) Kids and adults dress in costumes.

December

Boston Ballet (Late November to early January) The *Nutcracker* at the Wang Center is staged until early January.

Tree lighting (1st week) Boston Common trees remain lit throughout December.

Boston Tea Party reenactment (Sunday prior to December 16) Costumed actors march from Old South Meeting House to the waterfront and dump bales of tea into the harbor.

First Night (December 31) New Year celebrations begin early and continue past midnight, culminating in fireworks over the harbor. Purchase a special button that permits entrance into events citywide.

WORK

If you're not a US citizen, apply for a work visa from the US embassy before you leave home. If you're caught working illegally, you'll be deported and barred from the US for at least five years. Visas vary with your length of stay and the type of work you do. It's best to already have a job offer from an employer who considers your qualifications to be unique and not readily available in the US.

Getting There & Away

AIR

Boston has one major airport and two minor ones within an hour's drive. Depending on where you are coming from, it may be cheaper (but certainly less convenient) to fly into New York City and take the train or bus to Boston. It's about four hours on the ground from New York to Boston.

Airports

On MA 1A in East Boston, **Logan International Airport** *(Map 1; ☎ 800-235-6426; ⓦ www.massport.com)* has five separate terminals that are connected by a frequent shuttle bus (No 11). The nonprofit **Traveler's Aid Society** *(☎ 617-567-5385; open noon-9pm daily)* maintains a booth at Terminal E, where all international flights arrive and depart.

A quiet alternative to Logan, the **Manchester Airport** *(☎ 603-624-6556; ⓦ www.fly manchester.com)* is just 55 miles north of Boston in New Hampshire.

Just outside Providence, Rhode Island, **TF Green Airport** *(☎ 401-737-8222; ⓦ www .pvdairport.com)* is also serviced by major carriers. Southwest Airlines, in particular, offers very competitively priced tickets. The airport is one hour south of Boston.

Buying Tickets

Some of the cheapest tickets must be bought months in advance, and some popular flights sell out early. Note that high season in Boston is mid-April to mid-October (summer) and the weeks before and after Christmas. In the States, check the weekly travel sections of the *New York Times, Los Angeles Times, Chicago Tribune* and *San Francisco Examiner*. **STA Travel** *(☎ 800-777-0112; ⓦ www.statravel .com)* has offices in major cities nationwide.

Cheap tickets are usually referred to by airlines as advance-purchase fares, budget fares, Apex and super-Apex. Airlines also release cheap tickets through selected travel agents (not through airline offices). These are often nonrefundable and require an extra fee for changing your flight.

In Boston, head to the **Boston Airline Center** *(Map 4, #59; no phone; 155 Federal St; open Mon-Fri)* to pick up tickets for major carriers.

Once you have a ticket, write down its number and the flight number and keep the information somewhere separate. This will help with replacement if the ticket is lost or stolen. Buy travel insurance early (see Travel Insurance in the Facts for the Visitor chapter).

Search these online reservations services for good fares:

Atevo Travel (ⓦ www.atevo.com)
Cheap Tickets (ⓦ www.cheaptickets.com)
Microsoft Expedia (ⓦ www.expedia.com)
Travelocity (ⓦ www.travelocity.com)

Visit USA Passes Many domestic carriers offer Visit USA passes to non-US citizens. The passes are actually coupons – each coupon equals a flight. You have to book each of these, including your return flight, outside the US. Unless you want to rely on last-minute flights booked over the Internet once you're in the States, this is cheaper than buying flights in the US.

Contact the bigger carriers like Continental, American Airlines and Delta in your home country. Some will let you fly stand-by, while others require you reserve flights in advance (and penalize you if you need to change the fare). When flying stand-by, call the airline a day or two before the flight and make a 'stand-by reservation.' This way you get priority over others who just appear at the airport and hope to get on the flight the same day.

Other Parts of the USA

Getting a flight into Boston should present no problems. To secure the cheapest fare, purchase tickets 14 to 21 days in advance. Ask about 'companion fares,' letting two people travel for the price of one. Given the competitive nature of the airline industry, generally when one carrier offers a deal, others quickly follow suit.

You can often find round-trip fares from the West Coast for $400, but don't be surprised if it's $550 during the summer. Flights from Miami average about $300; with a bit of flexibility, you'll find fares from Chicago for about $250, a bit more from Denver.

The DC–Boston and New York–Boston corridor, frequented by business travelers, is often more than $200. It might behoove you to fly from Baltimore to Providence on Southwest for as little as $80 round trip and take a bus.

Canada

Travel Cuts (*☎ 416-966-2887 in Toronto; 866-246-9762; W www.travelcuts.com*) has offices in all major cities. The Toronto *Globe & Mail* and *Vancouver Sun* carry travel agents' ads. In the summertime from Vancouver, expect to spend about C$800; from Toronto, it's more like C$450. **Air Canada** (*W www.aircanada.ca*) has good last-minute Web deals.

UK & Ireland

Check ads in *Time Out*, the *Evening Standard* and *TNT*. Also check the free magazines widely available in London – start by looking outside the main railway stations.

Good, reliable agents for cheap tickets in the UK include **Trailfinders** (*☎ 020-7938-3939; W www.trailfinders.co.uk; 194 Kensington*

Major Airlines

The following airlines serve the Boston area:

US-Based Airlines

Air Tran (☎ 800-247-8726; W www.airtran .com)
America West (☎ 800-235-9292; W www .americawest.com)
American Airlines (☎ 800-433-7300; W www .americanair.com)
Continental Airlines (☎ 800-525-0280; W www.continental.com)
Delta Air Lines (☎ 800-241-4141; W www .delta.com)
Midwest Express (☎ 800-452-2022; W www .midwestexpress.com)
Northwest Airlines (☎ 800-447-4747; W www.nwa.com)
Southwest Airlines (☎ 800-435-9792; W www.iflyswa.com)
US Airways (☎ 800-428-4322; W www.usair ways.com)
Virgin Atlantic (☎ 800-862-8621; W www .virgin-atlantic.com)

International Airlines

Aer Lingus (☎ 800-223-6537; W www .aerlingus.com)
Air Canada (☎ 888-247-2262; W www.air canada.ca)
Air France (☎ 800-237-2747; W www.air france.fr)
Air New Zealand (☎ 800-262-1234; W www .airnewzealand.com)
Alitalia (☎ 800-223-5730; W www.alitalia.it)
British Airways (☎ 800-247-9297; W www .britishairways.com)
Iceland Air (☎ 800-223-5500; W www.ice landair.com)
KLM (☎ 800-374-7747; W www.klm.com)
Lufthansa (☎ 800-645-3880; W www.luft hansa.com)
Olympic Airways (☎ 800-223-1226; W www .olympic-airways.gr)
Qantas Airways (☎ 800-227-4500; W www .qantas.com.au)
Swissair (☎ 877-359-7947; W www.swissair .com)
TAP, Air Portugal (☎ 800-221-7370; W www .tap-airportugal.pt)

High St, London W8 7RG) and **STA Travel** *(☎ 020-7581-4132; *W* www.statravel.co.uk; 86 Old Brompton Rd, London SW7 3LQ).*

Most British travel agents are registered with the **Association of British Travel Agents** *(ABTA; *W* www.abta.com),* which are bonded under agreements such as the Air Transport Operators License (ATOL); if you buy a ticket from such an agent and the airline then goes out of business, ATOL guarantees a refund or an alternative.

A round-trip air ticket on British Airways from London to Boston in January might cost £250. In July, the same ticket would cost £500. On Aer Lingus from Dublin to Boston in January, you can expect to pay £300, in July £525.

Continental Europe

Most major European airlines serve Boston, many with nonstop service. In January/July, for a round-trip ticket expect to pay *from* €450/715 from Amsterdam; €475/740 from Paris; €430/575 from Madrid; €430/760 from Frankfurt.

NBBS, the Dutch Student Travel Service, is probably your best bet, but check out W www.budgettravel.com/amsterta.htm for a complete list of Dutch travel agents near you.

STA Travel *(☎ 49-69-703035; *W* www.sta travel.de; Frankfurt)* and **Travel Overland** *(☎ 89-272-76300; *W* www.travel-overland .de; München)* have many popular offices throughout Germany.

For great student fares from France, contact **Usit** *(☎ 33-1-42-44-14-00 in Paris; *W* www.usitconnections.fr),* which has many outlets in Paris and around the country. For Usit locations around the world check out W www.usitnow.ie.

Australia & New Zealand

Neither Qantas nor Air New Zealand have direct services to Boston; you'll have to change planes and carriers in Los Angeles or San Francisco. From Auckland to Los Angeles, it takes 12 to 13 hours; from Sydney to Los Angeles 13½ to 14½ hours. Add another five to eight hours to Boston, depending on the connections (or lack thereof). From the Australian east coast, typical round-trip fares start at about A$3200 to Boston (A$500 less during the US winter). On Air New Zealand, expect to spend about NZ$3250 to Boston.

STA Travel *(☎ 1300-360-960, 03-9207-5900; *W* www.statravel.com; 224 Faraday St, PO Box 75, Carlton South, Melbourne, Vic 3053, Australia • ☎ 0508-782-872, 09-309-0458; 229 Queen St, Shop 2b, Auckland, New Zealand),* which sells tickets to everyone but has special deals for students and travelers under 30, has offices in major Australian and New Zealand cities. In Australia, don't forget to peruse the Saturday editions of newspapers like the *Sydney Morning Herald* and the *Age.* Kiwis, pick up your *New Zealand Herald.*

Asia

Hong Kong is the discount plane ticket capital of the region, but its bucket shops can be unreliable. Ask other travelers for advice before buying a ticket. The dependable **STA Travel** *(*W* www.statravel.com)* has branches in Hong Kong, Tokyo, Singapore, Bangkok and Kuala Lumpur.

Northwest and Japan Airlines have daily flights to the West Coast where you can get a connecting flight to Boston. Airfares as low as HK$18,700 may be available from Hong Kong to Boston, including a West Coast connection, but more normal fares might hover around HK$21,800.

Central & South America

Most flights from Central and South America go via Miami or Dallas–Fort Worth, though some fly via New York. You can sometimes get incredible deals through discount brokers in Latin America, but they come and go quickly. By scheduled air, typical round-trip fares from major Central American cities, available through websites like W www.expedia.com, are about US$500.

From Rio de Janeiro, Brazil, economy fares often have to be purchased two weeks in advance and minimum stay restrictions apply. You can probably find a flight from Rio for around US$900 in July.

From Caracas, Venezuela, look for prices of around US$650 year-round.

BUS
Boston has a streamlined **bus station** *(Map 4, #65; no phone; 700 Atlantic Ave)* at Summer St, adjacent to the South Station train station and above the Red Line.

Regional Transit
Bonanza Bus Lines *(☎ 617-720-4110, 800-556-3815; W www.bonanzabus.com)* provides service between Boston and Cape Cod, Providence, Hartford, Albany and New York City. **Plymouth & Brockton** *(☎ 508-746-0378, 508-778-9767; W www.p-b .com)* provides frequent service to most towns on Cape Cod, including Hyannis and Provincetown.

Greyhound
Greyhound *(☎ 617-526-1800, 800-231-?222 for reservations; W www.greyhound .com)*, the only nationwide bus company, has reduced local services, but still runs cross-country. Buses depart for New York City throughout the day. Express buses take about 4½ hours and cost $42 one-way, $79 round trip (children are half-price). Long-distance bus trips are often available at bargain prices by purchasing or reserving tickets three days in advance.

TRAIN
Amtrak
Amtrak *(☎ 800-872-7245; W www.amtrak .com)*, the national railway system, stops at South Station, Back Bay Station (Orange Line) and North Station (Green Line).

Express service (4½ to 5 hours) to New York City costs $128 to $152 round trip, depending on the day and time. Service to Manhattan on the high-speed Acela Express train (3½ hours) rules, but you'll have to pay a premium for it: $204 to $254 round trip.

Special advance fares are the cheapest option. While round trips are the best bargain, these might end up costing the same as flying. 'Explore America' fares, the best value, enable you to travel anywhere within 45 days, with up to three stopovers, but you must reserve the entire trip in advance.

For non-US citizens, Amtrak offers USA Rail Passes that must be purchased outside the US (check with a travel agent). Sleeping accommodations cost extra.

Commuter Rail
Head to **North Station** *(Map 3; ☎ 617-222-3200, 800-392-6100; W www.mbta.com; 150 Causeway St)*, accessible via eponymous Green and Orange Line T stations, for excursions to Salem, Gloucester and Rockport (on the Rockport line), and Concord (on the Fitchburg line).

Head to **South Station** *(Map 4; ☎ 617-222-3200, 800-392-6100; Atlantic Ave at Summer St)* for excursions to Plymouth. See the Excursions chapter for information on getting to other nearby areas.

CAR & MOTORCYCLE
From western Massachusetts, the Massachusetts Turnpike ('Mass Pike,' or I-90, a toll road) takes you right into downtown. After paying a toll in Newton, drive east 10 more minutes on the pike and pay another $1; then the fun begins.

There are three exits for the Boston area: Cambridge, Copley Square (Prudential Center) and Kneeland St (Chinatown). Then the turnpike ends abruptly. At that point, you can head north or south of the city on the I-93 Expressway or directly past South Station, into downtown.

From New York and other southerly points, take I-95 north to MA 128 to I-93 north, which cuts through the heart of the city. From northerly points, take I-93 south across the Tobin Bridge, which merges into the Central Artery.

HITCHHIKING
Hitchhiking is never entirely safe, and we definitely don't recommend it. Travelers who decide to hitchhike should understand that they are taking a small but potentially very serious risk. People who choose to hitchhike will be safer if they travel in pairs and let someone know where they are planning to go.

In Massachusetts, hitchhiking is illegal on state highways and the Mass Pike, including rest stops and anywhere on or near exit ramps.

Getting Around

Boston is a small city and your feet will often prove faster than the subway, especially if you have to change lines. If you're thinking about driving, think some more; in fact, keep thinking until you change your mind.

TO/FROM THE AIRPORT
Logan International Airport
Downtown Boston is just a few miles from Logan International Airport, and is accessible by subway (the T), bus, water shuttle, van shuttle, limo, rental car and taxi.

Subway (The T) The MBTA subway (☎ 617-222-3200, 800-392-6100; W www.mbta.com), or the T, is the fastest and cheapest method of transport from the airport. If you are heading to the Red Line, take the Blue Line to Government Center, then take the Green Line Park St for the Red Line (going Blue–Orange–Red Line involves much more trekking). Free, well-marked shuttles connect terminals to the airport Blue Line station. Purchase a $1 token and you'll be downtown within 30 minutes. The subway operates from about 5:30am to about 12:30am daily.

Bus There is a direct **bus** (☎ 800-235-6426) between Logan and the South Station Transportation Center, bay No 25. Participating carriers include Bonanza Bus Lines, Concord Trailways and Plymouth & Brockton. Buses depart all Logan terminals from 7:45am to 10:15pm. From South Station, buses operate from 5:55am to 9:15pm. Buy tickets onboard at Logan or at the South Station counter. Buses cost $9 for adults, nothing for children under 12.

Water & Van Shuttle Accessible via free shuttle buses from each terminal, the **Airport Water Shuttle** (☎ 617-439-3131, 800-235-6426) whisks passengers to Rowes Wharf (Map 4, #43), Atlantic Ave, in seven minutes. Purchase tickets onboard; one-way costs $10 for adults, $5 for seniors, nothing for children under 12. (Round trips cost adults $17.) The shuttle runs from 6am to 8pm weekdays.

Check with your hotel for door-to-door airport van shuttles.

Car & Taxi If you're driving from the airport to downtown or points north, the Sumner Tunnel ($3 toll) will dump you into the North End, where there are immediate on-ramps for I-93 (the Central Artery) north. To and from the airport, use the Ted Williams Tunnel ($3 toll) for points south of Boston. To or from points west, the Mass Pike connects directly with the Ted Williams Tunnel. When you're heading to the airport from downtown Boston, take the Callahan Tunnel. All three tunnels are off I-93 and free when heading inbound.

Plentiful but pricey, taxis line up at every terminal on demand; traffic snarls can easily translate into a $20 fare (plus tip) to downtown.

Manchester Airport
Vermont Transit (☎ 800-231-2222) offers two buses daily (12:20pm and 2:35pm) from the airport to Boston's South Station. One-way fares are $13 for adults, $7 for children.

TF Green Airport
Bonanza Bus Lines (☎ 888-751-8800) departs from this Rhode Island airport for South Station hourly from 9am to 9pm, with an additional early bus at 5:15am and a late one at 1am. Tickets cost $14 for adults, $8 for children.

SUBWAY (THE T)
The **MBTA** (☎ 617-222-3200, 800-392-6100; W www.mbta.com) operates the USA's oldest subway, built in 1897, known locally as 'the T.' There are four color-coded lines – Red, Blue, Green and Orange – that radiate from the principal downtown stations. These central stations are called Park St, Downtown Crossing, Government Center and State. The Park St station has an information booth. When traveling away from any of

these stations, you are heading outbound. Trains operate from about 5:30am to 12:30am daily.

Night Owl service (ie, late night buses), which runs from about 12:30am to 2:30am on Friday and Saturday, picks up where the trains leave off: buses run parallel to most subway stops. You can only catch these buses on Cambridge St outside the Government Center station. Fares are $1. (Socially, it's a great singles scene; olfactory-wise, it's a brewpub.) Because of an impending budget crisis, the Night Owl service may be suspended. Inquire about it before counting on it.

The new Silver Line, a so-called 'rapid' bus, starts at Downtown Crossing and runs along Washington St in the South End to Roxbury's Dudley Square. Fares are 75¢. The Silver Line Transitway, an underground route from South Station to the South Boston Waterfront, was scheduled to open in late 2003 at the time of writing. Don't expect a connector between Downtown Crossing and South Station until 2010, though!

On the Green Line, the 'B' trains head along Commonwealth Ave through Boston University toward the Boston College terminus. 'C' trains follow Beacon St to Cleveland Circle after passing through Brookline's Coolidge Corner. 'D' trains skirt the Fenway and Riverway before stopping at Brookline Village and ending at Riverside. On Huntington Ave, 'E' trains are useful for Northeastern University and the Museum of Fine Arts.

Purchase tokens at all stations (adults $1, children 50¢) except those west of Symphony ('E' branch) and Kenmore ('B,' 'C' and 'D' branches) on the Green Line, which are aboveground stops. If you're aboveground on the Green Line heading outbound, it's free. When you head inbound, though, you must have exact change to board these trains. Some fares heading inbound are higher than $1.

If you are exiting the Red Line at Braintree, you must deposit an additional token. When boarding at the Braintree station, the fare is $2.

CAR & MOTORCYCLE

A car is the last thing you want or need in Boston. But, for convenience, you may

T Visitor Passes

Visitor passes for unlimited travel are available for one week ($22), three days ($11) and one day ($6). Purchase passes at the Boston Common Visitors Information Center and the following T stations: Park St, Government Center, Back Bay, Alewife, North Station, South Station, Hynes and Airport. Bostix (Faneuil Hall Marketplace and Copley Square) also sells passes. For longer stays, monthly passes ($35) are available from the first of the month to the 15th.

want to rent one for a Cape Cod or Cape Ann excursion.

Driving

Not only are streets a maze of confusion, choked with construction and legendary traffic jams, but Boston drivers have their own rules. (For instance, at yellow traffic lights we accelerate rather than brake. When merging into another lane, we don't make eye contact with the driver in the other lane.) Yes, driving is often considered a sport – in a town that takes its sports very seriously.

Parking

Folks on Beacon Hill pony up $150,000 to own a space at the Brimmer Street Garage. There's a reason: supply and demand. And you'll be affected by it, too. Since on-street parking is limited, you could end up paying $25 to $35 daily to park in a lot.

Some lots are cheaper than others. The cheaper ones include:

Along Northern Ave (Map 6) $7 daily
Farnsworth Street Garage (Map 6) Near the Children's Museum. $12 daily
Transportation Building (Map 6) Stuart St. $14 daily
Winthrop Square Garage (First Federal Parking; Map 4) Cnr Devonshire & Federal Sts. $11 daily

For early or late specials, head to:

Boston Harbor Garage (Map 4) Near the New England Aquarium. In by 9am, out by 7pm. $17
Dock Square Parking (Map 3) Near Faneuil Hall. In by 9am, out by 7pm. $17

Government Center Garage (Map 3) Congress
St. In by 10am, out by 7pm. $14
Radisson Hotel Garage (Map 6) Stuart St. After
5pm on weekdays. $12

If you need a space, any space, the **parking
lot** beneath Boston Common (access via
Charles St South) is rarely full. Other than
that, look for the blue 'P' signs around town
and cross your fingers.

The best time to secure an on-street meter
is 8am or 9am. But be sure to have lots of
quarters on hand. Tickets for parking violations begin at $25.

Rental
You'll need to have a valid driver's license,
to be at least 25 years of age and to present a
major credit card. Expect to pay $175 to $275
weekly for a compact car, plus miscellaneous
taxes and surcharges. Boston has the nation's
highest one-day rental fees.

Basic liability coverage is required by
law and included in the rental. While collision insurance is optional, seat belt use is
mandatory for drivers and passengers.

All major rental-car agencies are at the
airport. Downtown rental-car companies
include:

Avis (Map 3, #55; ☎ 617-534-1420, 800-331-
1212) 3 Center Plaza at Government Center
Budget (Map 6, #8; ☎ 617-497-1800, 800-527-
0700) 24 Park Plaza
Enterprise (Map 5, #53; ☎ 617-262-9215, 800-
736-8222) Prudential Center, 800 Boylston St,
ground floor
Hertz (Map 6, #8; ☎ 617-338-1500, 800-654-
3131) 24 Park Plaza
National (Map 10, #37; ☎ 617-661-8747, 800-
227-7368) 1663 Mass Ave, between Harvard
and Porter Squares
Rent a Wreck (☎ 617-576-3700, 800-535-1391)
161 Broadway, Somerville
Thrifty (Map 4, #57; ☎ 617-330-5011, 800-367-
2277) 125 Summer St at High St, near South
Station

TAXI
Taxis do not cruise Boston streets in droves
like they do in New York. But they are usually plentiful enough if you walk to a major

hotel. If you miss the last T, expect to spend
about $16 from Harvard Square to Copley
Square. From the North End or Faneuil Hall
to Kenmore Square, it'll cost you about $12
without much traffic.

Expect buckets of trouble hailing a cab
during bad weather and between 3:30pm and
6:30pm weekdays. Try these taxi companies:
Independent (☎ 617-268-1379) and **Metro
Cab** (☎ 617-242-8000). For lost and found
items call **Boston Police** (☎ 617-536-8294)
for the hackney and carriage division.

BICYCLE
Daredevil Bostonians cycle around town, but
for the most part there are no bike lanes, so
use caution if you take to the city streets on
two wheels. For information on biking and
renting bicycles in Boston, see Activities in
the Things to See & Do chapter. Also see
Maps in the Facts for the Visitor chapter.

You can take your bike on any MBTA
subway line, except the Green Line, from
10am to 2pm and after 7:30pm weekdays
(anytime on the weekend).

ORGANIZED TOURS
You can get a good sense of the city by taking advantage of tours by foot, trolley or
boat. Also see the Things to See & Do chapter, and the special section 'America's
Walking City,' for a close look at neighborhoods and historic sites.

Walking Tours
Boston is easily the country's preeminent
walking city. Perhaps that explains the proliferation of special-interest walking trails.

The 2½-mile **Freedom Trail** (W www.the
freedomtrail.org) is the granddaddy of
walks. Sixteen colonial- and revolutionary-
era sites are connected by red sidewalk
bricks (or a painted red line) that begin near
the Park St T station. It takes one hour to
walk it nonstop, a few hours to take in some
sites. The **National Park Service** (NPS; Map
4, #6; ☎ 617-242-5642; 15 State St) offers
free ranger-led walking tours of the Freedom Trail daily from mid-April to December. Self-guided tour maps are also
available.

Boston by Boat

As the harbor has become cleaner and more integral to Boston's renewed sense of self, the number of boats has proliferated. In fact, if you let your imagination roam a bit, the harbor might feel like the Grand Canal in Venice (in the summer). For recommended trips out to the Boston Harbor Islands State Park, see the Things to See & Do chapter.

MBTA Water Shuttle

This boat (☎ 617-222-3200) plies the waters between Lovejoy Wharf (Map 3, #1), Charlestown Navy Yard (Map 11, #12) and Long Wharf (Map 4, #12). Another route takes you between Lovejoy Wharf, the federal courthouse (Map 4, #60) and the World Trade Center (Map 4, #68) on weekdays. Boats run year-round and one-way tickets cost $1.25; buy tickets onboard.

Boston Harbor Cruises

This company (Map 4, #3; ☎ 617-227-4321; W www.bostonharborcruises.com; 1 Long Wharf) operates year-round boats to the USS Constitution in Charlestown for $1.25. For more information on Boston Harbor Cruises, see Boat Tours later in this chapter. Also see Activities in the Things to See & Do chapter.

City Water Taxi

This service (☎ 617-422-0392) makes on-demand taxi stops at about 15 waterfront points. Since it costs $10 no matter where you're going, it really makes sense only for the airport. That said, though, some stops are useful because of their proximity to lodging places; they include Lovejoy Wharf (Map 3, #1), Charlestown Navy Yard (Map 11, #12), Sargents Wharf (Map 3, #17) and the southern end of Christopher Columbus Park (Map 3). Service operates between April and October.

Africans arrived in Boston as slaves in 1638, a mere eight years after the city was founded, but by 1776 there were more free blacks in Boston than there were slaves. The histories of Boston and the free black community on Beacon Hill are woven together through a dozen stories and 19th-century sites on the 1½-mile **Black Heritage Trail**. Take an excellent free tour given by **NPS** (☎ 617-742-5415) rangers from late May to early September.

Five separate **Women's Heritage Trails** (☎ 617-522-2872; W www.bwht.org) mark Boston women's contributions to various causes. The trails are not marked, so to explore, purchase a $10 booklet from the **NPS** (☎ 617-242-5642).

If you've had your fill of Paul Revere and John Hancock, it might be time for some talk-story about immigrants, the working class and people of color. The 90-minute **MyTown tours of the South End** (Map 6, #37; ☎ 617-536-8696; W www.mytowninc.com), led by teens, cost $10 for adults, with a sliding scale for youth and students; call for times and days.

Boston by Sea (☎ 617-350-0358; W www.bostonbysea.org) is a land-and-water trail that theoretically spans 43 miles from Milton to Revere, but the most accessible portion runs between the Charlestown Navy Yard and Fan Pier. Pick up self-guided tour maps at the NPS and Boston Common Visitors Information Center.

Trolley Tours

These tours offer ease and flexibility because you can hop on and off as you like at about 18 sites, catching the next trolley that comes along (if it has room). The narration is a mix of the arcane, an endless list of Boston firsts, bad jokes, substantive information, drivel, more entertainment than scholarly erudition and a lot of tidbits that elicit a quizzically uplifting 'huh?'

Except for the color of their **trolleys** (orange and green ☎ 617-269-715 • blue

The Big Dig

The depression of the Central Artery and creation of a third harbor tunnel from Boston to the airport is quite simply the largest public works project ever undertaken in the history of the US. Ever. But nothing else about the massive Central Artery/Tunnel (CA/T) project is simple, except perhaps the moniker 'the Big Dig' (☎ 617-951-6400; W www.bigdig.com). And by the time you read this, the project just might be finished! (Well, the current projections are 2005.)

The $15 billion project has been compared to the digging of the Panama Canal, the English Channel Tunnel (Chunnel) and the Alaskan Pipeline. The goal: build an eight- to 10-lane highway below a six-lane one without disrupting the nearly 200,000 cars that use the highway daily, and without disrupting 29 miles of underground utility lines (owned by 31 different companies) that handle upwards of 17 million phone calls per day. The CA/T project has been likened to performing open-heart surgery on someone while they are running a marathon. It's been an impressive feat, marred by relatively few setbacks, considering the magnitude of the project. And there's no escaping it.

When the raised Central Artery opened in 1959, physically and psychologically dividing the city, it carried 75,000 vehicles daily. In 2000 the highway was crumbling and had an accident rate four times the national urban interstate average. 'Rush hours' were ten hours long. The consequences of doing nothing would have been ugly: traffic would have been practically at a standstill during every waking hour by 2010.

So urban planners set about to widen and depress the artery. And for the last 15 years or so, Bostonians have endured daily road closures and unusually elevated levels of dirt, dust and noise. The payoff: direct access from the Mass Pike to Logan Airport, a swath of prime parkland from Chinatown to the North End (unfortunately the last piece of the project), and a magnificent new city symbol, the Lenny Zakim-Bunker Hill Bridge across the Charles River. Incredibly impressive, it's the world's widest cable-stayed bridge and the first with an asymmetrical design.

☎ 617-269-3626 • white ☎ 617-742-1440), all operators offer essentially the same services for the same price. White trolleys, though, offer multilingual narration. Tickets cost $23 to $25 for adults and $22 for seniors and students. The **trolley starting point** (Map 4) is across from the New England Aquarium, but you can also purchase tickets at the **Trolley Shop Store** (cnr Charles & Boylston Sts).

Boat Tours

Ninety-minute narrated sight-seeing trips on Boston Harbor are operated by **Boston Harbor Cruises** (Map 4, #3; ☎ 617-227-4321; W www.bostonharborcruises.com; 1 Long Wharf) from May through October for $17 for adults, $14 for seniors and $12 for children.

Massachusetts Bay Lines (Map 4, #1; ☎ 617-542-8000; W www.massbaylines.com; Rowes Wharf) and **Bay State Cruise Co** (Map 4, #68; ☎ 617-748-1428; W www.baystate cruisecompany.com; 200 Seaport Blvd) have entertainment cruises with DJs or bands for $16 to $20, from mid-June to mid-September.

The **Schooner Liberty Clipper** (Map 4, #4; ☎ 617-742-0333; W www.libertyfleet.com; Long Wharf) makes a two-hour, 12-mile sail around the harbor daily from June through September. Departures are at noon, 3pm and 6pm. Tickets are $30 for adults, $18 for children.

Boston Duck Tours (☎ 617-723-3825; W www.bostonducktours.com) offers unusual land-and-water tours using modified WWII amphibious vehicles. The tours are one of Boston's most popular attractions, and tickets sell out by noon on weekends. Boats depart daily April through November; call for departure location and times. Tickets cost $23 for adults, $20 for seniors and students, and $13 for children.

Things to See & Do

Boston's 18th-century historic sites are perched side-by-side with 19th-century architectural gems, 20th-century museums and other postmodern cultural diversions. They are all woven into this chapter by neighborhood and are accessible by subway. With the exception of the Fenway, Boston's neighborhoods are small enough to walk in a few hours without straining yourself. In this book, Cambridge and Somerville's Davis Square, though separate areas, are treated as Boston neighborhoods. Outlying neighborhoods are all accessible via the subway. Recreational activities are discussed at the end of this chapter.

As for an overview of the neighborhoods, **Beacon Hill** *(Map 2)* is the stuff of Boston postcards and an earlier century. It's absolutely lovely, rich with noble architecture, glowing lanterns and cobblestone streets. It also boasts a few pubs and cafés along Charles St, dense with shops, when you need a break. One of the two most walkable areas in Boston, Beacon Hill arguably provides the most bang for the buck; see the 'America's Walking City' special section for a walking tour of this area. It also has a rich African-American history and abuts lots of green space. Put it on your shortlist of places to visit, no matter how much time you have.

Government Center *(Map 3)* is drab save for Faneuil Hall, a tourist emporium thick with outdoor cafés and shops. Government Center also boasts the oldest city block. The **North End** *(Map 3)*, heavy with Italian accents, authentic cafés and warrens of streets, is worlds away from its adjacent counterpart. It's the *other* most walkable neighborhood; see the 'America's Walking City' special section for a walking tour of the North End. You'd be remiss not to venture within its confines.

You'll encounter two worlds within **Downtown & Waterfront** *(Map 4)*, a sprawling and bustling territory. The former contains a number of important Freedom Trail sites, an outdoor pedestrian mall, the financial district, and lots of colonial buildings wedged in between modern office buildings. The waterfront hugs the harbor and is still feeling the effects of the Big Dig. This area will be radically transformed over the next few years as the enormous construction project that's underway here comes to a graceful conclusion (with parkland where the elevated expressway currently stands, or once stood, depending on when you read this). Harbor tours depart from here, and there are a few worthy museums as well.

Back Bay *(Map 5)*, chock-a-block with elegant brownstones, is most enchanting from late April to early June, when magnolia and dogwood trees are in bloom. Although it's home to successful young professionals and blue-blood Bostonians, Back Bay also has a fringe student population that tempers its tendency toward stodginess. (During the Great Depression, when many families couldn't afford to maintain these lavish single-family houses, the buildings were subdivided into apartments or converted into dormitories.) You'll undoubtedly end up wandering along Newbury St, Boston's most fashionable, stopping to sip a coffee. But make time to reflect at the dramatic Christian Science Mother Church pool, too, or dignified Copley Square. The Prudential Center observatory is here as well. For a complete Back Bay walking tour, see the 'America's Walking City' special section.

The **Theater District** and **Chinatown** *(Map 6)* areas are fairly self-explanatory: one is full of theaters, the other is a community of Chinese immigrants. Nearby, huge swaths of vibrant **South End** *(Map 6)* have been claimed by artists, gay men and young professionals (sending real estate prices soaring). South of Washington St is less gentrified, as housing projects and halfway houses rub elbows with converted condos. The South End neighborhood is predominantly convivial; residents hang out on front porch stoops on warm summer evenings and restaurant-hoppers cruise Tremont St year-round.

Kenmore Square, the Fenway & Brookline *(Map 7)* encompasses three distinct areas. The Kenmore Square area is thick with rowdy bars, dance clubs, inexpensive but nondescript eateries and dormitories disguised as brownstones. It's the epicenter of Boston University (BU) student life and Boston baseball. When you need some breathing room, the Fenway is filled with lots of green space (the Emerald Necklace) and major cultural institutions such as the Museum of Fine Arts (MFA).

Although it seems to be part of Boston proper, Brookline is a distinct entity, with a separate city government. Off the beaten tourist path, it combines lovely, tranquil residential areas with lively commercial zones, including **Coolidge Corner** and **Brookline Village**. Both have deeply rooted Jewish and Russian populations; there are more synagogues and kosher eateries here than anywhere in Boston. They both also feature cafés, eclectic shops and a number of fine restaurants in all price ranges.

Cambridge explorations center around distinct 'squares.' Although **Harvard Square** *(Map 8)* has lost its grungy edge – independently owned shops continue to be gobbled up by national chains – it's still worth your while to check out the overflowing cafés, shops, bookstores, restaurants and street musicians. The 'pit,' the brick plaza above the T station, is a mecca for skateboarders with baggy pants, and homeless teenagers. Dominated by Harvard University and colonial sites, the surrounding streets also abound with street performers and tourists. Brattle St is arguably the loveliest street in the whole city.

Kendall Square *(Map 9)* is alive and well thanks to the high-tech and biotech industries that have moved into its renovated brick warehouses. The One Kendall Square complex, at Hampshire and Broadway Sts, is its social nucleus, with restaurants, bars, coffeehouses and a nearby cinema.

Getting under the skin of 21st century Boston means getting into the neighborhoods; **Inman Square** *(Map 9)* epitomizes this in the same way that Brookline's Coolidge Corner and the waterfront's Fort Point Channel do. **Central Square** *(Map 9)*, formerly gritty and funky, is now home to

Seven Days In Boston

Day 1	Wander the cobblestone streets of Beacon Hill
Day 2	Visit the American Collection at the Museum of Fine Arts (MFA)
Day 3	Navigate the Harbor Islands, including Little Brewster's lighthouse
Day 4	Drink in the North End's sites, sounds and aromas
Day 5	Tour the ivory towers of Harvard and MIT
Day 6	Walk the Freedom Trail and Black Heritage Trail
Day 7	Tour the Emerald Necklace by bicycle

yet another Starbucks café. Although transformed, Central Square has retained enough cool music clubs, ethnic eateries and shops to keep it interesting. It's still the nexus for Cambridge's alternative scene, such as it is.

Mass Ave, Porter Square & Davis Square *(Map 10)* will give you a sense of the region sans tourist attractions. Mass Ave to Porter Square is lined with offbeat shops and restaurants that feed residents on either side of it. Davis is one of the hipper neighborhoods in metro Boston, with good cafés, alternative theater and lively nightlife.

Charlestown *(Map 11)*, best explored in conjunction with the North End, boasts good views of downtown Boston as well as a trio of important historical sites: the Charlestown Navy Yard, USS *Constitution* and Bunker Hill Monument. Thanks to the Big Dig, it now has a number of fine parks, too. Quaint streets are lined with gas lanterns, as well as attached brick row houses, wooden residences and stone houses that have been restored by young urban professionals. This influx of new blood has caused a tad of lingering tension between the blue-collar 'townies' and their new neighbors. Great for plain old wandering, the streets leading up to Monument Square are the best.

BEACON HILL (MAP 2)

Boston's anti-slavery activity is well documented via the neighborhood's Black

Heritage Trail. The city's Freedom Trail meanders through Beacon Hill as well (see Walking Tours in the Getting Around chapter).

There are two faces to Beacon Hill; Pinckney and Myrtle Sts, which run east–west along the crest of the hill, act as the dividing line. On the south slope, below Pinckney St to Boston Common, houses are grand and distinguished. On the north slope, above Myrtle St to Cambridge St, row houses are more modest. Charles St, which divides 'the flats' from the hill, is lined with antique shops, neighborhood haunts and fancy restaurants.

The area is bordered by Boston Common, Public Garden, Beacon and Cambridge Sts and Storrow Dr. The Park St and Charles/MGH T stops (Red Line) bring you to two different edges of Beacon Hill.

Built in 1810, the noble **Park St Church** *(Map 2; ☎ 617-523-3383; cnr Tremont & Park Sts; open 9:30am-3:30pm Tues-Sat mid-June–Aug, by appointment Sept–mid-June)*, with an elegant 217ft steeple, is both visually stunning and historically important. From this church's pulpit William Lloyd Garrison railed against slavery in 1829, and Katherine Lee Bates' hymn 'America' (the unofficial national anthem) was first sung on Independence Day in 1831.

The **Old Granary Burying Ground** *(Map 2; Tremont St)*, between Park and Beacon Sts, dates from 1660 (two others in Boston are even older) and is graced by exceptional headstone carvings. You'll find the remains of numerous revolutionary leaders, including Paul Revere, Samuel Adams, James Otis and John Hancock, interred here. Also buried here are Crispus Attucks (the freed slave who died in the Boston Massacre when British soldiers fired into a group of protesting colonists in 1770), Benjamin Franklin's parents (he's buried in Philadelphia), Peter Faneuil (of Faneuil Hall fame) and Judge Sewell, the only magistrate to denounce the hanging of the so-called Salem witches. The graveyard was so crowded with Revere's compatriots that when Revere died at the ripe old age of 83, there was barely room for him.

Highlights & Lowlights

The good stuff:

- Walking over the Longfellow Bridge at sunset
- Rollerblading along the Charles River on Sunday afternoon
- Looking for 17th-century gravestones
- Pondering globalism at the Christian Science Center's Mapparium
- Getting some perspective atop the Prudential Center observatory
- Exploring compact neighborhoods by foot
- Marveling at the Zakim Bridge from atop the Bunker Hill Monument
- Cheering in the bleacher seats at Fenway Park

The not so good stuff:

- Driving anywhere in town
- A dearth of parking spaces
- Early closing times at bars and clubs
- The wasteland called Government Center Plaza
- Lack of public funding for contemporary arts

The magnificent bas-relief **Robert Gould Shaw Memorial** *(Map 2, #23; Beacon St)*, across from the Massachusetts State House, was sculpted by Augustus St Gaudens after nearly 13 years of work. It honors the 54th Massachusetts Regiment of the Union Army, the nation's first all-black Civil War regiment, depicted in the 1989 film *Glory*. The soldiers, led by 26-year-old Shaw (the son of a wealthy Brahmin family), steadfastly refused their $10 monthly stipend for two years until Congress upped it to $13, the amount white regiments were paid. Shaw and half his men were killed in a battle at Fort Wagner, South Carolina. A highly recommended, free National Park Service (NPS) tour of the Black Heritage Trail departs from here (see Walking Tours in the Getting Around chapter).

The magnificent **First Harrison Gray Otis House** *(Map 2; ☎ 617-227-3956; 141 Cambridge St; adult/senior/child $5/4/2.50)* was the first of three houses designed at the turn of the 18th century for Mr Otis, who was at various times a real estate developer, US senator and Boston mayor. The Federal brick house is wonderfully symmetrical, if perhaps a bit severe. Note the squat 3rd floor, which is a hair's breadth higher than 6ft. The Society for the Preservation of New England Antiquities rescued the house after it had become a women's bath and rooming house. Tours are given hourly from 11am to 4pm Wednesday to Sunday.

Massachusetts State House

Within the golden-domed capitol (Map 2; cnr Beacon & Bowdoin Sts), the idiosyncrasies of governance and politics are played like a sporting match. Designed by Boston's beloved Charles Bulfinch and completed in 1798, this commanding structure was built upon Boston's highest peak, on grazing land owned by John Hancock. The corner stones were laid by Samuel Adams and Paul Revere; Revere returned four years later to cover the leaking dome with copper. Today, it's weatherproofed with 23-carat gold leaf.

Free 40-minute **tours** (☎ 617-727-3676) are offered between 10am and 3:30pm Monday through Friday; reservations are recommended. The tours include anecdotes about the history (like the fact that the state's constitution is the world's oldest existing constitution), art collection, architecture and local political personalities. You can also visit the legislative chambers when congress is in session. Note the carving of the 'Sacred Cod' in the House chambers; it stands as testimony to the importance of this now-dwindling species to the local economy. Interesting self-guided tours are possible from 9am to 5pm Monday through Saturday.

Front-lawn **statues** honor important Massachusetts figures, among them politician Daniel Webster; Civil War general Joe Hooker (while the general did 'encourage' women to 'entertain' his soldiers, the term 'hooker' did not originate with him); religious martyr Anne Hutchinson; Quaker Mary Dyer, who was hanged on Boston Common in 1660; President John F Kennedy; educator Horace Mann; and Senator Henry Cabot Lodge.

Museum of Afro-American History

This museum (Map 2, #13; ☎ 617-725-0022; W www.afroammuseum.org; 46 Joy St; admission free; open 10am-4pm daily summer, 10am-4pm Mon-Sat winter), which includes the African Meeting House and Abiel Smith School, is an excellent place to learn about Beacon Hill's African-American roots. The resource center has an extensive library, interactive computer programs and permanent exhibits, including a replica classroom.

The **African Meeting House** (☎ 617-723-8863) was built in 1806 by African-American tradesmen and is now the country's oldest standing black church. Abolitionists William Lloyd Garrison (who began the New England Antislavery Society here) and Frederick Douglass delivered stirring calls to action within this hall. The plain interior belies the passions roused within, but on a quiet day you can almost hear the fiery orations reverberating off the hallowed walls. When African Americans migrated from Beacon Hill to the South End and Roxbury in the late 19th century, the Irish and Jews, in turn, relocated here from the North End. For a while, the meeting house served an Orthodox Jewish congregation.

The **Abiel Smith School** was the country's first building constructed for the sole purpose of being a black public school.

Boston Common

Established in 1634, the 50-acre green (Map 2; between Tremont, Park, Beacon & Charles Sts) is the country's oldest public park. The Common has long been a place of amusements and protests, military trainings and concerts. While the park is certainly full of life, it's also full of monuments to more than 350 years of activity. The **Park St T Station**, a national landmark, is one of the subway's four original stations. **Flagstaff Hill**, great for sledding in winter, is crowned by a Civil War **Soldiers & Sailors Monument**. During the Revolutionary War, British troops camped here, and until 1830 the land was used for cattle grazing. The bronze **Boston Massacre Monument** memorializes the 18th-century colonists' quest for freedom from economic tyranny (see the boxed text

'Boston Massacre' later in this chapter). The 18th century also saw many public hangings at the **Great Elm Site**. Artist Gilbert Stuart is buried in the 1756 **Central Burying Ground**, near Tremont and Boylston Sts.

Although there is still a grazing ordinance on the books, today the Common serves picnickers, sunbathers, people-watchers and squirrel-feeders. The **Frog Pond**, site of the city's first public water system in 1848, hosts winter skating and summertime splashing (see Activities later in this chapter). Shakespearean drama is performed each August at the **Parkman Bandstand**; see the boxed text 'Free Outdoor Fun' in the Entertainment chapter. Colorful characters are often heard spouting off from atop a soapbox, real or imagined, near the Park St T station.

The **Boston Park Rangers** (☎ 617-635-7383), who offer free tours of the Common and Public Garden, are based at the **Visitors Information Center** (Map 2, #36; Tremont St; open 8:30am-5pm Mon-Sat, 9am-5pm Sun), near West St. The center has public restrooms.

Public Garden

The Public Garden (Map 2; between Charles, Boylston, Beacon & Arlington Sts) is a 24-acre botanical oasis of cultivated flower beds, clipped grass, ancient trees, ornamental flowering species and a tranquil lagoon ringed by weeping willows. Until it was filled in the early 19th century, it was (like the rest of Back Bay) a tidal salt marsh. You can't picnic on the lawn like you can on the Common, but this formal French-style park has plenty of benches. Pick one in front of the **swan boats** (adult/child $1.75/1), pedal-powered vessels that ferry children and adults around the pond while ducks swim alongside squawking for bread crumbs. Boat rides are available from mid-April to late September. (Children accustomed to animated computer games will likely get antsy after about 30 seconds; some adults might too.)

Hidden among notable specimen trees you'll find the **Ether Fountain** (it's a curious thing to memorialize an intangible substance), the **George Washington Statue** (whose replica sword is stolen every year by enthusiastic fraternity freshmen), the **George Robert White Memorial** (in honor of a generous Boston benefactor) and the **Make Way for Ducklings** statues (commemorating the children's book).

GOVERNMENT CENTER & NORTH END (MAP 3)

This 'neighborhood' covers two wholly distinct areas, one sprawling (by Boston standards) and one densely compacted. Government Center contains disparate elements such as Boston's most touristed destination (Faneuil Hall and its adjacent marketplace) and its least visited (the Old West End). You'll find the oldest block in Boston (the charming Blackstone Block) and one of the newest areas (Government Center was built from the ground up in the 1960s). In between, the North Station area has lively bars, a hostel, a transportation center and a sports arena.

The North End boasts impressive colonial sites, lots of local color and an abundance of edible, Italian riches (think cannoli, pasta and red wine). Boston's most compact and original neighborhood is also still the most tight-knit quarter of the city. Long separated from the rest of the city by the Central Artery (John F Fitzgerald Expressway), this enclave is a world unto itself and hopes to remain that way. Put it high on your list of places to visit.

Many T stations are convenient to the area. For Faneuil Hall, get off at Government Center (Green and Blue Lines) or State (Orange and Blue Lines). North Station is on the Green and Orange Lines. From any of these T stations, you can also walk to the North End. Directions to the North End are impossible due to the ever-changing timetables and vagaries of construction. Hanover St is the main thoroughfare, and as you'll soon see, the narrow jumble of streets is not receptive to autos; you could crawl faster than drive in the North End. The area is encircled by Commercial St on the waterfront.

Government Center Area

This area, bound by New Sudbury, Court, Cambridge and Congress Sts, occupies the

Scollay Square of yore. Before it was razed in the early 1960s, the bustling area was home to bawdy clubs and seedy nightlife. Prior to its decline and pave-over, it had been the site of several important historic events. The first Quaker meeting was held here (remember, in Boston at that time Quakers, such as Mary Dyer, were hanged); the *Liberator*, an anti-slavery newspaper, was published from this site; John and Abigail Adams lived here with their son John (both men were later US presidents), as did Zabdiel Boylston, the inventor of the smallpox vaccine; Alexander Graham Bell invented the telephone in his office here; and Thomas Edison invented the stock ticker from the very same office. Ah, if only today's inhabitants were so distinguished!

Erected in the 1960s, **City Hall Plaza** *(Map 3)* is a cold 56-acre concrete plaza surrounded by federal and state office buildings. Designed by IM Pei (who also designed the Kennedy Library and John Hancock Tower), it's home to the fortresslike **Boston City Hall**, a top-heavy mass of concrete, brick and glass. There have been plans afoot for years to create a more inviting City Hall Plaza, but city planning, mired as it is in local politics, creeps at a snail's pace. The high-rise **John F Kennedy Federal Building** anchors the northern edge of the plaza. The plaza is well suited to large public gatherings and summertime performances (see the boxed text 'Free Outdoor Fun' in the Entertainment chapter).

The plaza's high points are the gracefully curved brick **Sears Crescent** *(Map 3; cnr Court & Tremont Sts)*, with its 227-gallon **steaming kettle** *(Map 3, #49)* on the western tip of the building. The sweeping curve of the modern **Center Plaza** *(Map 3; Cambridge St)*, mirrors the Sears Crescent nicely. There is a tiny opening through the building that peers onto Pemberton Square and the grand French Second Empire Suffolk County Courthouse.

The **Old West End** *(Map 3; north of Cambridge St)*, once a teeming maze of row houses and narrow streets, was razed in the 1950s and replaced with wider roads, massive concrete government buildings and clusters of high-rise apartment buildings. Consequently, there's nothing much to recommend here except the **Ether Dome** *(Map 3, #33;* ☎ *617-726-2281; usually open 8am-6pm)*. The domed operating room is where ether was first used as an anesthetic in 1846. It's located of the 4th floor of Massachusetts General Hospital's 1823 Bulfinch building, the oldest hospital building in the complex. Mass General remains one of the world's finest teaching and research hospitals.

The **North Station area**, a little grid of narrow streets and brick commercial buildings off Causeway St, is noteworthy primarily because it comes as such a surprise. It is wedged between the expressway, the grand **Edward W Brooke Courthouse** *(Map 3; cnr New Chardon & Merrimac Sts)*, the **Fleet Center** sports arena and **North Station** *(Map 3; Causeway St)*. Between the car traffic and the elevated Green Line, it's a noisy and lively area, with pubs and sports bars. The **Sports Museum of New England** *(Map 3, #2;* ☎ *617-624-1234; 5th & 6th floors, Fleet Center, Causeway St; adult/senior/child $6/4/4)* houses interactive hockey and basketball exhibits featuring local sports legends such as Bobby Orr and Larry Bird.

Museum of Science This museum *(Map 3;* ☎ *617-723-2500;* Ⓦ *www.mos.org; Science Park, Charles River Dam; adult/senior/child $12/10/9; open 9am-5pm Sat-Thur, 9am-9pm Fri Sept-June, 9am-7pm daily July & Aug)*, is an educational fun house, especially for children. With more than 550 interactive exhibits, daily live presentations, and a discovery center for small children, you could spend an entire day here. Favorite exhibits include the world's largest lightning bolt generator, a full-scale space capsule, a 'virtual reality fishtank' of the undersea world and a 20ft model of a *Tyrannosaurus rex* dinosaur.

The museum also houses the **Hayden Planetarium** *(adult/senior/child $8/7/6)* and **Mugar Omni Theater** *(adult/senior/child $8/7/6)*. The planetarium boasts a state-of-the-art projection system that casts a heavenly star show, programs about black holes and other astronomical mysteries, and evening laser light shows with rock music. The Omni, a five-story wraparound theater, makes you feel as if you're actually experiencing whatever is projected around you:

the Grand Canyon, Antarctica or even the inside of a human body.

Combination tickets to the museum, planetarium and the Omni save about $3. Use the Science Park stop on the Green Line.

Blackstone Block Named after Boston's first settler, there's no other place in Boston where you can step back in time so easily. This tiny warren of streets, bounded by Union, Blackstone, Hanover and North Sts, dates back to the 17th and 18th centuries. Established in 1826, **Ye Olde Union Oyster House** *(Map 3, #42; 41 Union St)* is Boston's oldest restaurant. Around the corner in Creek Square, the c. 1767 **Ebenezer Hancock House** *(Map 3, #39; 10 Marshall St)* is a gem (it now houses offices). Ebenezer, a mason and bricklayer, was John Hancock's brother. At the base of the souvenir shop next door, the 1737 **Boston Stone** *(Map 3, #37)* served as the terminus for measuring distances to and from 'the Hub.' The addition of the 1982 **Bostonian Hotel** *(Map 3; North St)* could have been disastrous to this historic block, but its intimate scale fits perfectly and the architects preserved all the old streets, including the adjacent Scott Alley, a narrow covered passageway. The open air **Haymarket** *(Map 3, #41)* takes place on Blackstone St (see the boxed text 'Farmers Markets' in the Shopping chapter).

Check out the two lifelike bronze **James Michael Curley statues** *(Map 3, #46; North St)*, between Union and Congress Sts. One likeness wasn't enough to capture the controversial mayor's irrepressible spirit. Just beyond, the 1995 **New England Holocaust Memorial** *(Map 3, #44; cnr Union & Congress Sts)* is comprised of six glass columns etched with 6 million numbers in memory of those who perished during the Holocaust. Inside each tower is a pit, representing a major Nazi death camp, with smoldering coals sending plumes of steam up through the glass towers. While the presentation is particularly dramatic at night, its placement across from boisterous bars is quite disconcerting.

Faneuil Hall Marketplace Between North and Congress Sts, **Faneuil Hall** *(Map 3;*

☎ *617-242-5675; open 9am-5pm daily)*, pronounced 'fannel' or 'fan-yul,' was first constructed as a market and public meeting place in 1740 by Boston benefactor and merchant Peter Faneuil and was enlarged by Bulfinch in 1899. Over the years, numerous orators have held forth here; the 2nd floor is still used for public meetings. The **Ancient & Honorable Artillery Co of Massachusetts** *(Map 3, #50; ☎ 617-227-1638; 4th floor; open 9am-3:30pm daily)*, which was chartered in 1638, maintains a strangely interesting collection of antique firearms, political mementos and curious artifacts.

Dock Square *(Map 3)*, between the hall and Congress St, is graced with a statue of Sam Adams. Also, note the outlines of Boston's 1630 shoreline that are sandblasted in the pavement.

East of Faneuil Hall, four granite buildings comprise the **Faneuil Hall Marketplace** *(Map 3; ☎ 617-338-2323)*. The central Greek revival **Quincy Market** was the heart of Boston's produce and meat industry for almost 150 years, while the **North Market** and **South Market** buildings flanking it were commercial warehouses. All were redeveloped in the 1970s into today's colorful, festive shopping and eating mecca. Behind them, **Marketplace Center**, built in 1985, insulates the area from the waterfront.

North End

Wandering through the maze of streets today, it's hard to imagine anyone living here besides ancestors of the current Italian-American residents. But others did. The North End was a fashionable Tory enclave prior to the American Revolution. When the Loyalists decamped for Nova Scotia, free blacks settled around Copp's Hill, calling the area 'New Guinea.' After they relocated to Beacon Hill in search of better employment opportunities, successive waves of Irish, Eastern European Jews, Portuguese and Italians settled here and opened small businesses in the 19th and early 20th centuries.

Paul Revere House Originally built in 1680 in the wake of the fire of 1676, this small clapboard house *(Map 3, #27; ☎ 617-523-1676;*

THINGS TO SEE & DO

www.paulreverehouse.org; 19 North Square; adult/senior/student/child $3/2/2/1; open 9am-5:15pm daily mid-Apr–Oct, 9:30am-4:15pm daily Nov–mid-Apr, closed Mon Jan–Mar) violated building codes by not using brick. The house has survived and is worth a visit – and not just because it's the oldest house in Boston. The hourlong self-guided tour provides a great history lesson. A blacksmith (and goldsmith, silversmith, copper engraver and false-teeth maker), Revere was one of two horseback messengers who carried advance warning of the British march into Concord and Lexington on the night of April 18, 1775 (for more about these towns see the Excursions chapter). Revere was the father of 16 children. He owned the house for 30 years but lived here only for 10 years during the revolutionary period. Behind the house, the family well stood next to the outhouse – you can imagine the unhealthy results!

For a small additional fee, you can also visit the **Pierce-Hichborn House** *(Map 3, #28)* next door.

Old North Church Also called Christ Church, this 1723 place of worship *(Map 3; ☎ 617-523-6676; W www.oldnorth.com; 193 Salem St; open 9am-6pm Mon-Fri, 9am-5pm Sat & Sun, closed for funerals)* is Boston's oldest church and a beloved national historic landmark. It's best known as the place where sexton Robert Newman hung two lanterns from the steeple on the night of April 18, 1775, as a signal that the British would march on Lexington and Concord via the sea route. The 175ft steeple, made in three tiers, houses the oldest bells (1744) still rung in the US. Today's steeple is a 1954 replica, since severe weather toppled two prior ones. The 1740 weather vane is original. Inside, tall boxpews, many with brass nameplates of early parishioners who had to purchase their pews, fill the graceful interior. The pews were designed to retain the warmth generated by boxes filled with heated bricks in winter. The brass chandeliers used today were first lit on Christmas in 1724. Note the candles – there is no electric lighting in the church. This remains an active church; the grand organ is played at the 11am Sunday service.

Great Molasses Flood

Imagine a 50ft-high wave of the sticky liquid – over 2 million gallons of it – flowing down Foster and Commercial Sts at 35mph, swallowing warehouses, smashing houses and smothering 21 people and 100 horses. It happened. At about noon on January 15, 1919, a 90ft-tall tank of molasses exploded at the Purity Distilling Co, a munitions manufacturer. It was impossible to stop the 14,000 tons of gooey stuff. Various rumors circulated: the Germans did it; political anarchists did it; there was alcohol in the tank (the disaster happened during Prohibition). In the end, a structural problem with the tank was determined to be the cause. Trying to clean it up was nightmarish; even with the aid of high-pressure fire hoses and saltwater (to 'cut' the molasses), traces of molasses remained for years. Old-timers say that on certain days, the breeze still resurrects the smell.

Old North sponsors the show **Paul Revere Tonight** *(adult/child $12/8; 8pm Thur & Fri mid-June–Oct)*, in which a costumed actor portrays Revere.

At the back of the adjacent gift shop, a tiny **'museum'** displays such oddities as a strand of George Washington's hair and a vial of liquid purported to be tea from the Boston Tea Party. Often overlooked are several quaint courtyards located to the left of the church entrance.

Copp's Hill Burying Ground There are excellent views of the waterfront and Charlestown Harbor from the city's second-oldest cemetery *(Map 3; Hull or Charter Sts)*, established in 1660 and home to an estimated 10,000 souls. The oldest graves, located just beyond the crest of the hill, belong to cobbler William Copp's children. (Copp was the original purchaser of the land.) Look around for rebel activist Daniel Malcolm's headstone, used for target practice by the British. (Take the path to the crest, turn left and walk toward Snowhill St until you reach the large tree on the left; Malcolm's grave is to the left of the tree.) During the Battle of Bunker Hill on June 17, 1775, British troops rained artillery onto Charlestown from here. There are upwards of a thousand free blacks from the late 18th and early 19th centuries buried here, along with politically powerful religious leaders Increase (father), Cotton (son) and Samuel (grandson) Mather. Their graves are near the Charter St gate.

DOWNTOWN & WATERFRONT (MAP 4)

The downtown financial district has been extolling the stuff of work-a-day worlds for a long time: family trust funds have been managed on State St since the 17th century, and the area has been a bustling commercial center ever since.

Boston's waterfront has long played a vital role in the city's development, but not since colonial times has it felt so vibrant and full of promise. When the Big Dig concludes in 2005, the distinct downtown and waterfront districts will be reunited by parkland; the area will look and feel completely different. There is perhaps no other modern US city engaging in such a radical transformation of its core. Until then, you'll still want to navigate the extensive shoreline for harbor tours, museums and great views of downtown.

Downtown is bound by Essex, Tremont and State Sts. For downtown, use the State T stop (Blue and Orange Lines) for northern points, and Park St (Green or Red Lines) or Boylston (Green Line) for western and southern sights. The waterfront hugs the shoreline from the North End to South Boston. For the waterfront, use the Aquarium T stop (Blue Line) or South Station (Red Line). A myriad of boats ply the waterfront (see the boxed text 'Boston by Boat' in the Getting Around chapter).

Downtown

Plenty of buildings illuminate the area's lengthy history, but since most of the streets were laid out in the 17th and 18th centuries, getting around can be confusing. Our map will come in quite handy! Major Freedom Trail sites, all worth seeking out and highlighted here, grace this area, but there are a

Italian Festivals

North End social clubs each have a patron saint whom they honor yearly by hoisting its life-sized likeness onto a wooden platform and carrying it through the streets. Residents toss confetti from balconies, along with dollar bills that are pinned to banners streaming off the saint.

You can count on a festival almost every weekend in July and August. Some festivals, though, are bigger than others, particularly St Anthony's in late August. Although still quite traditional, many North Enders escape these weekends, complaining that the events are too commercial. Nonetheless, don't miss a chance to attend if you're in the area. Most festivals have outdoor bands and street vendors selling greasy food.

few other notable sites as well. We'll start with the latter.

Named King St until the revolution, **State St** was the most important byway during colonial times. Starting in 1710, crewmen and cargo docked at Long Wharf (which, prior to landfill reclamation, extended all the way to the Custom House) and traveled straight up to the Old State House and then down Washington St. What Wall St is to New York, State St was to colonial Boston.

The lower portion of the **Custom House** (Map 4), begun in 1837, resembles a four-sided Greek temple. In 1913 the federal government, having exempted itself from local height restrictions, decided something more grand was needed and financed a 500ft tower to crown it. Bostonians were aghast at the city's first skyscraper, a whopping 16 stories tall, but have since grown to love it, especially its 22ft illuminated clock. Today, the most memorable building in Boston's skyline is – gasp! – a Marriott luxury time-share condo. Free 30-minute daily tours at 10am and 4pm are offered on the **observation deck** (☎ 617-310-6300). The 1st floor has a small free **exhibit of maritime art and artifacts** from the famed Peabody Essex Museum (see Salem in the Excursions chapter). Go inside to check out the **lobby rotunda**.

Omni Parker House (Map 4, #16; ☎ 617-227-8600; 60 School St), the grand dame of Boston hotels, hosted literary luminaries such as Hawthorne, Whittier, Emerson and Longfellow back in the mid-19th century. They gathered here to exchange ideas at their 'Saturday Club.' But the list of notable guests doesn't stop there: Charles Dickens slept here, Ho Chi Minh worked in the kitchen, JFK announced his presidency here and John Wilkes Booth stayed here 10 days before assassinating President Lincoln. (Booth was visiting his thespian brother who was performing nearby; his visit also included some practice at a local rifle range.) The hotel's bar, the **Last Hurrah** (☎ 617-227-8600), is a swank place for a drink. A bowl of warm roasted nuts accompanies your libations.

Diagonally across School St is a marker for the site of the country's first public school (1635), **Boston Public Latin School** (Map 4, #17). A hopscotch sidewalk mosaic, *City Carpet*, commemorates the site of the school where Franklin, Emerson and Charles Bulfinch were educated.

Province House Steps (Map 4, #21; off Province St) are all that remain of the former 1679 residential mansion of the royal governor of Massachusetts Bay. (The steps actually led to gardens.) From here, General Gage ordered that Redcoats head to Lexington and Concord (see the Shot Heard Round the World section in the Facts about Boston chapter). These little steps make Boston Boston. All around, for those with keen eyes and interest, are vestiges of 17th-century Boston.

Dreams of Freedom (Map 4, #23; ☎ 617-338-6022; ⒲ www.dreamsoffreedom.org; 1 Milk St; adult/senior/student/child $7.50/6.50/6.50/3.50; open 10am-6pm daily) isn't as powerful and moving as Ellis Island, but it's still well worth a visit. It chronicles the history of immigrants from Puritans in 1620 to waves of Irish and Italians, and more recently Vietnamese and Portuguese. The intimate gallery space personalizes the emotional stories with interactive and high-tech exhibits.

Boston Bricks (Map 4, #37; Winthrop Lane), a narrow brick passageway near handsome Winthrop Square, is a delightful dose of public art. Each brick depicts themes, events and sites unique to Boston: the Underground Railroad, the molasses flood, graveyards, rowers, Boston Latin, smoots, Scollay Square, fish, swan boats and the Boston stone. Return at the end of your Boston visit and see how many you recognize.

Post Office Square (Map 4; between Congress, Franklin & Pearl Sts), a delightful vest-pocket park with specimen trees and plenty of benches, is the best place to rest. At its northern edge, **Angell Memorial Park** once served as a watering spot for horses. Its pond sculpture (complete with bronze water lilies and pond life) is dedicated to George Angell, a founder of the Society for the Prevention of Cruelty to Animals (SPCA). While you're here, peek in at **Alexander Graham Bell's laboratory** (Map 4, #40; 185 Franklin St; admission free; open daily), off the lobby of the adjacent Verizon Building. Check out the telephone inventor's re-created workshop and the life-sized mural that pays homage to an entire lineage of telephone employees.

King's Chapel & King's Chapel Burying Ground

The compact granite church (Map 4; ☎ 617-227-2155; 58 Tremont St; open 10am-4pm Sat Sept-Apr; 10am-4pm Mon, Thur & Fri, 1pm-3pm Sun May-Aug) you see today was designed by Peter Harrison and built in 1754 around the original 1688 wooden structure to avoid disrupting services. When the external building was complete, the wooden church was taken apart and tossed out the windows. After the revolution, it became the country's first Unitarian church. If the church seems to be missing something, it is: building funds ran out before a spire could be added. The church houses the largest bell ever cast by Paul Revere, as well as a lovely sounding organ. **Classical recitals** are given at 12:15pm Tuesday year-round. Donations of $2 are suggested.

The adjacent burying ground contains the graves of John Winthrop, the first governor of the fledgling Massachusetts Bay Colony; William Dawes, who rode with Revere to

Harvard University, Cambridge

Beacon Hill and Charles River from Longfellow Bridge

Old State House, Downtown

Trinity Church, Back Bay

Faneuil Hall Marketplace, Government Center

warn of the British march on Lexington and Concord; Elizabeth Pain, the model for Hawthorne's Hester Prynne in *The Scarlet Letter*; and Mary Chilton, the first woman to set foot in Plymouth. It's probable that for every grave marker, there are an additional 15 unmarked graves.

Old Corner Bookstore At the corner of School and Washington Sts, this c. 1718 building *(Map 4, #18)* once housed Boston's most illustrious publishing company, Ticknor & Fields, publisher of books by Thoreau, Emerson, Hawthorne, Longfellow and Harriet Beecher Stowe. Between 1845 and 1865, the authors often held lively discussions and meetings here. Today, it houses the Boston Globe Store, which sells front-page reprints of historic events covered in the eponymous newspaper.

Old South Meeting House This brick meeting house *(Map 4, #22; ☎ 617-482-6439; W www.oldsouthmeetinghouse.org; 310 Washington St; adult/senior/student/child $5/4/4/1; open 10am-4pm daily Nov-Mar, 9:30am-5pm daily Apr-Oct)*, with a soaring steeple, was built in 1729, but another building stood here as early as 1670. (Ben Franklin was baptized in the first building.) The largest hall in pre-revolution Boston, Old South was the scene of a typically feisty town meeting where colonists decided to protest the British tea taxation (see the Tempest in a Teapot section in the Facts about Boston chapter, and the Waterfront section later in this chapter). Phillis Wheatley, a former slave and the nation's first recognized African-American poet, worshiped here. When this congregation moved to Back Bay in 1875, Ralph Waldo Emerson and Julia Ward Howe gathered support to convert the church into a museum.

Old State House The location of this 1713 building *(Map 4, #5; ☎ 617-720-3290; W www.bostonhistory.org; 206 Washington St; adult/senior/student/child $5/4/4/1; open 9am-5pm daily)* is significant. It once commanded a waterfront view down State St and stood at the head of Washington St, the city's only 18th-century thoroughfare. The site is best

Boston Massacre

On March 5, 1770, Sons of Liberty Sam Adams, John Hancock and about 40 other protesters provoked the British soldiers with snowballs, curses and trash. Panicked British soldiers fired on the angry mob. Five townspeople were killed, sparking anti-British sentiment. The troops were moved quickly to Castle Island (in present-day South Boston). A propagandist and jack-of-all-trades, Paul Revere helped fan the flames by widely disseminating an engraving that depicted the scene as an unmitigated slaughter. Interestingly, John Adams and Josiah Quincy, both of whom opposed the heavy-handed authoritarian British rule, represented the accused soldiers in court. The lawyers firmly believed that all accused were entitled to a fair trial. (Seven of the nine soldiers were acquitted, and the remaining two had their hands branded as a sign they were guilty of manslaughter.)

known for its balcony, from where the Declaration of Independence was first read to Bostonians on July 18, 1776. Note the rooftop replica lions and unicorns, symbols of the English Crown. The originals were torn down after the Declaration of Independence was read. The first governor of Massachusetts, John Hancock, was inaugurated here. Inside, a museum operated by the Bostonian Society is definitely worth a visit. It houses revolutionary memorabilia pertinent to Boston's (and thus the nation's) history.

A cobblestone traffic island across from the balcony of the Old State House marks the **Boston Massacre site** *(Map 4, #6)*; see the boxed text.

The highly informative **National Park Service Visitors Center** *(Map 4, #6; ☎ 617-242-5642; 15 State St)* is nearby.

Waterfront

East of Atlantic Ave, the waterfront becomes more accessible with each passing year. A public path, officially designated the 'HarborWalk,' runs along the outer edge of most wharf buildings from Columbus Park to the new federal courthouse.

To escape Faneuil Hall crowds or the cramped North End, head to **Columbus Park**, just north of Long Wharf. There you will find plenty of benches, moored sailboats, a grassy knoll, a trellised archway draped with wisteria and a cobblestone walkway.

Rowes Wharf, shared by the Boston Harbor Hotel and ferry boat terminals, is one of Boston's most beautiful commercial developments. Head through the enormous domed, arched gateway to the terminal's octagonal glass pavilion, undoubtedly the country's most elegant ferry waiting room.

New England Aquarium Teeming with sea creatures of all sizes, shapes and colors, this giant fishbowl *(Map 4; ☎ 617-973-5200; W www.neaq.org; Central Wharf; adult/senior/child $15.50/13.50/8.50, senior noon-4pm Mon Jan-late May free; open 9am-5pm Mon-Fri, 9am-6pm Sat & Sun)* is equally popular with adults and children. Harbor seals and sea otters, frolicking in a large entrance observation tank, introduce the main indoor attraction: a three-story, cylindrical saltwater tank. It swirls with more than 600 creatures great and small, including turtles, sharks and eels. Leave time to be mesmerized by the *Echo of the Waves* sculpture, not to mention the Coastal Rhythms exhibit, which explores the lives and habitats of animals at water's edge. Sea lion shows take place four or five times daily.

The Aquarium also has an IMAX theater. If you've never encountered IMAX, now's the time. Adventure documentaries such as *Sharks!*, *Volcano* and *Everest* are shot with technology designed to make you feel smack in the middle of the action. It's so realistic that it causes motion sickness and scares the wits out of young children. Call for show times and advance ticket purchase.

Fort Point area Beyond the Summer St or Congress St Bridges over Fort Point Channel is a district of old brick warehouses, the center of the nation's wool trade until the 1960s. The core of this enclave stretches along and around the first few blocks of Congress and Summer Sts. Note the gracefully curving **Melcher St warehouses**. Most of these old buildings – until recently – bustled with a preponderance of artists and busy loading docks. But as the area becomes more developed, the artists who revitalized it are being squeezed out and put on the endangered species list.

The nucleus for the Fort Point Arts Community is their **gallery** *(Map 4, #73; ☎ 617-423-4299; 300 Summer St)*, and the **A St Diner** *(Map 4, #74; cnr Melcher & A Sts)*, a neighborhood institution with Formica tables, red benches, and kitschy and avant-garde art. It serves a mix of artists, businesspeople and construction workers. You want to know what's happening to this district? Step into this microcosm.

South Station *(Summer St)*, when it was built in 1900, was the world's largest railroad station. Decades of heavy use took their toll, but a late-1980s renovation brought the magnificent gateway back up to par. Today, the curved five-story building is formally called the South Station Transportation Center to include the abutting bus station. The grand terminal is alive with fast-food eateries, café tables, a newsstand and, on many summer afternoons, live concerts.

The **Leather District**, a little pocket of uniform brick buildings – along South and Lincoln Sts – was built after the great fire of 1872. Many of the five- and six-story buildings have Romanesque arches, big windows and carved ornamentation. They shelter some fine art galleries, a few funky restaurants and shops and increasingly pricey residential lofts.

Children's Museum The iconic giant white **milk bottle** on Fort Point Channel is the only sign necessary for this delightful museum *(Map 4, #67; ☎ 617-426-8855; W www.bostonkids.org; 300 Congress St; adult/senior/child 2-15 yrs/child 1 yr $8/7/7/2, admission 5pm-9pm Fri $1; open 10am-5pm Mon-Sun)*. Children of all ages can be entertained for an entire day with interactive educational exhibits. Highlights include bubble displays, dress-up areas, a two-story climbing gym and an exhibit on what it's like to be a Tokyo teen. (Be forewarned: it's crowded from 5pm to 9pm Friday!)

Boston Harbor Islands State Park

Until recently, Boston Harbor had the unenviable distinction of being the country's dirtiest harbor. After a massive, multimillion-dollar cleanup in the mid-1990s, the harbor is gaining a healthier reputation. It's a good thing, too, since there are more than 30 large and small islands that offer plenty of history, picnic spots, nature walks and fishing. A kiosk (☎ 617-223-8666; W www.bostonislands.com) on Long Wharf dispenses details on all islands overseen by the National Park Service and a number of state agencies.

Georges Island, the jumping-off spot for all other islands, features a 19th-century fort. It's the only island with fresh water and food. Lovell Island is the largest, good for walking along dunes, marshes and meadows. Look for wild raspberries on Bumpkin Island and for a variety of birds on Grape Island. Gallop's has a sandy beach, while Peddock's is the most diverse, with the remains of a c. 1900 fort. Allow a half day to visit Georges, and a whole day to visit the outer islands. Boston Light, the nation's oldest staffed lighthouse (1716), guards the harbor's entrance at Little Brewster Island; it's open only for tours.

Boston Harbor Cruises (Map 4, #3; ☎ 617-227-4320; W www.bostonharborcruises.com; Long Wharf), off Atlantic Ave, offers a regular ferry service from May through October. Purchase round-trip tickets (adult/senior/child $10/8/7) to Georges Island where you can catch free water taxis (another five to 10 minutes) to smaller islands. Boats run hourly. For information on island camping, see Downtown & Waterfront in the Places to Stay chapter.

For spectacular vistas of Boston's skyline and the harbor, consider a ranger-led **Boston Light Tour** (☎ 617-223-8666) on Little Brewster Island. Trips depart early June to mid-October from two locations: Fan Pier (Saturday and Sunday; adult/senior/student/child $25/20/20/15) and John Fitzgerald Kennedy Library & Museum (Thursday and Friday; adult/senior/student/child $29/22/22/15, including admission to the museum). Call for exact departure times (usually 10am and/or 2pm).

Beaver II & the Boston Tea Party Museum

This ship and museum (Map 4, #63; ☎ 617-338-1773; W www.historictours.com; Congress St Bridge) stand as testimony to the spirited colonists who refused to pay the levy imposed on their beloved beverage. In 1773, after a rabble-rousing town meeting at the Old South Meeting House, the rabble donned Native American garb as disguise, boarded the *Beaver* (the *Beaver II*, which you board today, is an approximate replica) and dumped all the tea overboard in rebellion. At the time of writing the ship and museum were temporarily closed due to fire. When it's open, costumed guides tell the story, and the adjacent museum offers multilingual information and a complimentary cup of tax-free (Salada) tea.

South Boston Waterfront Separated from Boston proper by the jellyfish-laden Fort Point Channel, this area has always afforded spectacular views of Boston, but until recently it had been neglected by city officials,

ignored by developers and inaccessible to the public. No more! The area's development presents the most important urban planning issues Boston has faced since the master plan for Government Center (or perhaps the filling of Back Bay). The development plan calls for thousands of units of housing, small-scale city blocks, mostly low-level buildings, condos, offices, parks, hotels, a $700 million convention center and a new Institute for Contemporary Art on the water's edge.

The sweeping **Moakley Federal Courthouse** occupies the most prominent site on **Fan Pier**. Walk around it to get a good sense of Boston's links to the past and visions of the future. On the water side, there is a lovely park with brick and granite walkways. Downtown views are stunning from here.

As the old makes way for the new, the retail lobster establishment **James Hook & Co Lobsters**, established in the 1920s, clings to life between the Moakley and Northern Ave Bridges. So does the Barking Crab (see the Places to Eat chapter).

Discounts & Freebies

If you're planning on blitzing Boston museums, **City Pass** (W *www.citypass.net*) can save you some cash. The pass is valid for nine days and admits you to the John F Kennedy Library, New England Aquarium, Harvard Museums of Natural History, Prudential Center Skywalk, Museum of Fine Arts and Museum of Science. Priced at $30.25 for adults and $18.50 for children aged 3 to 17, the pass saves you 50% off the total cost of admission.

The following places and/or tours are always free: tours of the Black Heritage Trail, State House, Boston Common and Public Garden, as well as entry to the Museum of Afro-American History (all on Map 2); tours of the Custom House observation deck and a visit to Alexander Graham Bell's laboratory (Map 4); tours of the Christian Science Church and entry to the Mary Baker Eddy Library for the Betterment of Humanity, plus lectures and programs at the Boston Public Library (Map 5); entry to the galleries at MassArt and the grounds of Arnold Arboretum (Map 7); entry to the Semitic Museum (Map 8); entry to the List Visual Arts Center (Map 9); entry to the Mt Auburn Cemetery (Map 10); and entry to the USS *Constitution* Museum and lots of tours within the Charlestown Navy Yard, as well as climbing the Bunker Hill Monument (Map 11).

The following offer free (or discounted) admission on certain days to certain groups: New England Aquarium (Map 4; free for seniors on Monday afternoon from January to late May); Institute for Contemporary Art (Map 5; free from 5pm to 9pm on Thursday); Photographic Resource Center (Map 7; free on Thursday); Isabella Stewart Gardner Museum (Map 7; $3 for students on Wednesday); Museum of Fine Arts (Map 7; voluntary contribution suggested from 4pm to 9:45pm on Wednesday); Fogg Art Museum, Busch-Reisinger Museum and Arthur Sackler Museum (Map 8; all free from 10am to noon on Saturday); Harvard Museums of Natural History (Map 8; free from 9am to noon on Sunday).

BACK BAY (MAP 5)

During the 1850s, when Boston was experiencing a population and building boom, Back Bay was an uninhabitable tidal flat. To solve the problem, urban planners embarked on an ambitious and wildly successful 30-year project: to fill in the 450-acre marsh (using the dam that had been dotted with mills running from Beacon Hill to Brookline), lay out an orderly grid of streets (including service alleys), erect magnificent Victorian brownstones and design high-minded civic plazas. It would take one day to fill enough land for two house lots – one day, that is, of 35-car trains hauling gravel every 45 minutes between Boston and a nearby quarry. The hard labor was done by Irish immigrants. The result, Back Bay, is one of Boston's architectural treasures.

The area is bounded by the Public Garden and Arlington St to the northeast, Mass Ave to the southwest, the Charles River to the northwest and Stuart St and Huntington Ave to the southeast. Cross streets are laid out alphabetically from Arlington St to Hereford St. Back Bay's alphabetical grid street pattern is easy to decipher. Hallelujah! Take the Green Line T to Copley for Copley Square (or the Orange Line to Back Bay), to Hynes/ICA for the hip end of Newbury St and to Prudential ('E' line) for the Christian Science Center.

Comm Ave Mall

A solid link in Frederick Law Olmsted's Emerald Necklace (see the boxed text 'Emerald Necklace' later in this chapter), this grand boulevard – the Champs Élysées of Boston – connects the Public Garden with the Back Bay Fens. The grassy nine-block parkway is dotted with a diverse selection of public sculptures (almost one for every block), benches for relaxing and stately trees. Unfortunately, the trees on the mall are succumbing to the virulent Dutch elm disease. As they do, they're being replaced with more disease-proof varieties. A two- or three-block stroll down the mall is a great introduction to the neighborhood's stately brownstones.

Gibson House Museum

To appreciate the opulence of 19th-century Back Bay mansions, visit this house *(Map 5, #3; ☎ 617-267-6338; 137 Beacon St; open for tours only Wed-Sun May-Oct, Sat & Sun Nov-Apr)*. Interestingly, the exterior of this splendid five-story Victorian brownstone barely merits a glance. Inside, though, it's filled with a charming mishmash of bric-a-brac, mementos and antiques. **Tours** *(cost $5, child under 12 free)* are given at 1pm, 2pm and 3pm. The **Victorian Society** *(☎ 617-789-3927)* is headquartered here.

Newbury St

International boutiques and galleries get tonier as you get closer to the Public Garden (see Newbury St in the Shopping chapter). Approaching Mass Ave, you'll see more nose rings, platform shoes and dyed hair. Newbury St is fun at night when shops are closed but the well-lit windows are dressed to the nines, and when darkness cloaks your less-than-Armani attire.

Institute for Contemporary Art

Although the ICA *(☎ 617-266-5152; 955 Boylston St; adult/senior/student/child under 12 $7/5/5/free, admission 5pm-9pm Thur free; open noon-5pm Wed & Fri, noon-9pm Thur, 11am-5pm Sat & Sun)* doesn't have a permanent collection, it livens up Boston's conservative art scene by showcasing avant-garde art by well-known national artists and unknown regional artists. The quirky space, within a renovated 19th-century police station, isn't always conducive to highlighting art at its best. That's one reason the ICA is planning a move to the waterfront in 2006.

Christian Science Church

Known to adherents as the 'Mother Church' *(Map 5; ☎ 617-450-3790; w www.tfccs.com; 175 Huntington Ave; admission free; open 10am-4pm Mon-Sat, 11:30am-4pm Sun)*, this is the international home base for the Church of Christ, Scientist (Christian Science), founded by Mary Baker Eddy in 1866.

The grand 1894 classical revival basilica, which can seat 4000 worshippers, boasts the largest organ in the Boston area. (The amazing 13,000-pipe organ was made in Boston.) The expansive, formal plaza has a 670ft-long **reflecting pool**. Tours run from 11:30am to 3:30pm daily, except on Sunday when there is only one tour at 11:30am.

Next door, you'll definitely want to visit the **Mary Baker Eddy Library for the Betterment of Humanity** *(Map 5, #67; ☎ 617-450-7000, 888-222-3711; w www.marybakereddy library.org; admission free; open 10am-9pm Tues-Fri, 10am-5pm Sat, 11am-5pm Sun)*, a four-story structure with a nice airy **café**. The 1st floor contains the Hall of Ideas, which includes a fountain of water and words, with quotes from great global thinkers. It also boasts the truly unique **Mapparium**, one of Boston's hidden treasures. The Mapparium is a room-sized, stained-glass globe that you can walk through on a glass bridge. Geopolitical boundaries are drawn as the world appeared in 1935. The acoustics, which were a surprise to the designer, are a wonder: no matter how softly you whisper into the ear of your companion, everyone in the room will hear you perfectly!

Second-floor galleries deal with the 'search for the meaning of life,' both on a personal and global level. Kids will enjoy the interactive kiosks. The offices of the internationally regarded daily newspaper the *Christian Science Monitor* (w www.csmoni tor.com), which Eddy founded at age 87, are also housed here. You can peer into the newsroom and delve into a notion of journalism that explores questions that matter. The heart of the library's collections, Eddy's papers and transcripts, are on the top floors and accessible by permission. The whole place is a wonderfully contemplative, inspiring place.

Copley Square

This high-minded square – set between Dartmouth, Clarendon and Boylston Sts, and St James Ave – is surrounded by significant historic buildings, including Trinity Church and the Boston Public Library.

The magnificent **New Old South Church** *(Map 5; ☎ 617-536-1970; 645 Boylston St;*

Mary Baker Eddy

Mary Baker Eddy (1821–1910) grew up in New Hampshire a sickly, pious, stubborn child with a great love of study. Her first husband died before she gave birth to their first child. Alone, penniless and in poor health, she was forced to marry again. During that time, she began studying homeopathy and other alternative methods for wellness. As she lay alone one day in 1866, bedridden, she began to read a biblical account of how Jesus had healed the sick. By the time she put down the book, she was healed. For three years, she retreated to formulate Christian Science principles, a belief system based on a rational understanding that the mind is an inalienable part of the greater goodness that is God.

Mary Baker Eddy taught that by consciously working to gain 'the mind of Christ,' humans can enter into a state in which spirit is more powerful than – and in command of – material things, including the human body. Gaining this spiritual state involves patience, humility, repentance and tribulation, and includes among its tasks the cure of human illness through prayer.

Science & Health, which details her philosophy, was published in 1875 to mixed reviews. 'Critics took pleasure in saying that the book was wholly original, but would never be read,' Eddy noted wryly. To date, the book has sold more than 9 million copies.

In 1879, Eddy and a small group of adherents founded the Church of Christ, Scientist, which, unusual among sects at the time, encouraged the full equality of men and women. In 1881, Eddy founded the Massachusetts Metaphysical College in Boston to train practitioners in Christian Science healing arts. Men and women were equally welcome, and the training provided hundreds of women with careers, allowing them a measure of financial self-sufficiency – something Eddy prized.

open 9am-7pm daily mid-June–early Sept; 9am-4:30pm Mon-Fri, 9am-2pm Sat & Sun early Sept–mid-June) is referred to as the 'new' Old South because up until 1875, the congregation worshiped in their original home, now called the Old South Meeting House. Please note that hours can be variable.

Duck into the 1912 **Fairmont Copley Plaza Hotel** (Map 5; cnr St James Ave & Dartmouth St), with Boston's most opulently appointed lobby. Crystal chandeliers, veined marble and other lavish touches abound in the lobby, restaurant, bar, 'oval room' and grand ballroom. This plaza hotel was designed by the same architect who did New York's famed Plaza Hotel.

Next door, the 62-story **John Hancock Tower** (200 Clarendon St) was constructed with more than 10,000 panels of mirrored glass. Because it reflects more sky and clouds than land, the building isn't nearly as intrusive as its mass would suggest. Designed in 1976 by IM Pei, the tower suffered serious initial problems: inferior glass panes were installed and when the wind whipped up (which it does frequently here), the panes

popped out, plummeting hundreds of feet to the ground. The area was quickly cordoned off and all the panes were replaced. Luckily, no one was ever hurt (but the engineers' egos took a drubbing). A sophisticated early-detection glass monitoring system was added to warn of future stress problems. Recalling that Back Bay is one great landfill, the building's weight also caused water table problems (flooded basements) for the tower's neighbors.

Copley Square has plebeian-sized, down-to-earth elements, too. Since the finish line for the Boston Marathon fronts the Boston Public Library and runners end up in a staging area here, the square honors the athletes who compete. Don't overlook the **Boston Marathon Monument** (Map 5, #58), embedded in the sidewalk on Boylston St near Dartmouth St. The **Tortoise & the Hare** (Map 5, #59), a bronze cast by sculptor Nancy Schon (who cast *Make Way for Ducklings* in the Public Garden), honors the philosophical differences between sprinters and slow-and-steady long-distance runners. There's also a refreshing fountain and a

Farmers Market *(open 11am-6pm Tues & Fri June-late Oct).*

Trinity Church

Designed by Henry Hobson Richardson from 1872 to 1877, this church *(Map 5; ☎ 617-536-0944; 206 Clarendon St; open 8am-6pm Mon-Sat, services only Sun)* is one of the nation's truly great buildings. But for all his creative work, the Harvard-educated Richardson was paid less than one percent of the final construction costs. (The project did come in at almost four times over the original estimated cost of $200,000; what's an artist to do?) The granite exterior, with a massive portico and side cloister, uses sandstone in colorful patterns. The grand but compact French and Romanesque building rests on 2000 wooden pilings, typical of massive Back Bay buildings, which must be kept submerged in water in order to maintain their strength and integrity.

Boston Public Library

The esteemed BPL *(Map 5; ☎ 617-536-5400; w www.bpl.org; 700 Boylston St; open 9am-9pm Mon-Thur, 9am-5pm Fri & Sat, 1pm-5pm Sun)* dates from 1852 and lends credence to Boston's reputation as the 'Athens of America.' True to the exterior's inscription, all of its fine lectures and programs are free.

The library contains great works of art and special collections, including John Adams' personal library. Frequent tours of various collections are given, including the rare book collection (which, for some reason, boasts a lock of John Hancock's hair). The 3rd floor features John Singer Sargent's unfinished Judaic and Christian murals, which were criticized for anti-Semitic messages. Many wished he hadn't departed from his usual portraits.

The original McKim building, inspired by Italian Renaissance palazzi, features enormous bronze doorways by Daniel Chester French flanked by iron gates and lanterns. From there a palatial marble staircase leads to the absolutely splendid **Bates Hall Reading Room**, restored in mid-1990 to its original glory. (The whole library is undergoing a long-term renovation project.) Even the most mundane musings are elevated by the barrel-vaulted, 50ft coffered ceilings. Some of the furniture dates from the library's 1895 opening.

Although more than 2 million people visit annually, most bypass the walled-in tranquil Italian-style **courtyard** garden, which has a reflecting pool and trees.

THEATER DISTRICT, CHINATOWN & SOUTH END (MAP 6)

'Midtown Cultural District' is a fancy name, used mostly by the mayor's office, for the Theater District, home to large and smaller-scale performance venues. Its neighbor Chinatown is a thriving, colorful and tight-knit community. The South End National Historic District, distinct from its aforementioned neighbors in style and substance, boasts the country's largest concentration of Victorian row houses. Side streets retain their London-style architectural flavor with side-by-side residences, steep stoops and tiny ornamental gardens. After 150 years and a recent infusion of upwardly mobile gay style, it's returned to the fashionable state that early developers intended.

Chinatown is bordered by Essex, Hudson, Tremont and Marginal Sts. The Theater District is roughly bordered by Tremont, Boylston and Charles St South. The South End is contained by Huntington Ave, Mass Ave, Albany St and the Mass Turnpike. Columbus Ave and Tremont St, lined with au courant restaurants, are the principal commercial streets.

The Chinatown T station is on the Orange Line; the Boylston T station, closer to the Theater District and Bay Village, is on the Green Line. From South Station (Red Line), it's just a five-minute walk to Chinatown. The South End is served by the Back Bay stop (Orange Line); Silver Line buses operate along Washington St.

Theater District

During the 18th century, waterfront wharves and marshy shoreline made up the area around Stuart and Washington Sts, but by the mid-1800s, thanks to a landfill, it was terra firma. Actors from England and Europe performed on stages so close together that underground tunnels were built between them, allowing patrons to go from one to another without getting wet during rainstorms. In the 1940s, Boston had over 50 theaters. The area today is tiny by New York standards, but the opulent palaces that remain have recently received long-needed face-lifts.

The 1925 **Wang Center for the Performing Arts** (268 Tremont St), opulent, baroque, gilded and cavernous, was modeled on the Paris Opera Comique. The Wang then became a movie palace before falling into a state of disrepair to be bailed out by early computer innovator An Wang.

Next door the colonial revival **Wilbur Theater** (246 Tremont St) premiered Thornton Wilder's *Our Town* and Tennessee Williams' *A Streetcar Named Desire*, starring a youngster named Marlon Brando.

Across the street, the illustrious **Shubert Theatre** (265 Tremont St), with Florentine doors, a marble entryway and Ionic columns, originally hosted *The King and I*, *Camelot* and Richard Burton's *Hamlet*. Its chandelier replicates one that's in Le Petit Trianon at Versailles. Nearby, the small **Charles Playhouse** (76 Warrenton St) was originally built as a church and wasn't converted into a theater until the late 1950s.

The beaux arts **Emerson Majestic Theatre** (219 Tremont St) was restored to its ornate majesty and luster by Emerson College in 1983. The lavish space in the high rococo style, decked with marble and neoclassical friezes, showcases many nonprofit and multicultural performance troupes.

Around the corner, the **Colonial Theatre** (106 Boylston St), ingeniously enveloped by an office building, is still resplendent with all the gilded ornamentation, mirrors and frescoes it had in 1900.

Boylston Place (off Boylston St), a tiny pedestrian-only alley marked by Greek tragedy and comedy masks, is lined with bars and nightclubs (see the Entertainment chapter). Daytime action takes place within the adjacent, massive and drearily named **State Transportation Building** (10 Park Plaza). Look for an atrium courtyard with fast-food vendors, free lunchtime concerts and art exhibits.

Chinatown

This tiny area is overflowing with ethnic restaurants (many open until 4am), bakeries, markets selling live animals, import and textile shops, and phone booths topped with little pagodas. The enormous **Chinatown Gate** (Map 6, #20; near cnr Beach & Hudson Sts) guards the entrance. In addition to the Chinese, who began arriving in the late 1870s, this community of 8000 also includes Cambodians, Vietnamese and Laotians. **Beach St**, **Harrison Ave** and **Tyler St** are the most colorful.

Bay Village

A charming and tight-knit gay neighborhood, Bay Village is certainly worth a stroll. It's wedged inside Stuart, Arlington, Marginal and Charles St South. With its early-19th-century attached brick houses, the quiet enclave resembles a scaled-down Beacon Hill. Buildings of particular note include **1 Bay St** (built in the 1830s), **115 Broadway** (note its Art Deco details) and the **Fayette St row houses**. The **Park Plaza Castle** (Map 6; cnr Arlington St & Columbus Ave), built in 1897 for an organization founded to guard the governor of Mass Bay Colony, it's now used as an exhibition and convention space for the Park Plaza Hotel.

South End

In the mid- to late 1800s, when South End tidal flats had been filled, the area offered a fashionable and spacious alternative to Beacon Hill. But by the end of the century, the middle class had fled to new suburbs like Brookline and the upper class jumped ship for Back Bay. The neighborhood slumped until the 1970s, when landlords began converting the elegant but decrepit brownstones from rooming houses to condos.

Historically, the South End has been Boston's most ethnically, racially and economically diverse neighborhood. Sammy Davis Jr, and Louis Mayer (of Metro-Goldwyn-Mayer movie mogul fame) both grew up here, as did Lebanese immigrant and poet Kahlil Gibran. Martin Luther King Jr and Coretta Scott King lived here while MLK was a Boston University theology student.

Community Activism

The South End has a rich and deeply rooted history of community activism. As early as 1968, activists feared gentrification would bring displacement. To dramatize Boston's lack of affordable housing, community leader Mel King and nearly 100 others staged a protest on the parcel that **Tent City** *(Map 6)*, a mixed-income housing project, would eventually occupy at Dartmouth St and Columbus Ave. Built in 1988, Tent City was the first development to link high-end commercial projects with more affordable ones that benefit all community members; in order to build Copley Place, developers had to build Tent City.

The primarily Puerto Rican housing project **Villa Victoria** *(Map 6, #69)*, between West Dedham and West Brookline Sts, was built during the 1970s in response to another community's fears of displacement. Although the buildings are not particularly aesthetic, the thriving enclave emphasizes outdoor spaces, shops and barrier-free walkways for the wheelchair-bound.

Deep in the South End, between Harrison Ave and the expressway, the **Pine St Inn** *(Map 6)* provides social services and shelter for homeless individuals. Housed in the former Fire Dept Headquarters, modeled after the Palazzo Vecchio in Florence, Italy, the organization is highly visible in more ways than one.

Renamed in honor of onetime slave and Underground Railroad organizer Harriet Tubman, the **United South End Settlements** *(Map 6, #75)*, also known as the Harriet Tubman House, houses an energetic social service agency at Columbus and Mass Aves.

Despite skyrocketing real-estate prices, it remains a fairly diverse neighborhood.

Columbus Ave Area Paved and landscaped, perfect for strolling or urban jogging, the **Southwest Corridor Park** *(Map 6)* is almost 5 miles long. It runs from behind the Copley Place mall on Dartmouth St to the Forest Hills T station near Arnold Arboretum. Walk northeast from Mass Ave for rewarding views of the Back Bay skyline. **St Botolph St** *(Map 6)* is also pleasant for walking. Triangular **Columbus Square** *(Map 6; cnr Columbus Ave & Warren St)* has two statues honoring activism and freedom: the **Harriet Tubman Statue** (she spoke in Boston often, galvanizing abolitionists) and the **Emancipation, 1913 Statue**, erected on the 50th anniversary of the Emancipation Proclamation.

Tremont St It might as well be dubbed 'restaurant row' for the amount of fashionable eateries along this stretch of Tremont. You'll also want to stroll the particularly quaint and tranquil streets and parks (most completed in the 1850s and 1860s) just off Tremont, including the elliptical **Union Park** *(Map 6)* between Tremont St and Shawmut Ave. The narrow Rutland Square, just north of Tremont

St, is really just a strip of grass and flowers that is surrounded by an iron gate, but the intimate scale brings the whole street together.

A contemporary arts scene also thrives at the **Boston Center for the Arts** *(BCA; Map 6; ☎ 617-426-5000; 539 Tremont St)*. The BCA houses theaters and exhibition spaces, including the **Cyclorama** *(Map 6, #55)*, an enormous domed performance venue. Around the corner, ballerinas practice pirouettes at the spiffy **Boston Ballet Center** *(Map 6, #53; ☎ 617-695-6950; 19 Clarendon St)*; call about special tours. The Boston Ballet performs at the Wang (see the Entertainment chapter).

South of Washington St In 17th- and 18th-century Boston, Washington St was the only through road. And for most of the 20th century, the Washington St El, one of the country's first elevated trains, followed alongside it. When the Orange Line was rerouted underground in the 1980s, the El was demolished, leaving a wide scar and destroying the link between the area's minority communities and economic opportunity downtown. For years, blighted Washington St was ignored, but no more. In the wake of a red-hot real estate market, developers' interest in the area has been reignited and it gets tonier by the minute. The street, by the way, is now served by the new Silver Line Transitway.

The large brick warehouses between Harrison Ave and Albany St have long housed artists in walk-up flats. In mid-September South End Open Studios provides public access to this artistic enclave.

When the 1875 **Cathedral of the Holy Cross** *(Map 6; cnr Washington & Union Park Sts)* was built, it was America's largest Catholic cathedral, as big as Westminster Abbey. It's definitely worth a look. Throughout 2002, this was the site of almost daily protests against Cardinal Bernard Law, America's most senior bishop. As presiding archbishop, he was accused of having a major cover-up role in the scandal that enveloped the Catholic community in Boston involving sexual abuse by priests. In December 2002 the pope accepted Law's resignation as archbishop.

KENMORE SQUARE, THE FENWAY & BROOKLINE (MAP 7)

This enormous area is really three separate neighborhoods. The lively, student-oriented Kenmore Square is dominated by Fenway Park (home of the Boston Red Sox), sports bars and the behemoth BU, which stretches along Comm Ave. A half-dozen other area colleges add to the mix.

South of Kenmore Square is the Fenway, named for its centerpiece, the Back Bay Fens or 'the Fens.' The Fens is just one section of an interconnected park system (see the boxed text 'Emerald Necklace' later in this chapter). Barely west of the Fens, a little cluster of streets is lined with low-quality student housing (with nicely maintained exteriors) and modestly priced restaurants. You'll also find two renowned museums – the Museum of Fine Arts and the Isabella Stewart Gardner Museum – in the Fenway, along and just off Huntington Ave.

Brookline Village ('D' branch Green Line) and Coolidge Corner ('C' branch Green Line), both in the town of Brookline, lie ten minutes east of Kenmore Square via public transportation. There aren't sites, per se, in Brookline; these villages will simply yield an insider's view of Boston neighborhoods.

Consider having a meal, catching a movie or doing some window shopping here.

Kenmore Square Area

Over the years, Kenmore Square has been a transient home for '60s hippies, '70s and '80s punk rockers and modern-day students and panhandlers. These days it's also been spiffed up with a new hotel. There's not much to do in the square itself, but it's easy to find: look for the mammoth 60-sq-ft **Citgo sign** *(Map 7, #29)* that has marked the spot since 1965. Two blocks away, **Lansdowne St** is Boston's 'club central' – the strip is lined with boisterous bars and nightclubs.

West of Kenmore Square, the experimental **Photographic Resource Center** *(Map 7, #25; ☎ 617-353-0700; 832 Comm Ave; adult/ senior/student $3/2/2, admission Thur free; open noon-5pm Tues-Sun, noon-8pm Thur)*, in BU's Morse Auditorium, is one of the few centers in the country devoted exclusively to this art form. It has a well-stocked **library** *(open Tues, Thur & Sat)*.

A few blocks further west, BU's main research library, **Mugar Memorial Library** *(Map 7; ☎ 617-353-3696; 771 Comm Ave)*, has outstanding **special collections** *(open 9am-4:45pm Mon-Fri)* and 20th-century archives that balance pop culture and scholarly appeal. There are several rotating exhibits on the 1st, 3rd and 5th floors: you may see Bette Davis' Oscar statue for the 1935 film *Dangerous* (Davis grew up in nearby Somerville and Newton); works by President Teddy Roosevelt and the poet Robert Frost; as well as the most extensive collection of BU alumnus Dr Martin Luther King Jr's papers. It's quite a remarkable assemblage.

Isabella Stewart Gardner Museum

The Gardner *(Map 7; ☎ 617-566-1401; W www.gardnermuseum.org; 280 The Fenway; adult/senior/student/child under 18 $10/7/ 5/free, student Wed $3, adult Sat & Sun $11; open 11am-5pm Tues-Sun)* is a magnificent Venetian-style palazzo built to house 'Mrs Jack' Gardner's collection, but was also her home until her death in 1924. A monument to one woman's exquisite taste for acquiring unequaled art, the Gardner is filled with

Fenway Park

Boston's most cherished landmark? Site of Boston's greatest dramas and worst defeats? That's easy. To many Bostonians, it's not Bunker Hill or the Freedom Trail, not Harvard or MIT, but tiny old Fenway Park, home of baseball's Red Sox. It's where names such as Babe Ruth, Ted Williams, Yaz and Jim Rice are uttered as reverently as any hero from Boston's colonial history. Pitcher Pedro Martinez, shortstop Nomar Garciaparra and batting champ Manny Ramirez are the new stars in this constellation, adding to their legacies game by game.

Red Sox fans are nothing if not loyal, despite the team's failure to win a World Series in more than 80 years. Much of the team's ill fate is attributed to the legendary Curse of the Great Bambino, the 1918 sale of their best young pitcher, Babe Ruth, to the hated rival New York Yankees. The Red Sox have not won a World Series since that season, while Babe Ruth and the Yankees went on to achieve success and fame throughout the century. Many believe the sale of Ruth to be among the worst transactions in professional sports history. Yes, it's time to 'reverse the curse.'

Fenway Park is a baseball mecca. One of the last survivors of old-style baseball parks, the field itself has a devoted following beyond that of the team. Only Wrigley Field in Chicago rivals it in age and uniqueness. Baseball played in Fenway is made special by the unique geometry of the park. Thanks to its downtown location, an economy of space gives the Fenway Faithful an intimate proximity to the playing field. Fenway also has the one and only Green Monster, a towering left-field wall that compensates for the relatively short distance from home plate. The Green Monster consistently alters the regular course of play – what appears to be a lazy fly ball could actually drop over the Monster for a home run, and what appears to be a sharp double into the gap may be played off the wall to hold the runner to a single.

Park **tours** (☎ 617-236-6666; adult/senior/child $8/7/6) are offered from Gate E on Landsdowne St hourly (9am to 2pm weekdays when there isn't a game), from April to September. For more information on attending games, see Spectator Sports in the Entertainment chapter.

almost 2000 priceless objects, primarily European, including outstanding tapestries and Italian Renaissance and 17th-century Dutch paintings.

Mrs Jack's will stipulated that the collection not change one iota after her death. That helps explain a few notably empty spaces on the walls: in 1990 the museum was robbed of nearly $200 million worth of paintings, including a beloved Vermeer. The walls on which they were mounted will remain bare until the paintings are recovered (highly unlikely). The palazzo itself, with a four-story greenhouse courtyard, is a masterpiece, a tranquil oasis, alone worth the price of admission. The Gardner has a nice café that's open for lunch.

Huntington Ave

Dubbed 'Avenue of the Arts,' a concentrated area of major and minor artistic and cultural venues, Huntington Ave extends

from **Horticultural Hall** (a grand 1901 English baroque building at 300 Mass Ave) and **Symphony Hall** (across the street) to the Massachusetts College of Art, or MassArt. The **Museum of Fine Arts, Boston**, a prominent cultural institution on Huntington, houses a world-renowned collection (see the boxed text 'The MFA in Half a Day').

The **Northeastern University** campus stretches out along Huntington Ave between Gainsborough and Ruggles Sts. With 20,000 undergrads and 5000 graduate and law students, Northeastern's Curry Student Center is always busy.

MassArt (Map 7; ☎ 617-232-1555; W www .massart.edu; open 10am-6pm Mon-Fri, 11am-5pm Sat), more formally known as the Massachusetts College of Art, was the country's first four-year independent public art college (and it remains the country's only one!) In 1873, state leaders decided the new textile mills in Lowell and Lawrence needed a

The MFA in Half a Day

The Museum of Fine Arts' *(MFA; Map 7;* ☎ *617-267-9300, www.mfa.org; 465 Huntington Ave)* encyclopedic collections are second in this country only to New York's Metropolitan Museum of Art. The main museum is tricky to navigate, but the West Wing, designed by IM Pei in 1981, is a breeze.

Particularly noteworthy are the MFA's holdings of American art, which include more than 60 portraits by John Singleton Copley, 50 by Gilbert Stuart and many by Winslow Homer, John Singer Sargent, Edward Hopper and the Hudson River School. American decorative arts, including furniture, are also well represented. Hunt for the American silver collection, which includes Paul Revere's *Liberty Bowl*. For a real adventure, head to the dusty, musty basement galleries of colonial American art and artifacts. You'll feel like you've stumbled into a 17th-century flea market.

The museum has one of the world's most comprehensive collections of Japanese art, from porcelain to woodblock prints to painted silk screens and samurai regalia. Don't miss the dimly lit templelike room displaying six massive and awesome Buddhas.

When the museum joined forces with Harvard for a 1905 archaeological expedition at the Great Pyramids at Giza, they hauled back a world-famous collection of mummies and related objects. The refurbished galleries provide the royal treatment these treasures deserve. You'll also find one of the most significant collections of Nubian art outside the Sudan.

The collection of European paintings dating from the 11th to the 20th centuries is outdone by only a handful of museums around the globe. Check out the huge stash of French impressionist paintings, including 36 by Claude Monet. Look for Donatello's relief *Madonna of the Clouds*, one of the few rare, authentic works of his displayed in this country.

When it's time to rest, head to Tenshin-En (Garden of the Heart of Heaven), a tranquil Japanese garden, or the early-20th-century European garden, aka Fraser Garden Court. When it's time to eat, the outdoor Calderwood Courtyard café serves light meals, while the pleasant ground-floor café is best for tea and cake. There is also an inexpensive and unassuming basement-level cafeteria. Skip the fancier restaurant. Check to see what's on at Remis Auditorium, which hosts films and lectures. Concerts are held in the courtyard.

The museum is open 10am to 4:45pm weekdays (until 9:45pm Wednesday); the West Wing stays open until 9:45pm Thursday and Friday. Admission is $15 for adults for two visits in a 30-day period, $13 for seniors, and students under 17 are free (except during regular school hours – they wouldn't want kids skipping school to come to the museum!). A 'voluntary contribution' is suggested from 4pm to 9:45pm on Wednesday.

steady stream of designers, so they figured they'd better educate some. From the beginning, women have comprised more than half the student body. MassArt fosters 'a holistic notion that art is at the core of an ability to envision a future.' There are two professional **galleries** (the main one is at 621 Huntington Ave; admission free) and more than seven other informal on-campus galleries.

Brookline

Brookline is a 'streetcar suburb,' a historical term describing its development after electric trolleys were introduced in the late 1800s. Its main historic attraction is the **John F**

Kennedy National Historic Site *(Map 7, #2;* ☎ *617-566-7937; 83 Beals St; adult/child $3/free; open 10am-4:30pm Wed-Sun May-late Oct)*. JFK spent the first three years of his life in this modest three-story house, until 1920. Matriarch Rose Kennedy oversaw its restoration and furnishing in the late '60s. From the Coolidge Corner T station, walk north on Harvard St for several blocks to Beals St. Mandatory guided tours are offered every half hour prior to 3pm.

CAMBRIDGE

Cambridge, a city of 100,000, is known around the globe as the home of intellectual heavyweights Harvard University and MIT. With upwards of 25,000 students, it's a diverse and youthful place, to say the least. Shabby-chic charm predominates, but there are still enclaves of fabulously expensive residences belonging to the politically connected and well-heeled, as well as immigrant and working-class neighborhoods.

Founded in 1638, Cambridge was home to the country's first college (Harvard) and first printing press, putting an early lock on the city's reputation as a hotbed of ideas and intellectualism.

Cambridge has long been a bastion of progressive politics. Cantabrigians, as residents are called, vehemently opposed the Vietnam War early on; they produced a booklet on how to survive a nuclear war before anyone else did; they embraced the environmental movement before recycling became profitable; and they were one of the first communities to ban smoking in public buildings.

One April Fool's Day not long ago, pranksters put up an official-looking sign that read: 'People's Republic of Cambridge. Passports Please.'

Life on the 'other side' of the river (it's always about perspective, isn't it?) is centered on squares (pardon the pun): Harvard, Kendall, Inman, Central, Porter and Davis.

Harvard Square (Map 8)
When people refer to 'the Square,' they mean the four- or five-block area radiating from the intersection of Mass Ave and JFK St. In fact, the Square isn't a square at all, but rather a triangle of brick pavement above the Harvard T station, where you'll find the 1928 national landmark **Out of Town News**, with a worldwide selection of magazines and newspapers. The adjacent **information kiosk** has lots of good resources. Note the 21ft sculpture *Omphalos*, Greek for 'navel' – an apt metaphor for a community that thinks of itself as the center of the universe. Across Mass Ave, chess players hang out all day at the outdoor **Au Bon Pain** café.

Across from the T station, **the Coop** (Harvard Cooperative Society; Map 8, #35; ☎ 617-499-2000; 1400 Mass Ave) is the country's oldest college cooperative. It was founded in

1882 in response to students' perception that local merchants were price fixing and gouging. (There are highly sought after public restrooms here.)

Find the curved building at Brattle and JFK Sts, and then look for the 2nd-floor sign 'Dewey, Cheetam & Howe'. This is the epicenter of *Car Talk's* **Click and Clack** (Map 8, #39; ☎ 617-876-6632; w www.cartalk.com), the two wisecracking brothers Tom and Ray Magliozzi. They host a hilarious National Public Radio talk show about car repairs (and life repairs) that broadcasts from 'our fair city.'

The Harvard T stop on the Red Line is directly below the Square.

Harvard University
Founded in 1636 by the Massachusetts Bay Colony to educate men for the ministry, Harvard is America's oldest college. (No other college came along until 1693.) The original Ivy League school has six graduates who went on to become US president, not to mention dozens of Nobel laureates and Pulitzer prize winners. It educates 6500 undergraduates and about 12,000 graduates yearly in 10 professional schools. Its seal, *Veritas*, is Latin for 'truth.' At $17.5 billion, it has the largest endowment of any university.

The **Holyoke Center** (Map 8; ☎ 617-495-1573; w www.harvard.edu; 1350 Mass Ave) has reams of information (some for free and some for a fee – Harvard didn't grow that big endowment by giving it away). Free hour-long tours are given at 10am and 2pm weekdays (at 2pm on Saturday) year-round from here. There are additional tours in summer.

Museums The **Carpenter Center for the Visual Arts** (Map 8; ☎ 617-495-3251; 24 Quincy St; open 9am-11:30pm daily) houses studios, the excellent Harvard Film Archive (see Cinema in the Entertainment chapter) and two galleries devoted to modern art and photography. Its photography collection is worth seeking out.

The **Fogg Art Museum** (Map 8; ☎ 617-495-9400; w www.artmuseums.harvard.edu; 32 Quincy St; open 10am-5pm Mon-Sat, 1pm-5pm Sun) concerns itself with no less than the

Emerald Necklace

Widely considered the father of landscape design architecture, Frederick Law Olmsted made an indelible mark on Boston's urban landscape, linking green space from Boston Common to Franklin Park, some 7 miles distant. His firm spent nearly 20 years on the project, between 1878 and 1896. The **Frederick Law Olmsted National Historic Site** (☎ 617-566-1689; 99 Warren St), off Brookline Ave in Brookline, is open for tours; call for times and directions. One of the best ways to see this area is by bike; see Activities later in this chapter.

Back Bay Fens

The Muddy River's winding banks are choked with phragmites, a tall invasive reed that frequently serves as camouflage for sexual encounters. In recent years, there have been a number of gay-bashing incidents; don't linger in the Fens after dark. The Fens features the beloved Community Gardens, the elegant Kelleher Rose Garden and open grassy areas where college students sunbathe. Combine a visit with the MFA or Gardner Museum ('E' branch Green Line).

Jamaica Pond

The idyllic spring-fed pond, on the west side of the Jamaicaway, is more than 50ft deep and great for boating (☎ 617-522-6258), fishing, jogging and picnicking. Take the 'E' branch of the Green Line to the corner of Centre and Pond Sts and walk down Pond.

Arnold Arboretum

The 265-acre arboretum (☎ 617-524-1717; W www.arboretum.harvard.edu; 125 The Arborway) is a gem, planted with more than 14,000 botanical specimens, including exotic trees and flowering shrubs. Dog walking, Frisbee throwing, bicycling and general contemplation are encouraged, but picnicking isn't. It's free and open daily from dawn to dusk. Take the Orange Line to Forest Hills and walk a quarter-mile northwest to the Forest Hills gate (follow the signs).

Franklin Park & Franklin Park Zoo

At 500-plus acres, the park is an underutilized resource. That's partly because of its location – bordering an iffy (by night) neighborhood – and partly because it's large, the layout is confusing and parts are disconcertingly deserted. Still, on weekend afternoons the park is full of families from the nearby multiethnic neighborhoods of Jamaica Plain, Dorchester and Roxbury. The park, providing a slice of city life most tourists never experience, is bordered by Seaver St, Blue Hill Ave, Morton St (MA 203) and Forest Hills St. Take the Orange Line to Stony Brook, Green St or Forest Hills and head east for a few blocks until you reach the park's western edge. Keep your wits about you and don't linger longer than the sun.

The 70-acre zoo (☎ 617-541-5466; W www.zoonewengland.com; Blue Hill Ave at Columbia Rd; adult/senior/child $9.50/8/5; open 10am-5pm Mon-Fri, 10am-6pm Sat & Sun Apr-Sept; 10am-4pm Oct-Mar) boasts a Tropical Forest pavilion with lowland gorillas, a mixed-species Bongo Congo and an Australian Outback Trail, with wallabies, emus and kangaroos. Take the Orange Line to Forest Hills, then the No 16 bus, which departs every 15 minutes and takes about five minutes to reach the zoo.

history of western art from the medieval era to the present. There is also a selection of decorative arts. Free tours are given at 11am Monday to Friday (except during summer when they are given only on Wednesday). Tickets, which include admission to the Busch-Reisinger and Arthur Sackler Museums, cost $6.50 for adults and $5 for seniors and students. Admission is free to those under 18. The Fogg, Busch-Reisinger and Sackler are free 10am to noon on Saturday and share the same opening hours.

Entered through the Fogg, the **Busch-Reisinger Museum** specializes in Northern European art. Free tours are given at 1pm Monday to Friday.

The **Arthur Sackler Museum** *(Map 8; ☎ 617-495-9400; 485 Broadway)* is devoted to ancient, Asian, Islamic and later Indian art. It boasts the world's most impressive collection of Chinese jade as well as fine Japanese woodblock prints. Free tours are given at 2pm Monday to Friday.

The university operates four distinct museums in the **Harvard Museums of Natural History** *(Map 8; ☎ 617-495-3045; [W] www .hmnh.harvard.edu; 24 Oxford St; adult/senior/ student/child $6.50/5/5/4, admission 9am-noon Sun free; open 9am-5pm daily)*, including the Peabody Museum, which are devoted to archaeology, botany, minerals and zoology. Although it seems to be more geared to teaching than to visitors, the eclectic collection might pique your interest. The **Museum of Comparative Zoology** has impressive fossils. The **Botanical Museum**, perhaps the most well known of the museums, houses more than 3000 handblown-glass reproductions of flowers and plants. The **Mineralogical & Geological Museum** boasts a 1642lb amethyst geode from Brazil and a gallery devoted to rough and cut gemstones of New England. (Better yet, hit their museum shop, Harvard Collections; see Art & Crafts in the Shopping chapter.)

Adjacent to the Museums of Natural History, the multicultural **Peabody Museum of Archaeology & Ethnology** *(Map 8; ☎ 617-496-1027; [W] www.peabody.harvard.edu)* boasts a strong collection of North American Indian artifacts. The Hall of the North American Indian traces how native peoples responded to the arrival of Europeans. The museum has the same hours and prices as the Museums of Natural History.

The small **Semitic Museum** *(☎ 617-495-4631; 6 Divinity Ave; admission free; open 10am-4pm Mon-Fri, 1pm-4pm Sun)* has changing exhibits from its Near East archaeological and photographic collections.

Widener Library Behind this mass of Corinthian columns and steep stairs are more than 5 miles of books. Widener was built in memory of rare-book collector Harry Elkins Widener, who had the misfortune of returning from England aboard the *Titanic*. Apparently Harry gave up his seat in a lifeboat to retrieve his favorite book from his stateroom. When he returned, all the lifeboats were full. The Widener family made two stipulations to their library grant: that the building's exterior mortar or bricks not be altered (Harvard circumvented this by connecting the library to another with a glass breezeway) and that a reading room like Harry's be built and fresh flowers placed in it daily. Legend states that the bequest also required that students pass a swimming test. (The myth asserts that the Wideners were convinced young Harry would have lived had he known how to swim.) The library, unfortunately, is not open to the public.

Other Harvard Sights Between Brattle and Garden Sts, and Appian Way and Mason St, the modest but lovely **Radcliffe Yard** is home to the principal buildings of Radcliffe College, founded in 1879 as the sister school to the then all-male Harvard. The two colleges merged in 1977, and in 1999 Radcliffe ceased to exist except as a network of research institutions (including one for the study of women, gender and society). Within Radcliffe Yard, the **Schlesinger Library** *(Map 8; ☎ 617-495-8647; open 9am-5pm Mon-Fri, 9am-8pm Wed when school is in session)* houses the country's preeminent collection of books, photos and oral histories pertaining to women.

The distinguished **Harvard Graduate School of Business** *(B-School; Map 8; ☎ 617-495-6000)* is across the Charles River. Head south on JFK St, cross the Larz Anderson Bridge and head left onto the campus. The B-School has a particularly noteworthy cylindrical chapel with an adjacent pyramid and tiered garden. Students tend to gather at Kresge Hall, where the dining room is located. Graduate Jim Koch, founder of Boston Beer Co (makers of Sam Adams), is credited with hatching the American craft-brewing industry.

As for the revered **Law School** *(Map 8; ☎ 617-495-3100; off Mass Ave)*: look for

Hasty Pudding Awards

Jodie Foster, Mel Gibson, Susan Sarandon, Tom Hanks, Sigourney Weaver and Robin Williams. Could a little pudding pot, a bunch of guys parading around in drag and an evening of roasting the celeb with embarrassing outtakes really draw these A-list types?…to little old Cambridge?…in February? You betcha. The **Hasty Pudding Theatrical Club** (**W** *www.hastypudding.org*) has toasted and roasted a 'Woman & Man of the Year' since 1951. Heads turned in 1981 when John Travolta said he was more honored to have received a pudding pot than an Academy Award nomination.

It all began back in 1795, when 21 students gathered in secrecy to 'cultivate the social affections and cherish the feelings of friendship' and 'in alphabetical order provide a pot of hasty pudding for every meeting.' Soon after, in response to increased 'rowdiness,' the group improvised a mock criminal court to try its members for 'insolence.' Over ensuing years, these productions became more and more elaborate, with the addition of costumes and scripts. In 1844, an upperclassman secretly produced an opera instead of a trial, and thus the Hasty Pudding show was born. To this day, men play both male and female roles (women are relegated to behind-the-scenes contributions) and the professional-quality shows feature no-holds-barred drag burlesque.

Austin Hall, a delightfully grand Romanesque structure designed in 1883 by HH Richardson. If the building is open, peek into the 2nd-floor Ames Courtroom (the original library), where students hold an annual mock trial presided over by a US Supreme Court Justice. (Many of the distinguished jurists, including Scalia, Souter, Bryer, Kennedy and Ginsberg, were schooled here.) The Austin lecture halls easily conjure images of a crusty Socratic professor bearing down relentlessly on his students, just as in the movie *Paper Chase*.

The **JFK School of Government** (*Map 8;* ☎ *617-495-8290; cnr Eliot & JFK Sts*), founded in 1936, changed its name to honor the slain president in 1966. The only portrait of JFK painted when he was alive hangs in the entrance. Despite its ultra-Democratic namesake, the school extols bipartisan principles. The C-SPAN broadcast, *ARCO Forum of Public Affairs*, which deals with weighty matters and looks so darn serious on TV, is actually produced in the cafeteria.

The **Loeb Drama Center** (*Map 8, #8;* ☎ *617-547-8300; 64 Brattle St*) is home to the professional, prestigious and nonprofit American Repertory Theater (see Theater in the Entertainment chapter), which presents unconventional adaptations of classics as well as new American plays. There isn't a single bad seat in the small auditorium and the productions are always entertaining and thought provoking.

Colonial Cambridge

The phrase 'George Washington slept here' is well worn in these parts. There's lots of colonial history in and around the **Cambridge Common** (*Map 8*), a public park since 1631. Washington pitched camp here from 1775 to 1776 and is said to have gathered a Continental Army under a giant elm. To this day, it still looks as if a few too many horses have been trampling on the grass.

On the little traffic island south of the common, where Mass Ave and Garden St intersect, look for bronze hoofprints embedded in the sidewalk. **Dawes Island** (*Map 8*) memorializes the 'other rider,' William Dawes, who rode through Cambridge to Lexington on April 18, 1775, to warn that the British were coming.

Christ Church (*Map 8, #5;* ☎ *617-876-0200; Zero Garden St*) was designed in 1761 by America's first formally trained architect, Peter Harrison (who also did Boston's King's Chapel). Although Washington's troops used it as a barracks after its Tory congregation fled, he ordered services be held here on New Year's Eve, 1775. The interior is simple, but elegant. When he was a Harvard student, President Teddy Roosevelt taught Sunday school here.

Indestructible Wafers

You know those little candies that show up around Valentine's Day imprinted with 'Love Ya' or 'Cutie Pie' or, in a nod to changing times, 'Fax me'? You know those little pastel-colored, chalky wafer candies? They're made by **NECCO Candy Co** (W www.necco.com), short for New England Confection Co. Although no longer manufactured in Kendall Square, they're still made in metro Boston (where they've been since 1884). In a bind, the wafers are great for practicing first communion or can act as substitutes for poker chips or checkers. Did you know that enough NECCO wafers are sold each year to go around the world once; that it takes 40 minutes to work your way through a roll of them, on average; that Martha Stewart is a fan (it makes sense – they match her paint chip palette); that 120 wafers are consumed around the world every second of every day of the year; that Admiral Byrd took 2½ tons of them to the South Pole in the 1930s for a two-year stay; that they have an indefinite shelf life (under dry conditions)? Ah, there's nothing like the confluence of kitsch and resourcefulness.

Within the revolutionary-era **Old Burying Ground** (Map 8; Church St) lie Harvard's first eight presidents. Around the corner the wooden **First Parish Church** (Map 8, #21; ☎ 617-876-7772; 3 Church St) houses the Nameless Coffeehouse (see the Entertainment chapter).

Brattle St One of the area's most prestigious residential addresses, Brattle St is lined with magnificent (and mostly private) 18th- and 19th-century mansions. Dubbed Tory Row in the early 1770s, it was generally home to wealthy British loyalists. But in 1775, Washington got his revenge by appropriating most of these houses for his patriot cohorts.

Head west out of the Square along Brattle St. The beloved 1890 **Brattle St Theatre** (Map 8, #26; ☎ 617-876-6837; 40 Brattle St) is one of the country's oldest movie houses.

Next door, the **Cambridge Center for Adult Ed** (Map 8, #24; ☎ 617-547-6789; 42 Brattle St), historically known as the Brattle House, is an 18th-century colonial clapboard gem. Margaret Fuller, feminist editor of *The Dial*, once lived here.

The former **Blacksmith House** (Map 8, #9; 54 Brattle St) is an apropos site to honor the blacksmith in Longfellow's poem. The sculpted steel Chestnut Tree Memorial is complete with an anvil and a set of blacksmith tools.

Designed in 1882 by HH Richardson, the private **Stoughton House** (Map 8, #4; 90 Brattle St) has been called 'perhaps the best suburban wooden house in America.' Parts of the adjacent and notable private **Henry Vassal House** (Map 8, #3; 94 Brattle St) may date from 1636; the chimney is a whopping 8 sq ft.

The c. 1685 **Hooper-Lee-Nichols House** (☎ 617-547-4252; 159 Brattle St; adult/senior/student $5/3/3; open for tours 2pm-5pm Tues & Thur), home to the Cambridge Historical Society, is decorated in various period styles. There's also an informative model that depicts Brattle St prior to the revolution. Inquire about the Cambridge Historical Society's excellent Brattle St walking tours offered June through October.

The **Longfellow National Historic Site** (Map 8, #2; ☎ 617-876-4491; W www.nps.gov/long; 105 Brattle St; adults/children $3/free; open for tours 10:30am-4pm Wed-Sun), a stately and immense home, is another of Washington's appropriations. The general liked it so much that he moved his headquarters here during the siege of Boston. Henry Wadsworth Longfellow lived here for 45 years from 1837 (when he first rented a room here) until 1882. (He received the house as a gift from his new father-in-law after marrying Frances Appleton in 1843.) During that time he wrote *Evangeline* and *Hiawatha*. The Georgian mansion, which contains many of Longfellow's books and other belongings, is under the auspices of the National Park Service.

Kendall Square (Map 9)

On your way to the movies, or a bar or restaurant, check out the public art at the **Kendall/MIT T Station** (Map 9; Main St). Celebrating the history of Cambridge and the

Charles River Esplanade

The Charles River, once lined with sawmills and leather manufacturers, was a smelly, marshy tidal estuary until the early 1900s, when the Charles River Dam was built. Today, both sides of the curvaceous Charles River are graced with grassy banks and paved byways, perfect for bicycling, in-line skating, jogging, walking and festivals. Sailing, rowing and sculling are popular pastimes. It's about 2 miles from the Museum of Science (on the Cambridge side) to the Larz Anderson Bridge. Storrow Dr snakes along the Boston side of the river, Memorial Dr along the Cambridge side.

Bridges

The **Longfellow Bridge**, nicknamed the Salt & Pepper Bridge because its towers resemble shakers, affords one of Boston's best skyline views. To prolong the view glimpsed on the Red Line between Charles/MGH and Kendall, walk across the bridge, preferably just prior to sunset.

Despite its name, the **Harvard Bridge** (Mass Ave) leads to MIT, not to its academic neighbor. The bridge is known for a bit of recent lore. While Oliver Reed Smoot was an MIT undergraduate between 1958 and 1962, he devised a new unit of measurement, the **'smoot'**. Smoot and his fraternity pals decided to measure the bridge using the young man as a yardstick (or a 'smootstick'). They purportedly lay Smoot on the ground, end over end, and marked their progress until they got from one side to the other. Turns out that the bridge measures 364.4 smoots and the markings are so popular they have been preserved.

According to [W] www.uselessfacts.net, the **BU Bridge** is the only place in the world where 'a boat can sail under a train driving under a car driving under an airplane.' What you do with that information is up to you.

Neither the **River St Bridge** nor the **Western Ave Bridge** is particularly notable, although it's useful to know that they lead to Central Square.

The charming **Weeks Memorial Bridge** offers the best vantage point during the Head of the Charles Regatta in late October. The course runs from the BU Bridge to a half mile beyond the Eliot Bridge (which is just beyond the Larz Anderson Bridge). The bridge connects the Harvard B-School to the main Cambridge-side campus. The **Larz Anderson Bridge** leads to Harvard Square.

Boston Shore

The most popular and picturesque portion extends from Mass Ave to Arlington St. On warm days, Bostonians migrate here to sunbathe, picnic, sail and feed water fowl gliding along the tranquil riverbank.

---

technological innovations of MIT, this is an enchanting, interactive sonic sculpture that you can activate by pulling levers mounted on the station platform walls. Aboveground, techies hang with skateboarders around the sculpture **The Galaxy** (Map 9, #56; Broadway and Main St), a stainless-steel globe with puffs of steam rising from beneath it.

Inman Square (Map 9)

Northwest of Kendall Square and east of Harvard Square (pretty much at the intersection of Prospect, Cambridge and Hampshire Sts), this residential neighborhood is just far enough off the beaten tourist path that its character should remain intact, in the short term at least. Home to a thriving immigrant community, primarily Portuguese, Inman has a diverse selection of restaurants.

Inman Square is a 15-minute walk from either Harvard or Central Square.

Central Square (Map 9)

This square (Mass Ave at Prospect and River Sts) has had an economically checkered history. It was developed in the late 1700s after the West Boston Bridge (now the Longfellow Bridge) connected Cambridge with Boston. As more bridges were built, funneling traffic into the square, it earned its name as a 'central' crossroads. In the late 1800s, City Hall was sited here, but after the

Charles River Esplanade

See Map 2 for sites along the Boston Shore. This stretch includes Storrow Lagoon and the **Hatch Memorial Shell** (Map 2), a 1940 Art Deco semicovered stage where free outdoor movies and concerts are held throughout the summer (see the boxed text 'Free Outdoor Fun' in the Entertainment chapter). Just west of the Arthur Fiedler Footbridge is the aluminum **Arthur Fiedler bust** (Map 2, #24), a modern 1984 sculpture of the maestro who led the Boston Pops for 50 years until 1979. Most of the little white sailboats tacking back and forth on the Charles originate from the **Community Boating** boathouse, just south of the Longfellow Bridge (see Activities later in this chapter).

Cambridge Shore
Graceful brick buildings topped with various colored spires line the banks just east of the Larz Anderson Bridge; these are Harvard houses or dormitories. The best views of downtown Boston are from anywhere between the Longfellow and Harvard Bridges. Memorial Dr is closed to cars on Sunday in the summer so rollerbladers have more room.

The most picturesque boathouse is Harvard's **Weld Boathouse** (Map 8), just east of the Larz Anderson Bridge, which the school leases from the state for an 'extravagant' $500 annually. The world's richest academic institution finagled an even better deal for the **Newell Boathouse** (Map 8), on the opposite shore. That costs $1 a year, and the lease on Newell extends through the year 2900. You'll also see the **BU Boathouse** (Map 7), just east of the BU Bridge, and the **MIT Boathouse**, just west of the Harvard Bridge. The MIT boathouse contains one of the nation's best rowing simulators, complete with honest-to-goodness water currents of 10mph.

Getting There & Away
There are a number of T stations within easy reach of the river. From east to west they include: Charles/MGH (Red Line); Kendall/MIT (Red Line, then a five-minute walk to the Longfellow Bridge); Hynes/ICA (Green Line then walk north on Mass Ave for the Harvard Bridge); Mt Fort station on the 'B' branch of the Green Line (for the BU Bridge); and Harvard Square station (Red Line for the Larz Anderson Bridge). From the corner of Beacon and Arlington Sts, you can walk across Storrow Dr via the Arthur Fiedler Footbridge.

There is street parking along parts of Memorial Dr (near MIT) but not Storrow Dr.

T was extended to Harvard Square, people bypassed Central. Buildings were torn down or reduced to low-rises during the Great Depression, and when suburban malls went up in the '70s and '80s, Central Square stores suffered. But as all things old become new again, this is, again, Central Square's time, with plenty of alternative clubs and pubs.

MIT
The **Massachusetts Institute of Technology** (MIT; Map 9; ☎ 617-253-4795, ⓦ www.mit.edu), a scientific mecca founded in 1861, is spread along Mass Ave east of Central Square and along the Charles River. Join one of the excellent guided campus **tours** to best appreciate MIT's scientific contributions, as well as the East Campus's truly exceptional public art (including work by Henry Moore, Alexander Calder, Alvar Aalto and Picasso). Free tours are given at 10am and 2pm Monday to Friday from 77 Mass Ave, Building 7 lobby.

The **List Visual Arts Center** (Map 9, #59; ☎ 617-253-4680; Weisner Bldg, 20 Ames St; admission free; open noon-6pm Tues-Thur, Sat & Sun, noon-8pm Fri) mounts rewarding and sophisticated shows that push the contemporary art envelope in painting, sculpture, photography, video, architecture and design, as well as other works that defy general categorization.

The **MIT Museum** (Map 9; ☎ 617-253-4444; ⓦ web.mit.edu/museum) has exhibition spaces all across campus. The main exhibition space (Map 9; 265 Mass Ave; adult/senior/student $5/2/2; open 10am-5pm Tues-Fri, noon-5pm Sat & Sun) boasts the world's largest collection of holographic images. An extensive nautical collection and photographs by and about stroboscopic legend Harold 'Doc' Edgerton are elsewhere (Map 9; 55 Mass Ave); inquire at the main exhibition space.

There are great Boston **skyline views** across the Charles River from Memorial Dr along the East Campus.

Mass Ave to Porter Square (Map 10)

So what happened to all those funky, quirky shops that were in Harvard Square before it was inundated with national chains? They fled north, north of the Law School that is. The stretch of Mass Ave up to Porter Square has some hip shops and more than a few restaurants and cafés. It takes about 25 minutes to walk from Harvard to Porter Square without stopping, but of course the main reason to walk it is to stop all along the way. You also can take the Red Line T to Porter.

Davis Square (Map 10)

Although Davis is in Somerville, it's just north of Cambridge and accessible via the T, so it's included here. Please forgive us, city of Somerville. Having said that, Davis Square is way more hip than any square in Cambridge. The working-class city of Somerville – where statues of the Virgin Mary overlook new BMWs, and Christmas light displays glow brightly enough to read by – is changing, and nowhere more than Davis Square. It's been transformed with trendy bars, cappuccino counters, gourmet restaurants and art. Davis Square showcases art by many of Somerville's artists, who are encouraged by City Hall. (Perhaps there was a kernel of truth in the catch phrase 'Somerville, the Paris of the '90s.') Somerville, and Davis Square in particular, are no longer the butt of jokes; it's hip to be this square.

Davis Square is directly above its eponymous Red Line T stop, at the intersection of Elm St and Highland and College Aves.

Mt Auburn Cemetery

On a sunny day, this delightful spot (Map 10; ☎ 617-547-7105; 580 Mt Auburn St; open 8am-5pm daily, until 6pm during daylight saving time) at Coolidge and Brattle Sts is worth the 30-minute walk west out of Harvard Square. Developed in 1831, its 175 acres were the first 'garden cemetery' in the US. Until then, the colonial notion of moving a body and rearranging grave markers around a cemetery was commonplace. Take an audio or walking tour for $5, or a free self-guided tour. Maps pinpoint the rare botanical specimens and notable burial plots, including those for Mary Baker Eddy (founder of the Christian Science Church), Isabella Stewart Gardner (socialite and art collector), Winslow Homer (19th-century American painter), Oliver Wendell Holmes (US Supreme Court Justice) and Henry W Longfellow (19th-century writer). Bus No 71 out of Harvard Square station (adjacent to the Red Line) runs past the cemetery.

CHARLESTOWN (MAP 11)

Charlestown was settled a year before Boston and then completely destroyed by the British during the revolution. Townspeople rebuilt quickly, and today most houses in the core date from the early 19th century. (Charlestown was incorporated into Boston in 1873.)

It's logical to combine this exploration with the North End. It takes about 15 minutes to walk from Commercial and North Washington Sts across the Charlestown Bridge. Turn right onto Constitution Rd to reach the Navy Yard or cross the oasis-like City Square and head into the heart of town. Or take a ferry from Long Wharf to the Navy Yard or a shuttle to Lovejoy Wharf (see the Getting Around chapter). Another alternative is to take the T Green or Orange Line to North Station and head across the Charlestown Bridge. If you are driving (gasp), there is free parking (gasp) on both sides of Constitution Rd.

Charlestown Navy Yard

The Navy Yard, where British troops landed to fight the Battle of Bunker Hill, offers more than a nice view of Boston's skyline. Its current mission is to interpret the art and history of naval shipbuilding. A mere museum on the topic might prove boring, but touring the USS *Constitution* and walking around the dry docks and impressive granite buildings makes for a fascinating history lesson. A thriving shipbuilding center from 1800 until the early 1900s, the Navy Yard was decommissioned in 1974. The area has been remarkably preserved and resurrected with shops, recreation areas, and residential and office space.

Begin your introduction to both the Navy Yard and Bunker Hill Monument at the **Bunker Hill Pavilion** *(Map 11, #11; ☎ 617-241-7575; Constitution Rd; open 9am-5pm daily Apr-Nov, 9am-6pm daily Jun-Aug)*. The 18-minute multimedia **Whites of Their Eyes Exhibit** *(adult/child $4/2; open 9:30am-4:30pm)* elucidates the battle quite nicely.

Free half-hour **tours** of the Navy Yard are offered at 11am daily during the summer from the pavilion. On your own, have a look at **Dry Dock No 1** *(Map 11)*, the country's oldest shipbuilding dry dock (1833); the hexagonal **Telephone Exchange** *(Map 11, #7)*, atypically intimate and ornate for a shipyard building; and the **Commandant's House** *(Map 11, #8)*, a brick Georgian-style mansion.

The **Ropewalk** *(Map 11)*, where all navy rope was made for 135 years, is more than 1000ft long. Its granite walls are 2½ft thick and have many isolated sections, all the better to snuff out frequent fires. It's the only remaining complete ropewalk in the US, but it's closed to the public. When metal workers invented 'die-lock' chain next door in 1926, it put the ropemakers out of business.

The NPS offers free guided 45-minute tours of a refurbished WWII destroyer, the **USS Cassin Young** *(Map 11; ☎ 617-242-5601)*, at 1pm, 2pm and 3pm (and a bit more often in the summer). You can always tour the main deck on your own. After all the walking around, **Shipyard Park** is a good place to relax.

USS Constitution A few notable facts about the USS *Constitution*: Paul Revere was paid almost $4000 to outfit her in copper hardware and sheathing; construction costs were 260% over budget (perhaps the Big Dig isn't doing so badly after all); the captain's son died on her maiden voyage; Oliver Wendell Holmes made a name for himself by penning a poem about her; for her last mission in 1853 she seized an American slave ship off the coast of Africa; and in 1886, Congressman John F 'Honey Fitz' Fitzgerald introduced a bill to permanently moor her in Massachusetts.

Outfitted in period uniforms, perky Navy personnel give free and entertaining 30-minute tours of the USS *Constitution*'s top deck, gun deck and cramped quarters. In order to maintain the ship's commissioned status, she is taken out onto Boston Harbor every 4th of July, turned around and brought back to the dock. **Tours** *(☎ 617-242-7511)* are offered from 10am to 4pm daily in summer and from 10am to 4pm Thursday to Sunday in winter.

Across from the ship, the **USS Constitution Museum** *(Map 11, #9; ☎ 617-426-1812; admission free; open 9am-6pm daily Apr-Oct, 10am-4pm daily Nov-May)* has colorful gallery displays for nautical buffs, interactive exhibits for kids and many informative short videos about ship life and the ship's battles (if you're into that kind of thing).

From City Square to Monument Square

Recent Central Artery construction in City Square unearthed the foundation for the Great House, widely believed to be John Winthrop's 1630 house. (He soon moved across the Charles to the Shawmut Peninsula.) After reading the informative dioramas, wander up Main St, detouring through **John Harvard Mall**, a gem of a walled, tree-covered brick plaza. A 1630 fort once crowned Harvard Mall, atop Town Hill; bronze plaques detail the specifics. Before the local minister – one John Harvard – died of consumption, he donated half his £800 estate and all 300 of his books to a young Cambridge college in 1638, which saw fit to name its school after him. (For that sum Harvard wouldn't name a park bench after you today!) Both **Harvard Square** and **Harvard St**, behind the mall, are also enchanting. From here, there are two scenic ways to reach Monument Square.

Follow **Main St** and turn right onto Winthrop St to check out the now-tranquil and pacifist **Winthrop Square** (militia trained here for 250 years) before following it around to the left. Or take Harvard St to **Monument Ave** or Pleasant St. The c. 1780 **Warren Tavern** *(Map 11, #4; ☎ 617-241-8142; cnr Main & Pleasant Sts)* was one of the first buildings constructed after the town was burned. It's still a fine place for a drink. The narrow streets surrounding Monument Square are picturesque, lined with restored mid-19th-century Federal and colonial houses.

Bunker Hill Monument

The area known today as Bunker Hill is actually Breed's Hill. Regardless of its name, the hill on which the memorial stands is the site of a crucial Revolutionary War battle that took place on June 17, 1775. Although won by the British, the colonists fought valiantly and British casualties were very high. According to oft-quoted legend, colonial colonel William Prescott, hoping to preserve the element of surprise, commanded his troops: 'Don't fire 'til you see the whites of their eyes.' The face-to-face combat that ensued was the bloodiest of the war. A battle re-enactment takes place every June. Musket firing demonstrations are given Thursday through Sunday (at 10:30am, 11:30am, 2:30pm and 3:30pm) in the summer.

Bunker Hill Monument *(Map 11, #2; ☎ 617-242-5641; admission free; open 9am-5pm daily)*, a 221ft granite obelisk rising from atop the hill, offers a fine view of Boston for those willing to climb 294 steps. The Marquis de Lafayette laid the cornerstone in 1825, but it took another 15 years of fund-raising to finish it. (Ironically, the battlefield itself was sold to finance the monument.) NPS park rangers are on hand year-round to give talks.

The Locks & Paul Revere Park

Immediately to the west of the Charlestown Bridge (site of a toll ferry benefiting Harvard College until 1786), the dam and locks control the water levels between the Charles River Basin and Inner Harbor. Upwards of

1000 pleasure boats and an inestimable number of fish pass through daily in the summer. No other section of the Charles River shoreline is hidden like it is here, severed from the rest of the city by industry. The locks provide a great vantage point for the Zakim Bridge. It's a gritty and noisy viewing station, but it provides a dose of reality after one too many trips to Faneuil Hall. The adjacent Paul Revere Park, a welcome oasis if you don't mind a perpetual snake of cars hulking above, is a link in an ongoing plan for 7 miles of area recreational pathways.

OUTLYING NEIGHBORHOODS

There are a number of other communities that exemplify the Boston area's contemporary diversity. All are within easy reach by subway.

South Boston

This tight-knit, predominantly white, working-class, Irish-Catholic community has lots of great harbor views and a number of Irish pubs along West and East Broadway. While this main thoroughfare is experiencing some gentrification, it remains the real thing. For a study in contrasts, stop into **Amrhein's** *(☎ 617-268-6189; 80 West Broadway)*, which has been here more than 100 years and serves hearty fare, onion rings and beer. **Boston Beer Garden** *(☎ 617-269-0990; 734 East Broadway)*, complete with café-style accordion doors that open onto the street, serves crab cakes and portobello mushrooms. Take the Red Line to Broadway.

From the Broadway T station, hop on Bus No 11 or walk 45 minutes along West Broadway (about halfway through it becomes East Broadway) to **Castle Island**, at Marine Park. Although no longer an island, it is the site of five-pointed **Fort Independence** *(☎ 617-727-5290, 617-628-5744; Day Boulevard)*, which you can tour for free in the summer. A fort has stood here, at the entrance to the Inner Harbor, since 1634; this one dates from 1801.

During the 1776 siege of Boston, from high atop a hill between G and Old Harbor Sts, George Washington and his troops set up cannons that ultimately convinced the British to go home. To reach the **Dorchester Heights Monument**, walk east along West Broadway from the Broadway T station, turn right onto Dorchester St and head up any of the little streets to the hill. (Or take Bus No 11 and get off near Dorchester St.)

John Fitzgerald Kennedy Library & Museum

Herein (☎ 617-514-1600; Columbia Point, Dorchester; adult/senior/student/child over 12 $8/6/6/4; open 9am-5pm daily) lies assorted memorabilia related to the 35th US president: papers, videotape, speeches and photographs. Check out the introductory film about JFK. The building was designed by architect IM Pei, also responsible for the dramatic John Hancock Tower in Back Bay. The monumental white and black structure successfully blends cylindrical elements with strong pyramid-like lines.

The library also serves as an archive for writer Ernest Hemingway's manuscripts and papers. About 95% of his works can be accessed if you're interested in research, but there is no exhibit space. What's the connection? Kennedy helped Mary Hemingway, Ernest's fourth wife and widow, get the manuscripts and papers out of Cuba during the first and most intense days of the embargo. When she died, she willed them here, because this library offers the public better access than most other libraries.

From the JFK/UMass Red Line station, catch a free shuttle to the museum or to campus.

Roxbury

In the mid-1950s the Nation of Islam founded **Muhammad's Mosque No 11** (☎ 617-442-6082; 10 Washington St). Malcolm X (then Malcolm Little) lived with his sister and two aunts from 1941 to 1946 in a little **house** (72 Dale St) about a mile away from the mosque. In 1998 the decrepit structure was saved from demolition and designated a historic landmark. The house is not open to the public.

ACTIVITIES
Bicycling

Although you have to be a kamikaze to ride on inner-city streets, people do. Ride defensively since autos drive offensively. Both

Revere Beach

Also known as the 'North Shore Riviera,' Revere Beach lives. Yeah, yeah...it's the country's first public beach, but who cares. Revere Beach is classic urban Boston. It's Baywatch, Boston-style. It's people-watching extraordinaire. Thanks to a colossal reclamation project, the formerly trashy wide beach now boasts fine white sand. But for some reason (go 'figga'), a whole lot of people prefer setting up lawn chairs on the concrete walkway and seawall.

Take the Blue Line to Revere Beach or Wonderland and walk east for one or two blocks. (Just follow the boom boxes.) One added bonus: you can sunbathe while watching the jets take off from Logan Airport – no wonder everyone has boom boxes! Head to nearby **Kelly's Roast Beef** (☎ 781-284-9129; 410 Revere Beach Blvd) for clams after getting fried yourself; it's the ultimate Ra-vee-ah dining experience.

sides of the Charles River are popular, but you can also ride along the Emerald Necklace (see the boxed text 'Emerald Necklace' earlier in this chapter). The more adventurous can invest in a Rubel BikeMap (see Maps in the Facts for the Visitor chapter).

For renting, try **Community Bicycle Supply** (Map 6, #48; ☎ 617-542-8623; 496 Tremont St; rentals Apr-Sept) or **Back Bay Bicycles** (Map 5, #13; ☎ 617-247-2336; 336 Newbury St; rentals year-round), at Mass Ave. In Cambridge, try **Ata Cycle** (Map 10, #32; ☎ 617-354-0907; 1773 Mass Ave; rentals year-round), between Harvard and Porter Squares, or **Bicycle Exchange** (Map 10, #19; ☎ 617-864-1300; 2067 Mass Ave; rentals year-round).

Definitely consider the 12–17-mile, 4-hour tour with **Boston Bike Tours** (Map 2; ☎ 617-308-5902; w www.bostonbiketours.com; Boston Common Visitor Information Center). Trips cost $25 and are offered mid-April to mid-October on most Sundays. They also have a number of other trips around desirable neighborhoods, with and without bike rental.

Also see Bicycle in the Getting Around chapter.

Colleges & Universities

Greater Boston has over 35 campuses, too many to mention here. In addition to the details about Harvard (Map 8) and MIT (Map 9) earlier in this chapter, this brief listing should help you get further information.

In the Fenway area, head to **Northeastern University** *(Map 7; ☎ 617-373-2000; W www.neu.edu; Huntington Ave)*, which boasts one of the country's largest work-study cooperative programs.

Down the street, **Massachusetts College of Art** *(Map 7; ☎ 617-232-1555; W www.massart.edu; Huntington Ave)* hosts regular gallery exhibits at 621 Huntington Ave.

Nearby in Kenmore Square, **Boston University** *(Map 7; BU; ☎ 617-353-2000, 353-2169; W www.bu.edu)* enrolls about 30,000 graduates and undergraduates, and has a huge campus and popular sports teams.

University of Massachusetts, Boston *(UMass; ☎ 617-287-5000, W www.umb.edu; Morrissey Blvd)* is on Columbia Point, surrounded by Dorchester Bay on three sides.

Other well-established universities in the outlying neighborhoods include Boston College, Wellesley College, Tufts University and Brandeis University.

Boston College *(☎ 617-552-8000; W www.bc.edu)*, on Comm Ave (MA 30) in Chestnut Hill, is the nation's largest Jesuit community. It boasts Gothic towers, a good art museum and excellent Irish and Catholic ephemera collections.

Wellesley College *(☎ 781-283-1000; W www.wellesley.edu; 106 Central St)*, a Seven Sisters women's college in Wellesley, sports a lovely green campus and the excellent Davis Museum & Cultural Center. Take the MBTA Commuter Rail, plus a 10-minute walk, or drive along the MA 16 to MA 135.

Tufts University *(☎ 617-628-5000; W www.tufts.edu)*, in Medford, has about 8500 students and a good basketball team. From the Davis Square T station, board the No 94 or No 96 bus to campus.

Brandeis University *(☎ 781-736-2000; W www.brandeis.edu; South St)*, a heavily Jewish school in Waltham, features the Rose Art Museum specializing in New England art. Take the MBTA Commuter Rail from North Station to the Brandeis/Roberts stop on the Fitchburg line.

Boating & Kayaking

The **Charles River Canoe & Kayak Center** has two locations: one branch *(☎ 617-965-5110; W www.charlesriver.us; 2401 Comm Ave; open Apr-Oct)* in Newton, MA 30 near I-95, and another *(☎ 617-462-2513; Soldier's Field Rd; open Apr–mid-Oct)* just a bit upstream from the Eliot Bridge. Canoes cost $11 hourly, rowboats and double kayaks are $14. Rowing shells are available for $25 per session, if you can demonstrate proficiency. The Newton center is across from a tranquil stretch of the Charles River. Take the T Green Line 'D' branch to Riverside and then it's a 20-minute walk; call for directions. The Soldier's Field Rd location is a 20-minute walk from the Harvard Red Line T station, on the opposite side of the river.

Community Boating *(Map 2; ☎ 617-523-1038; W www.community-boating.org; open Apr-Oct)*, at the Charles River Esplanade near the Charles St Footbridge, offers experienced sailors unlimited use of sailboats, kayaks and windsurfers for $100 for two days. But you'll have to take a little test to demonstrate your ability. For locals, a 45-day unlimited membership costs $75, including all the free lessons you need to gain confidence.

Also see Boat Tours in the Getting Around chapter.

In-Line & Ice Skating

Beacon Hill Skate *(Map 6, #32; ☎ 617-482-7400; 135 Charles St S)* rents in-line skates hourly ($8) and daily ($25). Glide to the Esplanade, or better yet, to Memorial Dr on the Cambridge side of the Charles River, which is closed to auto traffic from 11am to 7pm on Sunday in warm weather.

Ice skating on the **Boston Common Frog Pond Rink** *(Map 2)* is very popular – even for restrained Bostonians – from mid-November to mid-March. (It's less crowded during the week.) Skate rentals ($7), lockers ($1) and restrooms are available at the **pondside kiosk** (☎ 617-635-2120), which has a limited menu of hot food. Skating costs $3 if you're aged 14 or over.

Whale Watching Cruises

Whale sightings are practically guaranteed at Stellwagen Bank, a fertile feeding ground 25 miles out to sea. The big humpback whales are awesome, breaching and frolicking, and in the spring and fall, huge pods of dolphins make their way to and from their summers in the Arctic. Trips take about 4½ to 5 hours, with onboard commentary provided by naturalists. Dress warmly even on summer days.

The **AC Cruise Line** *(Map 4, #75; ☎ 617-261-6633; 290 Northern Ave)* offers family-friendly trips: up to four children are free when accompanied by two paying adults (adults/seniors $16/22). Trips depart at 10am on weekends from mid-April to mid-October. Make reservations.

Tickets for the **New England Aquarium Whale Watching tour** *(Map 4, #13; ☎ 617-973-5281; Central Wharf)* cost $28 for adults, $22 for seniors and students, and $18 to $20 children. Call for reservations and departure times from April to early November. Their catamaran cuts travel time by an hour.

Boston Harbor Cruises *(Map 4, #3; ☎ 617-227-4320)* also has daily whale watching tours departing from Long Wharf May through October. Tickets cost $29 for adults, $25 for seniors and $23 children.

AMERICA'S WALKING CITY

Boston's intimate neighborhoods are a tapestry of historical anecdotes, politics, personalities and architectural styles. They are bursting at the seams with their jumble of beautiful buildings and lively little museums. The best way to unravel their spirit is by feeling the uneven brick sidewalks beneath your feet. In between visiting revolutionary hangouts and Victorian gems, though, don't forget to check out the Bostonians all around you. It's really the intersection of the past with the present that makes the trajectory so interesting.

Beacon Hill: Bastion of Brahmins & Black History

Stately 19th-century brick townhouses, purple windowpanes, gas lanterns, precious courtyards, colorful window boxes and narrow alleyways – this is the stuff of Beacon Hill. It's Boston's most handsome and affluent residential neighborhood. Although seemingly exclusive, Beacon Hill has never been the domain solely of blue-blood Brahmins. Free African Americans settled here in the early 19th century; they were followed by Jewish and Irish immigrants. More recently, a number of the grand residences have been subdivided into small condos for young professionals and students. The Black Heritage Trail and the Freedom Trail both make their way along the streets of Beacon Hill; see Walking Tours in the Getting Around chapter for details of these tours. Also see Beacon Hill in the Things to See & Do chapter.

This tour will take about two hours. To begin, head into Beacon Hill on Joy St and turn left on **Mt Vernon St**, one of the Hill's loveliest streets. The **Nichols House Museum** (☎ 617-227-6993; 55 Mt Vernon St; open noon-4pm Tues-Sat May-Oct, noon-4pm Thur-Sat Nov-Apr, closed Jan) is one of the Hill's few former residences open to the public. The 30-minute tour ($5) is particularly engaging and is offered noon to 4pm.

Make your way to lovely **Chestnut St**, past **29A Chestnut St**, with rare and authentic purple windowpanes. Head up Willow St to glimpse Boston's narrowest and most photographed street, the cobblestone **Acorn St**, once home to coachmen who worked for the adjacent mansion dwellers.

On Mt Vernon St the private **Second Harrison Gray Otis House** (85 Mt Vernon St) is the second of three houses designed at the turn of the 18th century for Harrison Gray Otis, a real estate developer, US senator and Boston mayor. This house typified Charles Bulfinch's grand plan for this prestigious street in 1802. On land bought from painter John Singleton Copley for a mere $1000 per acre, Bulfinch envisioned a series of freestanding mansions set back from the road, but alas, a population boom and economic slump quashed the plan. Writer Henry James called this showy stretch of Mt Vernon St the 'most respectable street in America.' Indeed.

Inset: Lobster weather vane (photo by Neil Setchfield)

74

BEACON HILL WALKING TOUR

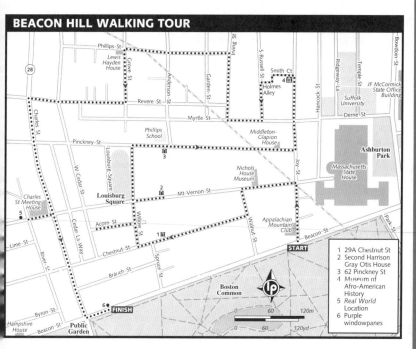

1 29A Chestnut St
2 Second Harrison Gray Otis House
3 62 Pinckney St
4 Museum of Afro-American History
5 *Real World* Location
6 Purple windowpanes

Head down the cobblestone **Louisburg Square** (pronounced Lewis-burg), an elegant cluster of multimillion-dollar brick row houses that face a private elongated park owned by the square's residents. There is not a single more prestigious address in Boston. Louisa May Alcott moved to No 10 after gaining literary success. Senator John Kerry and his wife Teresa Heinz live at the northern corner of the square at Pinckney St.

Turn right up **Pinckney St**, particularly lovely when bathed in late-afternoon light and anytime in spring when the trees are blossoming. During a 1920s renovation of **62 Pinckney St**, a secret closet door was discovered; it led to a tiny attic space where two spoons and tin plates were found. It is assumed that the original owner's wife, Susan Hilliard, a resolute abolitionist, provided a stopping point for runaway slaves on the Underground Railroad during the 1850s. (The house is private.) Across the street the **Phillips School** (formerly known as Boston English High School) was the first public grammar school in Boston to be racially integrated. Unfortunately, it was not integrated by gender as well. It's now condominiums. Continuing along, the small, c. 1795 clapboard **Middleton-Glapion House** (*5 Pinckney St*) is one of Boston's best-preserved colonial structures. It was built by an African-American coachman and his mulatto barber friend, whom you half expect to walk out the front door.

Pinckney St and parallel Myrtle St act as a dividing line between the stately south slope (where you've been walking) and the less conforming north slope. Take a left onto **Joy St**, the only through street connecting Beacon and Cambridge Sts. Joy St demarcated 19th-century white and black communities; whites lived on the south slope, blacks on the north. Head down Joy St to the **Museum of Afro-American History** *(46 Joy St)*, incorporating the African Meeting House and the Abiel Smith School, which served local families in the 1830s. At the time, there were 2000 African Americans on Beacon Hill, with more children than the school could accommodate.

At the end of Smith Court, pass through the narrow and winding **Holmes Alley** to South Russell St. Now turn around and come through it again, this time imagining yourself a slave fleeing 'slavecatchers' (bounty hunters who pursued runaway slaves across state borders and returned them to their owners). The alley was well known to slaves but not to traders; from South Russell St it looked like a dead end. In the mid-18th century the doors fronting the alley were left unlocked so fleeing slaves could hide at any time. If no doors were open, slaves would run to the end to blend into groups of free blacks congregating at the meeting house. Slavecatchers were so unsuccessful that they rarely returned to Boston after an initial visit; a few were even tarred and feathered.

Turn left up South Russell St, take a right onto narrow Myrtle St, a right onto Irving St and a left onto **Phillips St**, which was a hotbed of abolitionist activity in the 19th century. Its proximity to the Charles River proved key. The river, after all, could carry escapees faster than land-based routes could, and it didn't leave a trace of anyone's passage. The private **Lewis Hayden House** *(cnr Phillips & Grove Sts)* is Boston's most important abolitionist site, having served as refuge to many runaway slaves. In fact, an underground tunnel ran from the Charles River to Hayden's house. It's said that his house was never searched for fugitives because he kept a stash of gunpowder in the basement and threatened to blow up the house if its threshold was crossed. When slavecatchers came to his doorway, the militant Hayden, who himself had been born a slave (of Senator Henry Clay), would simply proclaim 'leave in peace or leave in pieces.'

Walk up Grove St then take a right onto Revere St to **Charles St** and the 'flats,' which Otis and Bulfinch filled in in the early 1800s after leveling peaks on the Hill. Charles St, by the way, was named after the Charles River, which in turn was named after King Charles I. The classically Federal **Charles St Meeting House** *(70 Charles St)*, designed by Asher Benjamin, provided a pulpit for abolitionist leaders William Lloyd Garrison, Frederick Douglass, Harriet Tubman and Sojourner Truth during the 19th century. At the corner of River and Mt Vernon Sts, the old **fire-house** was the site for MTV's 1997 *Real World*.

Take Charles St to the **Public Garden**, the country's first botanical garden. Head uphill on **Beacon St**, noting the houses with **purple windowpanes**. Most are reproductions, but at **63–64 Beacon St**, they're the real thing. Between 1818 and 1824, glass shipments from England to America were defective, resulting in the manganese oxide in the glass turning purple. Over time the panes have become a status symbol. From here, head into the **Boston Common**, the country's first public park.

North End: Patriots, Pasta & Paisani

This warren of streets and alleys retains the old-world flavor brought by European immigrants. Notice the storefront social clubs and listen for passionate discussions in Italian by old-timers. Ritual Saturday morning shopping takes place at speciality stores selling handmade pasta, cannoli, biscotti, fresh cheeses, cuts of meat, flowers, and a little of this or that – all within a ¼-mile radius of Boston's oldest colonial buildings.

NORTH END WALKING TOUR

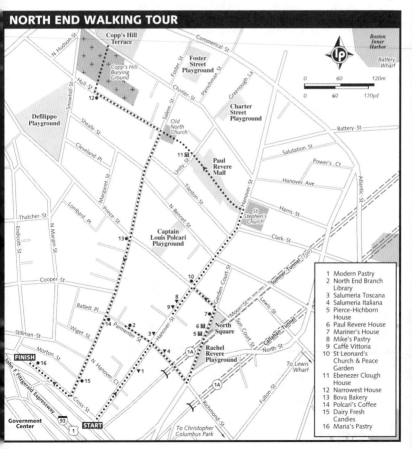

1 Modern Pastry
2 North End Branch Library
3 Salumeria Toscana
4 Salumeria Italiana
5 Pierce-Hichborn House
6 Paul Revere House
7 Mariner's House
8 Mike's Pastry
9 Caffè Vittoria
10 St Leonard's Church & Peace Garden
11 Ebenezer Clough House
12 Narrowest House
13 Bova Bakery
14 Polcari's Coffee
15 Dairy Fresh Candies
16 Maria's Pastry

When you get tired or hungry, there are dozens of cafés and more ristoranti per block than anywhere else in the city. Depending on how long you linger at sites and cafés, this tour will take you one to three hours.

Hanover St is the main commercial thoroughfare, lined with tiny shops, cafés, restaurants and double-parked cars. Two businessmen – Eben Jordan of Jordan Marsh department store fame and Rowland Macy of Macy's department store glory – got their starts here with small dry-goods shops. On the right at **Modern Pastry** (☎ 617-523-3783; 257 Hanover St; open daily), sample the colorful, fruit-shaped marzipan. Modern has plenty of tempting sweets, but other places do too, so pace yourself. Just across Parmenter St on the left is **Salumeria Toscana** (☎ 617-720-4243; 272 Hanover St; open daily), a gourmet Italian deli with a spellbinding array of olives. Pop into the **North End Branch Library** (☎ 617-227-8135; 25 Parmenter St; closed Sun) to check out the impressive plaster model of Venice's Doge's Palace. Then retrace your steps to Hanover St and head down Richmond St to **Salumeria Italiana** (☎ 617-523-8743; 151 Richmond St; closed Sun), an old-fashioned deli and grocery shop. Here you'll find fixings for an Italian-style picnic: salami, prosciutto di Parma, cheese, classic white bean spread, fresh bread and olives.

Turn left for **North Square**, one of Boston's quintessential little triangular paved 'squares'. Look for the 1710 English Renaissance brick **Pierce-Hichborn House** (☎ 617-523-1676; 29 North Square; adult/senior/student/child $3/2/2/1) home of Paul Revere's boatbuilder cousin. The three-story house has a central staircase, unusual for its time. (The house is open only for guided tours, usually at 12:30pm or 2:30pm. Call the morning of your visit.) Next door is the 1680 **Paul Revere House** (19 North Square), which has been changed on numerous occasions over the past 300 years (see Paul Revere House in the Things to See and Do chapter). The 1838 **Mariner's House** (11 North Square) still houses homesick seamen on shore leave. In ye olden days, mariners kept an eye on the sea from atop the cupola. (The shoreline was much closer in the mid-18th century.) Now that the refurbished boarding house has Internet access, sailors log onto Ⓦ www.weather.com.

LEE FOSTER

Left: Paul Revere House, North End

Former mayor John F 'Honey Fitz' Fitzgerald (JFK's grandfather), whose family emigrated from Ireland during the potato famine, was born nearby on little Ferry St in 1863. His father owned small grocery stores on North and Hanover Sts. Honey Fitz referred to his days in the 'dear old North End' so affectionately and repeatedly that residents were known as 'Dearos' during his years of political prominence. Honey Fitz's daughter Rose (JFK's mother) was born near North Square at 4 Garden Court St in 1890.

From North Square you could dip into the Christopher Columbus Park or walk along the sturdy granite wharf buildings that have been converted to expensive condominiums. In the mid-19th century, the famed clipper ship trade revolved around **Lewis Wharf**, where an 18th-century incident inspired Edgar Allan Poe's *Fall of the House of Usher*. Supposedly, when the Usher house was demolished in 1800, two skeletons were found clutching one another behind a locked gate leading to a tunnel. Legend has it that an elderly husband had discovered his young wife in the arms of a sailor and he locked them in.

From North Square follow Prince St (of pasta fame) to Hanover St. Across the street to the left, **Mike's Pastry** *(300 Hanover St)* has fantastico cannoli, if you know how to order; see the boxed text 'Just Desserts' in the Places to Eat chapter. The lobster tail, filled with sweet, whipped marscapone cheese, is another decadent option. For the best cup of cappuccino, go next door to **Caffè Vittoria** *(296 Hanover St)*; see the boxed text 'Cafés' in the Places to Eat chapter. Fortified with caffeine and sugar, head back across Prince St to the Roman Catholic **St Leonard's Church & Peace Garden**, built by Italian immigrants in 1873. The garden is always peaceful, but is particularly worth visiting in the spring and at Christmastime.

Continue on Hanover St to the 1804 **St Stephen's Church**, Boston's only remaining church designed by the renowned Charles Bulfinch. The elaborate facade is made of stone, brick and wood; Revere cast the belfry bell in 1805. Originally a Unitarian church, it was sold to the Catholic diocese in 1862 to serve the North End's Irish-Catholic community. Rose Kennedy was baptized here.

Across the street the shady **Paul Revere Mall** (called 'the prado' by locals) could very well have been snatched brick for brick from Italy. It not only serves as a perfect frame for the Old North Church, but is a lively local meeting place for all generations. And it's also a rare outdoor place to rest while contemplating the imposing equestrian statue of Revere. Pass through the promenade to the 1712 **Ebenezer Clough House** *(21 Unity St)*, one of Boston's few remaining early-18th-century houses. Clough, a Sons of Liberty member who participated in the Boston Tea Party, was a mason who worked on the adjacent **Old North Church** (see Old North Church in the Things to See & Do chapter). Note the little refurbished courtyards, terraces and memorial gardens between the Clough House and the church.

Head up Hull St to **Copp's Hill Burying Ground** (see Copp's Hill Burying Ground in the Things to See & Do chapter). Across from the entrance to the graveyard, the **Narrowest House** (44 Hull St) measures a whopping 9½ft wide. The c. 1800 house reportedly was built, out of spite, to block light from the neighbor's house and to obliterate the view from the house behind it. If the northern cemetery gate is locked, peer over **Copp's Hill Terrace** for a view of Charlestown and the last two Freedom Trail sites – Charlestown Bridge and the USS *Constitution*. If you intend to visit Charlestown by foot, this might be a good time to do it. Otherwise, return to Salem St and head downhill.

Salem St has long been the domain of shopkeepers, and it remains the North End's most interesting commercial street. Stop in at the **Bova Bakery** (134 Salem St; open 24 hr) and the aromatic **Polcari's Coffee** (☎ 617-227-0786; 105 Salem St; closed Sun), purveyor of coffee, nuts, grains and spices, all self-serve from bins, baskets and tubs. The tiny **Dairy Fresh Candies** (☎ 617-742-2639; 57 Salem St; open daily) specializes in domestic and imported nuts, chocolates, candies and dried fruit.

Around the corner **Maria's Pastry** (☎ 617-523-1196; Cross St; open daily) is considered the neighborhood's most authentic pastry shop. Sample the *biscotti regina* (a twice-baked 'queen's cookie' with anise, lemon and sesame seeds), *ossa di mort* (translating as 'dead man's bones,' a sweet anise-flavored cookie) and *torrone* (a nougaty-chocolatey-almondy treat).

Back Bay: From Lowly Landfill to High-Minded Aesthetic

You could easily spend a day strolling down shady Comm Ave, window-shopping and sipping a latte on chic Newbury St, visiting grand churches or taking in remarkable and unified French-influenced Victorian architecture. This dense tour is an amalgam of residential and commercial sites, and does not include the dozens of speciality shops you'll find on Newbury St; see the Shopping chapter for those. Without stopping too much, expect to spend about two hours. You can find more detailed descriptions of many of the following sites in the Things to See & Do chapter.

Start at the **Arlington St Church** (☎ 617-536-7050; open 9am-5pm Mon-Thur year-round). Back Bay's first public building (the neighborhood was filled and constructed from east to west) features 16 commissioned Tiffany windows, a bell tower and an embellished steeple modeled after London's St Martin-in-the-Fields church. The Unitarian Universalist ministry is purely progressive. You have to walk through the office to see the church. Walk up Arlington, past the flagship **Ritz-Carlton Hotel**, neither outwardly showy nor glamorous, true to its pedigree.

The backbone of Back Bay is the Parisian-style boulevard, the **Commonwealth Avenue Mall**, planted with great elm trees. Head west on Comm Ave. On the right the Italianate **Baylies Mansion** (5 Comm Ave) is a relative newcomer, built in 1912. Occupied by the Boston Center for Adult Education (BCAE), its grand ballroom evokes images of Le Petite Trianon at Versailles. BCAE courses are the hottest singles ticket in town.

Newbury St, Back Bay

Townhouse, Beacon St, Beacon Hill

Antique shops, Charles St, Beacon Hill

ANGUS O'BORN

Modern Pastry Shop, North End

KIM GRANT

Christian Science Church, Back Bay

NEIL SETCHFIELD

John Hancock Tower, Back Bay

America's Walking City – Back Bay 81

AMERICA'S WALKING CITY

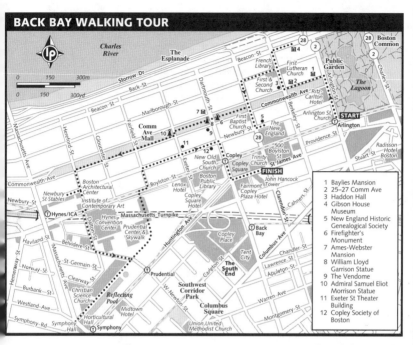

BACK BAY WALKING TOUR

1 Baylies Mansion
2 25–27 Comm Ave
3 Haddon Hall
4 Gibson House Museum
5 New England Historic Genealogical Society
6 Firefighter's Monument
7 Ames-Webster Mansion
8 William Lloyd Garrison Statue
9 The Vendome
10 Admiral Samuel Eliot Morrison Statue
11 Exeter St Theater Building
12 Copley Society of Boston

The Hooper mansion at **25–27 Comm Ave** is the only house in the neighborhood with a corner yard – and what a yard it is! On the opposite side of Berkeley St, the 11-story **Haddon Hall** caused all sorts of problems for its neighbors when it was built. Its weight affected the underground water table (remember, this is landfill) and caused adjacent basements to flood. After it was built, strict height restrictions were imposed (and occasionally violated).

Turn right onto Berkeley St. On the left is **First & Second Church**, which serves one of the country's oldest congregations (founded in 1630). It utilizes nicely what remains of the medieval-style facade (the church burned in 1968). Across the street the **First Lutheran Church** is plain on the inside but has a tranquil courtyard. On the northwest corner of Berkeley and Marlborough Sts, the **French Library** holds a festive annual Bastille Day celebration and is graced by blooming magnolia trees in May. Turn right onto Beacon St for the over-the-top Victorian **Gibson House Museum** *(137 Beacon St)*, which appears just as its last owner left it in 1957 (plus some dust).

Retrace your steps to Marlborough St, Back Bay's quietest, most civilized street, turn right and then turn left onto Clarendon St. On the far corner of Comm Ave and Clarendon St, the 1872 **First Baptist Church**, an early Romanesque HH Richardson design, has an Italian campanile and a striking frieze depicting the sacraments. The church's nickname, 'the Church of the Holy Bean Blowers,' comes from the angels blowing their trumpets from on high.

Think you might be related to Frederick Douglass or Mary Dyer? The private **New England Historic Genealogical Society** *(☎ 617-536-5740; 101 Newbury St; library open 9am-5pm Tues-Sat, until 9pm Wed)* contains millions of manuscripts and documents, dating back to the Puritans, that help people from all over the world trace their family tree. For $15 a day or $60 a year, you are granted access to everything but manuscripts.

Head back to the Comm Ave Mall and turn left down the middle of it. The somber **Firefighters' Monument** honors the nine men who died in the **Vendome** *(160 Comm Ave)* fire of 1972. Built in 1871, this former French Second Empire hotel was the most luxurious in Boston in its time, the first public building to have electricity. The interior is now gutted but the ornamental facade remains intact.

On the opposite corner of Comm Ave and Dartmouth St, the massive 1872 **Ames-Webster Mansion** has Back Bay's most grand interior. (Alas, subdivided into offices, it's not open to the public.) You'll have to imagine guests arriving under the porte cochere, making an entrance down a grand staircase, the likes of which are not often seen this side of the Atlantic, and dancing beneath richly paneled 18ft-high ceilings in a breathtaking hall some 60ft long.

Continuing down the mall, the **William Lloyd Garrison Statue** pays tribute to the extraordinary abolitionist. One block farther the **Admiral Samuel Eliot Morison Statue** is perhaps the most beloved on the strip. The seaman and historian is perched atop a boulder, as if on sea's edge. Continue down the mall and turn left onto Hereford St, then continue to **Newbury St**. Epitomized by café hounds and haute couture crowds, Newbury St is to Boston what Fifth Ave is to New York City, on a more intimate scale.

The **Boston Architectural Center** *(BAC; ☎ 617-536-3170; cnr Newbury & Hereford Sts; open 9am-10pm Mon-Thur, 9am-5pm Fri & Sat, noon-5pm Sun)*, adorned with a trompe l'oeil mural by Richard Haas, is best viewed from Boylston St or Newbury St near Mass Ave. The BAC has frequently changing exhibits on urban architecture and design. Next door, running almost the length of the block, the **Newbury St Stables** once accommodated horses and carriages for residents who didn't have their own stables.

Continue down Hereford St for the **Institute for Contemporary Art** *(955 Boylston St)*. Cross Boylston St, head down Dalton St, then turn left on Belvidere St and right at the **reflecting pool** of the monumental **Christian Science Church** and world headquarters complex. Next door, at the corner of Mass and Huntington Aves, are two grand buildings, **Horticultural Hall** and **Symphony Hall**.

Head back toward Boylston St by cutting through the **Prudential Center** plaza and mall. The 50th-floor **Prudential Center Skywalk** offers panoramic views of Boston (see the boxed text 'Bird's-Eye View' in the Facts for the Visitor chapter).

Take a right on Boylston St, a quick left on Fairfield St and a right on Newbury St. At the corner of Exeter St the HH Richardson Romanesque **Exeter St Theater Building** was built as a church in 1884, converted into a movie theater in 1914 and gutted for retail space in 1985. Continuing on Newbury St, the **Copley Society of Boston** (☎ *617-536-5049; 158 Newbury St; open 10:30am-5:30pm Tues-Sat)*, the oldest nonprofit art association in the country, has 1st-floor galleries.

Turn right onto Dartmouth St where you'll quickly encounter the late-19th-century **New Old South Church**. Somehow, it fits perfectly on the corner of **Copley Square**, itself surrounded by four monumental buildings. The venerable **Boston Public Library** consists of two distinct structures: the original 1895 McKim, Mead & White building fronting Dartmouth St, and the dignified, skylit 1971 Philip Johnson wing facing Boylston St. (Both buildings are named for their architects rather than a wealthy patron.) The extravagant **Fairmont Copley Plaza Hotel** anchors the corner of St James Ave, where the original Museum of Fine Arts was located from 1872 to 1909. HH Richardson's Romanesque masterpiece **Trinity Church**, often called one of the great monuments of American architecture, takes center stage. Or does the **John Hancock Tower**, a reflective 62-story glass skyscraper, dominate?

NEIL SETCHFIELD

Right: Trinity Church, Back Bay

Places to Stay

It's not cheap to sleep in Boston. Hotel construction and hotel rates are soaring faster than eagles on an updraft. Still, despite the arrival of many new properties (boutique beds geared toward business folks) and despite the fallout from 9-11 (when occupancy dipped precipitously), Boston hotels still enjoy astonishingly high occupancy rates. Room rates average about $200 nightly. In fact, the city is among the three tightest markets in the country for finding beds. Translation: hotels charge what they want because they can get it. Be strategic though, and you'll be able to feed and entertain yourself once you've caught a few z's. Call the reservation services before calling the hotel directly. Secure reservations six months in advance if you can. Stay on the outskirts of town. Visit during low season. Finally, if you can't find an inexpensive place, consider weekend jaunts in the city sandwiched by weekday overnights in the surrounding areas.

Price ranges for budget, mid-range and top-end accommodations are generally as follows: budget, less than $100; mid-range, $100 to $200; top end, $200 and up. Use our quoted prices, based on published 'rack rates,' only as a guideline. Rates fluctuate from hour to hour – oftentimes depending on who answers the phone! They certainly fluctuate daily and seasonally. The high season for hotel rates is roughly defined as April through October, although it's more accurately driven by occupancy and high-profile events. So New Year's or Valentine's Day, for instance, in late December and mid-February respectively, *should* be low season, but you'll probably find higher than expected rates. Simply asking about specials can often save quite a bit of money. And don't forget about the rooms tax (not applicable to B&Bs), currently a whopping 12.75%. Rates quoted do not include this tax.

BEACON HILL (MAP 2)
You can't beat this neighborhood for location and beauty. Almost everything, except

Boston's Best Beds

Best deal	Irish Embassy Hostel (p84)
Most quirky digs	Golden Slipper (p85)
Best rooms with a view	Custom House (p86)
Most gay friendly	Chandler Inn (p88)
Friendliest B&B	Gryphon House (p89)
Coolest covers	University Park Hotel at MIT (p90)

Cambridge, is within walking distance from here.

John Jeffries House *(Map 2, #2; ☎ 617-367-1866, fax 617-742-0313; ⓦ www.johnjeffriehouse.com; 14 David Mugar Way; singles $90, doubles & suites high season $110-145)* has 46 rooms and suites in a four-story, early-20th-century building owned by the Massachusetts Eye & Ear Infirmary. (You don't have to know someone having an operation to stay here.) Rooms are nicely decorated, and some still have original molding and hardwood floors; most have a kitchenette. Off-season doubles drop in price by $10 to $20.

Beacon Hill Bed & Breakfast *(Map 2, #18; ☎ 617-523-7376; 27 Brimmer St; rooms $225-275)*, Susan Butterworth's home, really gives travelers a taste of living on the hill (even though this is the flat part of the hill). She has only two rooms, but what rooms they are! Private bathrooms and full breakfast are included.

GOVERNMENT CENTER & NORTH END (MAP 3)
There's not much atmosphere around here, and the area around North Station can be filled with late-night sports fanatics, but prices compensate for it. Very few things can beat a waterfront North End location.

Irish Embassy Hostel *(Map 3, #9; ☎ 617-973-4841, fax 617-720-3998; ⓔ beantownh@aol.com; 232 Friend St; beds $25)* rents 82 beds in seven rooms (with four to 10 people per room) above its lively eponymous pub. For a very modest price you'll get an extremely tidy place; sheets, towels and bedding; admission to hear live bands in two pubs; an all-you-can-eat barbecue buffet dinner Sunday through Wednesday in summer (two to three nights year-round); and $1.50 beers. It can't be beat, but don't get too comfortable; there's a six-night maximum stay. There's no lockout either. The hostel is full by the official check-in time of 9am in summer, so make reservations as far in advance as possible.

Beantown Hostel (Map 3, #10; ☎ 617-723-0800, fax 617-720-3998; e beantownh@aol.com; 222 Friend St), operated by the nearby Irish Embassy Hostel, has 56 beds. Some rooms are single sex; some are mixed. They supply lockers; you supply locks. Prices and information are similar to the Irish Embassy's. One difference is Beantown's 1:45am curfew.

Shawmut Inn (Map 3, #6; ☎ 617-720-5544, 800-350-7784, fax 617-723-7784; 280 Friend St; rooms high season $116-146, low season $91-121, children under 12 free), a friendly, small hotel with many European guests, has 66 darkish rooms on five floors. All rooms have a microwave, coffeemaker and refrigerator in their kitchenette. Suites, with a foldout couch, are available for reduced weekly rentals. Rooms that face the elevated subway line are noisy, but the staff try to accommodate noise level preferences. Continental breakfast is included.

Holiday Inn Select – Government Center (Map 3, #36; ☎ 617-742-7630, 800-465-4329, fax 617-742-7804; 5 Blossom St; rooms $159-250, children under 19 free), on the back side of Beacon Hill, has 303 well-kept rooms with two double beds or one king. Other perks of this 15-story inn include a $13 all-you-can-eat breakfast buffet or $8 continental buffet, an adjacent supermarket and a small outdoor pool.

In the North End, the **Golden Slipper** (Map 3, #32; ☎ 781-545-2845; Lewis Wharf; doubles $175, each additional person $35), a 40ft docked wooden boat, offers an unusual and romantic set-up. While it's sweet and cozy, with a cabin separate from the sleeping quarters, this is no yacht. The shower is funky but

fully functional. As long as it's a calm night, you might enjoy cooking in the galley, too. The price includes an expanded continental breakfast delivered in a basket.

DOWNTOWN & WATERFRONT (MAP 4)
Budget
It's a rare opportunity to stay overnight on islands in a major metropolitan area. But you can do it in Boston. If that's not your (sleeping) bag, take in sunrise *and* room service from a prime waterfront location. This neighborhood is less foot-friendly and slightly more removed than others.

Boston Harbor Islands State Park (☎ 617-223-8666; w www.bostonislands.com) is managed by both the **Department of Environmental Management** (DEM; ☎ 781-740-1605 ext 205 for information, ☎ 877-422-6762 for reservations) and the **Metropolitan District Commission** (MDC; ☎ 617-727-7676; 98 Taylor St, Dorchester, MA 02122). It consists of 34 islands and there's camping on four: Peddock's, Lovell's, Grape and Bumpkin. Each island has about 10 to 12 individual sites and one group site that holds 50 people. Camping is allowed on Saturday from early May to mid-October and nightly from early June to early September. For more on each island, see the boxed text 'Boston Harbor Islands State Park' in the Things to See & Do chapter.

Here are the important do's and don'ts: do bring your own water and supplies; do carry in and carry out everything; do hang your food high, out of reach of animals; don't bring pets or alcohol; don't make open fires; don't expect anything more than primitive sites and composting toilets.

The MDC manages Peddock's and Lovell's Islands; call for reservations and then fax or write for free camping permits in advance. The DEM manages the wooded Grape and Bumpkin Islands; phone for a camping reservation.

Regular daytime ferry service is provided by **Boston Harbor Cruises** (Map 4, #3; ☎ 617-227-4321; w www.bostonharborcruises.com; 1 Long Wharf), off Atlantic Ave, from early May to mid-October. Purchase a round-trip ticket (adult/senior/child $10/8/7) to Georges Island where you then catch a free water taxi to the smaller islands (another 15 to 60 minutes, depending on where you're going). It's best to go out for a few days, island hop and come back to stay somewhere else in Boston.

Mid-Range & Top End
Although these places generally cater to business folks, they offer good deals on weekends to travelers.

Harborside Inn *(Map 4, #9; ☎ 617-723-7500, 888-723-7565, fax 617-670-2010; W www.hagopianhotels.com; 185 State St; doubles $119-220, suites for up to 5 people $310)*, a seven-story top-end place in a respectfully renovated 19th-century warehouse, has B&B-style rooms with hotel-style service. The 54 rooms have original exposed brick and granite walls, hardwood floors, area carpets and Victorian furnishings. They also have modern bathrooms, cable TV and free local calls. Windows are well insulated from street noise.

Wyndham Hotel *(Map 4, #28; ☎ 617-556-0006, fax 617-556-0053; W www.wyndham .com; 89 Broad St; doubles weekdays $199-249, weekends $129-249)* hosts business travelers during the week. But on weekends travelers have the place to themselves and pay a cheaper rate for state-of-the-art guest rooms and top-notch amenities.

Omni Parker House *(Map 4, #16; ☎ 617-227-8600, 800-843-6664, fax 617-227-9607; W www.omnihotels.com; 60 School St; rooms high season $199-309, low season $169-259)*, the country's oldest continually operating hotel, has 551 modern but charming rooms. Even though the lovely 1856 establishment sits smack dab in the middle of town, you may find yourself lazily luxuriating in one of its deep tubs. Ask for special promotions.

Marriott's **Custom House** *(Map 4, #8; ☎ 617-310-6300, 800-845-5279; W www .marriott.com; 3 McKinley Square; 1-bedroom suites $200-400)*, considered a blasphemous time-share takeover by some, offers perhaps the most stunning views in Boston. The 25-story tower, one of the city's most prominent landmarks, has 84 one-bedroom suites with

Hotel Discounts

One of the best ways to gain entry into an otherwise inaccessible mid-range or top-end hotel is to contact a hotel broker or reservation service. These service bureaus develop relationships with hotels during economic downturns that carry over into good times, too. These agencies have access to lower rates than you can get by calling the hotel directly.

Central Reservation Service of New England *(☎ 617-569-3800, 800-332-3026, fax 617-561-4840; W www.bostonhotels.net)* operates out of Terminal E at Logan International Airport. But try not to wait until you've landed to secure a place to stay.

Hotel Reservations Network *(☎ 800-964-6835; W www.hoteldiscount.com)* and **Citywide Reservation Services** *(☎ 617-267-7424, 800-468-3593, fax 617-267-9408; W www .cityres.com)* offer similar services.

Accommodations Express *(☎ 800-444-7666; W www.accommodationsexpress.com)* is worth a try if you can get through.

all the amenities and facilities you'd expect for the price.

Boston Marriott Long Wharf *(Map 4, #2; ☎ 617-227-0800, 800-627-7468, fax 617-227-2867; W www.marriott.com; 296 State St; doubles high season $239-339, low season $159-179)* is pretty small for a Marriott (only 400 rooms on seven floors) and its location is pretty special – on a real wharf jutting into Boston Harbor, just a block from Faneuil Hall and next door to the aquarium. All the usual Marriott amenities are included, and it's cheaper on weekends than weekdays.

BACK BAY (MAP 5)
There are lots of enormous, expense-account hotels around Copley Place, the Prudential Center and the Hynes Convention Center, geared toward conventioneers and business people. Fortunately this desirable neighborhood has a range of other places, too.

463 Beacon St Guest House *(Map 5, #2; ☎ 617-536-1302, fax 617-247-8876; W www .463beacon.com; 463 Beacon St; doubles*

$79-109)$, a well-situated six-story c. 1880 brownstone, has 20 guest rooms, most of which have a private bathroom and kitchenette. Rooms vary considerably in size; all have cable TV and phone.

Commonwealth Court Guest House *(Map 5, #4; ☎ 617-424-1230, 888-424-1230, fax 617-424-1510; W www.commonwealth court.com; 284 Comm Ave; rooms high season $99-130, low season $75-105, doubles weekly $625)* has 20 rooms with kitchenettes, cable TV and free local phone calls. Rooms aren't spiffy, but the location is great and the price is pretty darn good.

College Club *(Map 5, #6; ☎ 617-536-9510, fax 617-247-8537; W www.thecollege clubboston.com; 44 Comm Ave; singles $80-90, doubles $130-150)*, originally a private club for female college graduates, has 11 enormous rooms, open to both sexes. Some furnishings are a bit shabby (in a worn-out Ivy League sort of way) and the shared bathrooms are a bit scruffy, but all in all it's great value. A generous continental breakfast is included.

Newbury Guest House *(Map 5, #28; ☎ 617-437-7666, 800-437-7668, fax 617-670-6100; W www.hagopianhotels.com; 261 Newbury St; singles $110-175, doubles $125-190)* has 32 rooms with private bathroom in a four-story, c. 1882 renovated brownstone. Prices include a continental breakfast buffet. There is limited parking for $15, but you must reserve it in advance.

Copley Square Hotel *(Map 5, #55; ☎ 617-536-9000, 800-225-7062, fax 617-236-0351; W www.copleysquarehotel.com; 47 Huntington Ave; doubles high season from $295, low season from $169)* is a low-key European-style hostelry built in 1891. Although its age shows a little bit in the hallways and bathrooms, the 143 rooms are well equipped, the staff is friendly and room windows actually open! Ask about special packages.

Lenox Hotel *(Map 5, #54; ☎ 617-536-5300, 800-225-7676, fax 617-236-0351; W www .lenoxhotel.com; 710 Boylston St; rooms high season from $308, low season from $189)* is another early-20th-century hotel that's undergone recent renovations. A fancy old-worldish lobby gives way to soundproof guest rooms with classical furnishings, high ceilings, and sitting areas.

THEATER DISTRICT (MAP 6)

This centrally located neighborhood is bustling with activity day and night, but if you want to be in the thick of it, you can't do any better.

Milner Hotel *(Map 6, #30; ☎ 617-426-6220, 800-453-1731, fax 617-350-0360; W www.milner-hotel.com; 78 Charles St S; doubles $105-163)*, a five-story place built in 1918, has a tidy, tiny, tacky lobby. Regardless, it has a few things going for it: friendly staff, great location and even better prices. The rooms are small and drab, but you can get a quiet night's sleep. Somehow, it manages to be a charmer. Rates drop $15 to $30 off-season.

Tremont House *(Map 6, #31; ☎ 617-426-1400, 800-331-9998, fax 617-482-6730; W www.wyndham.com; 275 Tremont St; doubles $209-314)*, built in 1925 as the national Elks headquarters, retains an ornate and elegant lobby. Today its 322 rooms on 15 floors are smallish but contemporary. It's a comfortable and fun hotel, as befits any place sprinkled with elk heads. Nightclubs and theaters just outside the door add to the appeal.

Radisson Hotel *(Map 6, #24; ☎ 617-482-1800, 800-333-3333, fax 617-451-2750; W www.radisson.com; 200 Stuart St; doubles high season $204-339, low season $179-204)* and its central location are appreciated by both business travelers and tourists. This 24-story hotel has 356 rooms. Added bonuses include many rooms with private balconies, a fitness center and an indoor swimming pool.

SOUTH END (MAP 6)

Chichi, funky, slightly edgy and filled with excellent restaurants, this predominantly gay neighborhood is great for walkers.

Berkeley Residence YWCA *(Map 6, #46; ☎ 617-375-2524, fax 617-375-2525; 40 Berkeley St; singles/doubles/triples $56/86/99, weekly $280/430/495)* rents over 200 small rooms to women. Nightly rates include breakfast, and the maximum stay is 13 nights. For those on travel-study programs who want to stay three to four weeks, the weekly rate includes breakfast and dinner. Guests can use the library, TV room, laundry room and garden.

Copley House *(Map 6, #50; ☎ 617-236-8300, 800-331-1318, fax 617-424-1815; W www.copleyhouse.com; 239 W Newton St; studios & 1-bedroom apartments $80-135, weekly $475-750)* has accommodations in six area buildings, but everyone checks in at West Newton St. The studios and one-bedroom apartments are worn but service-able with fully equipped kitchenettes, cable TV and free local calls.

Copley Inn *(Map 6, #39; ☎ 617-236-0300, 800-232-0306, fax 617-536-0816; W www.copleyinn.com; 19 Garrison St; studios high season $125-145, low season $95-125, children under 12 free low season)*, a brick townhouse in a quiet residential neighborhood, offers 20 comfortable and modern guest studios.

Chandler Inn *(Map 6, #45; ☎ 617-482-3450, fax 617-542-3428; W www.chandlerinn.com; 26 Chandler St; singles $99-169, doubles $109-179)*, on a quiet side street, is popular with Europeans and gays and has 56 clean, albeit undistinguished, rooms.

Clarendon Square Inn *(Map 6, #57; ☎ 617-536-2229; W www.clarendonsquare.com; 198 W Brookline St; rooms $119-249)* has only three rooms (with private bathroom) but they're oh-so-urbane and stylish. Staying at the brick townhouse B&B, complete with lofty living room and roof-deck hot tub, will give you a great sense of gay, chichi South End living. Prices vary with the season.

Midtown Hotel *(Map 6, #49; ☎ 617-262-1000, 800-343-1177, fax 617-262-8739; W www.midtownhotel.com; 220 Huntington Ave; rooms high season $209-229, low season $119-189)* straddles Back Bay and the South End, just two blocks from the 4½-mile Southwest Corridor Park (great for walking). The two-story, 159-room hotel has a few perks: free parking, an enclosed outdoor pool and children under 18 stay free with their parents.

KENMORE SQUARE & THE FENWAY (MAP 7)

This area bustles with students and Red Sox fans. It also has a fair number of cheap places to stay (hostels) and some good mid-range

non-hotel options. If you're big on late-night clubbing, this neighborhood may be your best bet for stumbling home without the aid of a taxi.

Budget

You'll find the cheapest beds at **Boston International Hostel** *(Map 7, #49; ☎ 617-536-9455, fax 617-424-6558; W www.bostonhostel.org; 12 Hemenway St; dorm beds members/nonmembers $29/32)*. In addition to offering discount tickets to activities, the hostel offers walking tours, slide shows, free or cheap lectures, transportation to clubs and low-cost, high-speed Internet connections on two computers. Best of all, though, the staff acts as a concierge service.

Most dorm-style bunk rooms hold six people (same sex); some coed doubles are available. There is a 14-night maximum stay during any six-month period. US citizens can become members for $28 on the spot ($18 for international visitors). Try to reserve (with a credit card) at least three months ahead of time by phone, fax or email. If the hostel is full, the staff will guide you elsewhere. About 10 beds are set aside for 7:30am walk-ins; be there early. There is no lockout.

Fenway Summer Hostel *(Map 7, #26; ☎ 617-267-8599, 617-536-1027 reservations; W www.bostonhostel.org; 575 Comm Ave; beds $33-37)* is operated by Hostelling International. A Boston University dorm during the school year, its 250 beds are only rented from early June to late August. Sheets and towels are provided. Since the hostel was a hotel, all rooms have private bathrooms and only three beds each.

YMCA of Greater Boston *(Map 7, #61; ☎ 617-536-7800, fax 617-267-4653; W www.ymcaboston.org; 316 Huntington Ave, Boston, MA 02115; singles/doubles members $40/55, nonmembers $45/65, triples $81, quads $96)* rents 39 rooms to men, women and families with children 16 and older from June through August. From September through May, though, the Y accepts men only. Prices include breakfast and use of the excellent gym and pool. Reserve by mailing a deposit two weeks prior to your visit, or call to make a credit card reservation; very few rooms are available for walk-ins. If you're going to try to get lucky, show up at 11am.

Anthony's Town House *(Map 7, #19; ☎ 617-566-3972;* [W] *www.anthonystown house.com; 1085 Beacon St; rooms $70-90)* boasts friendly management and a late (noon) check-out. The Victorian-era brownstone, more reminiscent of a boarding house than a boudoir from a Henry James novel, has 10 rooms with shared bathroom. Room rates tend to attract professors, foreigners, and students and their parents.

Mid-Range & Top End

On the edge of the Fenway and bordering the South End and Back Bay, **Oasis Guest House** *(Map 7, #50; ☎ 617-267-2262, fax 617-267-1920;* [W] *www.oasisgh.com; 22 Edgerly Rd; doubles $90-140)* actually consists of four renovated bow-front brick townhouses. Most of the 30 modest rooms have queens and private bathroom, but the cheapest ones are smaller and share bathrooms. There's also a guest kitchen and living room. Parking costs $10 daily.

Buckminster *(Map 7, #28; ☎ 617-236-7050, 800-727-2825, fax 617-262-0068; 645 Beacon St; singles/doubles high season $109/209, low season $69/79)*, a 1903 pension-style hotel, has rooms ranging from small singles to suites that can accommodate larger families or groups. Each floor has its own laundry and kitchen facilities, fine if you're traveling with your own pots, pans and utensils. Rooms have air-con, TV and phone.

Howard Johnson Fenway *(Map 7, #44; ☎ 617-267-8300, 800-654-2000, fax 617-267-2763;* [W] *www.hojo.com; 1271 Boylston St; rooms high season $180, low season $115-140)*, only about 10 minutes from downtown on the T, has 94 standard rooms. Rates include parking.

Gryphon House *(Map 7, #32; ☎ 617-375-9003, fax 617-425-0716;* [W] *www.innboston .com; 9 Bay State Rd; rooms $179-234)*, an elegant five-story brownstone on a quiet side street, has eight B&B-style suites. Alongside gas fireplaces, TV, VCR, CD players, two phone lines and high-speed Internet connections, the rooms have retained late-19th-century period details. Each room has a

different theme. It's one of the nicest places to stay in the city. Period. Rates include continental breakfast and on-site parking.

BROOKLINE (MAP 7)

For more leafy pastures, head out to these Coolidge Corner digs, a Green Line ride away from downtown. If you value a little pocket change over being within walking distance of historical sites, this neighborhood is a great option.

Brookline Manor Guest House *(Map 7, #13; ☎ 617-232-0003, 800-535-5325, fax 617-734-5815; 32 Centre St; rooms $125-175)* has 35 mid-range rooms with private bathroom and continental breakfast; parking is $5 nightly.

Bertram Inn *(Map 7, #18; ☎ 617-566-2234, 800-295-3822, fax 617-277-1887;*

W *www.bertraminn.com; 92 Sewall Ave; rooms summer & fall $129-229, spring & winter $109-179)*, an honest-to-goodness B&B that sets out homebaked cookies in the afternoon, has 14 upscale Victorian-style rooms with period antiques and private bathroom.

CAMBRIDGE (MAPS 8, 9 & 10)

Places are scattered all around town, from the ultra-convenient Harvard and Central Squares to the less central (but cheaper) Inman Square and East Cambridge. Most are 'moderately priced' B&Bs.

Windsor House Bed & Breakfast *(Map 9, #20; ☎ 617-354-7916; 283 Windsor St; doubles $75-95)*, in Inman Square, is a 10- to 15-minute walk from the T. It has two homey guest rooms (one of which can sleep three people) and on-street parking. Owner Heidi Lyons, who has a room on the 2nd floor, sets out a particularly generous buffet-style breakfast.

Holiday Inn Express & Suites – Cambridge *(☎ 617-441-9200, 888-887-7690, fax 617-354-1313; W www.hiselect.com; 250 Monsignor O'Brien Hwy; rooms high season $127-149, low season $110-129)*, in East Cambridge, has 112 well-maintained rooms. Prices, which include local calls and a breakfast buffet, reflect its in-the-middle-of-nowhere location. Nonetheless, it's a two-minute walk from Lechmere Green Line or a short, direct bus trip from Harvard Square.

Irving House *(Map 8, #6; ☎ 617-547-4600, 877-547-4600, fax 617-576-2814; W www.irvinghouse.com; 24 Irving St; singles with shared/private bathroom $89/149, doubles $119/164, triples $179, children 7 & under free)*, in the Harvard Square area, is staffed 24 hours a day. It boasts 44 rooms and is good value made better by its prime location. With luck and timing, you might get one of the limited free parking spaces and use of a museum pass, too. Rates include continental breakfast.

A Friendly Inn *(Map 8, #7; ☎ 617-547-7851; 1673 Cambridge St; singles/doubles $97/117)* leaves itself open to constant evaluation because of its name. ('Friendliness reviews' vary depending on who's working.) Just a 10-minute walk from Harvard Square,

all rooms come with private bathroom, air-con, TV, phone and continental breakfast. There's also free parking, if you're silly enough to have a car anywhere near Harvard Square.

Mary Prentiss Inn *(Map 10, #30; ☎ 617-661-2929, fax 617-661-5989; W www.mary prentissinn.com; 6 Prentiss St; rooms high season $149-229, low season $129-169)*, on a quiet residential street off Mass Ave between Harvard and Porter Squares, has 20 upscale rooms and suites within a completely renovated neoclassical Greek revival gem. The outdoor deck is particularly nice in warm weather. Rates include full breakfast.

Harding House *(Map 9, #15; ☎ 617-876-2888, 877-489-2888, fax 617-497-0953; W www.irvinghouse.com; 288 Harvard St; singles with shared bathroom $89-99, doubles with private bathroom high season $165-210, low season $115-149, children 12 & under free)*, between Harvard and Central Squares, is a graceful 1860s Victorian B&B with 14 nicely appointed guest rooms. A couple of rooms can accommodate families. Hardwood floors, stained-glass windows and oriental carpets add to the period ambiance. Continental breakfast, free on-site parking and museum passes are included.

Best Western Hotel Tria *(☎ 617-491-8000, 800-528-1234, fax 617-491-4932; W www .hoteltria.com; 220 Alewife Brook Parkway; rooms high season $189-219, low season $139-169)*, in North Cambridge, is an easy 10-minute walk from the Alewife Red Line T station, and has 69 rooms on three floors. Friendly management, a small indoor pool, free parking, high-speed Internet connection, and continental breakfast are included. Always ask about specials. A health-food supermarket and movie theater are right next door.

University Park Hotel at MIT *(Map 9, #57; ☎ 617-577-0200, 800-222-8733, fax 617-494-8366; W www.hotelatmit.com; 20 Sidney St; doubles weekdays $199-279)*, near Central Square, is certainly the area's hippest place. It fuses art, design and science. An atom rotates within a sculpted carpet on the elevator; computer boards equipped with high-speed Internet connections are built into wood armoires; wash basins rise above marble sink tops in the bathroom. The 201 rooms and suites are awash with wood, chrome and ergonomically designed furniture. Rooms cost slightly less on weekends.

Marriott Residence Inn *(Map 9, #52;* ☎ *617-349-0700, 800-627-7468, fax 617-547-8504;* **w** *www.marriott.com; Broadway at Ames St; one-bedroom apartments $209-349)*, a Marriott property in Kendall Square with 221 suites, boasts studios and one- or two-bedroom apartments with full kitchens (although the place serves breakfast daily). This place is great for travelers looking for a full-facility base camp. Rates are based on length of stay and season.

CHARLESTOWN (MAP 11)

It's a tad inconvenient staying in Charlestown, but the price is right.

The excellent **Constitution Inn YMCA** *(Map 11, #3;* ☎ *617-241-8400, 800-495-9622, fax 617-241-2856;* **w** *www.constitution inn.com; 150 Second Ave; twins $99)*, Charlestown Navy Yard, is a short, scenic boat ride from downtown Boston. Although it accommodates active and retired military personnel, the Y accepts civilian guests, too. Strident antiwar types needn't be put off sleeping here, nor will you see a preponderance of crew cuts. What you'll find is a good fitness center, refrigerators in every room and a pool.

OUTLYING NEIGHBORHOODS

Boston has its share of adequate, cookie-cutter motel chains, most of which are in outlying neighborhoods and accessible via the T. Camping, as long as you're willing to commute by car, will save you big bucks in Boston.

Budget

Wompatuck State Park *(*☎ *781-749-7160, 877-422-6762 reservations; Union St, Hingham; sites for 2 people $10-15; open Apr–mid-Oct)* has 260 relatively undeveloped camp sites on 3500 acres. It's about 30 minutes south of Boston by car, as long as it's not rush hour. The park has excellent paved paths and mountain bike trails. Take I-93 south from Boston to MA 3 south to MA 228 (exit 14). Head 7 miles north on Free St to Union St.

Normandy Farms Campground *(*☎ *508-543-7600; 72 West St, Foxboro; sites for 2 people $26-40; open year-round)*, resembling a self-contained town more than a traditional camping ground, caters more to recreational vehicles (RVs) than tents. It has a big recreation room and four pools (one indoor), and over 400 open and wooded sites on 50 acres. A state park, great for walking, is just down the road. The camping ground is about 50 minutes from Boston by car; take I-93 south to I-95 south to MA 1 south for 7 miles; head east on Thurston St to West St.

Motel 6 *(*☎ *781-848-7890, 800-466-8356, fax 617-843-1929; 125 Union St, Braintree; singles/doubles/triples/quads $90/96/99/102)* is 15 miles south of the city, but you can be whisked hassle-free into Boston in 30 minutes via the T, which stops 50ft away. Rates are about $10 less off-season. Take the T Red Line to Braintree.

Newton Park Inn *(*☎ *617-527-9000, 800 670-7275, fax 617-527-4994; 160 Boylston St/ MA 9, Newton; doubles high season $90-117, low season $59-77)* is about 8 miles (30 minutes) west of downtown Boston on public transportation. Rates for its 144 simple rooms include free parking, use of an outdoor pool, continental breakfast and cable movies. Ride the T Green Line, 'D' branch to Chestnut Hill, and then it's a 15-minute walk.

Mid-Range

Howard Johnson Inn *(*☎ *617-287-9200, fax 617-282-2365;* **w** *www.bostonhotel.com; 900 Morrissey Blvd; doubles $99-169)*, right off the I-93, 5 miles south of the city, has 133 rooms across from a grocery store. Every 30 minutes a van shuttles guests from the JFK Red Line T station to the hotel.

Ramada Inn *(*☎ *617-287-9100, fax 617-265-9287;* **w** *www.bostonhotel.com; 800 Morrissey Blvd; doubles $99-149)*, right off the I-93, also 5 miles south of the city, is a 150-room, 3-story hotel with an outdoor pool. Every 30 minutes a van shuttles guests from the JFK Red Line T station to the hotel.

Best Western Terrace Inn *(*☎ *617-566-6260, 800-242-8377, fax 617-731-3543;* **w** *www.bestwestern.com/terraceinn; 1650 Comm Ave, Brighton; singles & doubles*

$109-169, triples & quads $139-209) is 2 miles west of Kenmore Square or 20 minutes from Boston Common via public transportation. Some of the 72 rooms have kitchenettes; all have TV, refrigerator and air con. Rates include parking. Hop on the T Green Line, 'B' branch to Mt Hood.

Holiday Inn Express (☎ *617-288-3030, 800-465-4329, fax 617-265-6543;* W *www .hiexpress.com/bos-express; doubles high season $129-189, low season $99-119),* in Dorchester, is about 3 miles south of downtown. Parking is free, the Red Line is eight blocks away on a well-lit street and a 24-hour grocery store is around the corner. The 118 standard motel-style rooms have aircon. Take the T Red Line to Andrew, or take exit 16 off I-93.

Places to Eat

Boston has outgrown its reputation for stodgy, bland, overcooked food. These days, you'll have to look hard to find old standards like 'New England boiled dinner' (corned beef, potatoes and cabbage, boiled together in a pot until all three ingredients achieve the same gray color, zero flavor and mushy consistency), 'seafood Newburg' (chunks of fish, scallops and shrimp in an overwhelmingly heavy cream sauce served on a pastry shell) and 'Boston baked beans' (navy beans and salt pork in molasses). Prepared by the right chef on a cold winter's day, some of these dishes might be categorized as trendy 'comfort food,' but they no longer define dining in Boston, thank goodness.

Eating cheaply doesn't have to mean eating badly. Moreover, if you want to splurge, you'll find some of the country's most highly regarded restaurants. For well-heeled Bostonians, dinner is not a prelude to an evening on the town; it's the evening's entertainment. Considering the cost of a concert or theater ticket, three hours with one of Boston's celebrity chefs is a bargain.

Expect to pay less than $10 for main meals at budget eateries, and from $10 to $20 per person at mid-range eateries. Top-end restaurants will set you back at least $20 per person, but they're all worth a splurge; reservations are recommended. Unless otherwise noted, all are open for lunch and dinner daily.

BEACON HILL (MAP 2)
Budget
Panificio *(Map 2, #10; ☎ 617-227-4340; 144 Charles St; breakfast $2-5, lunch mains $6-8, dinner mains $15-17)*, a cozy bistro, is particularly known for weekday breakfast and weekend brunch. Arrive early for frittatas and french toast if you intend to linger over coffee and a newspaper. Pastas are de rigueur

---

Succulent Seafood

For many, a visit to Boston is not complete without a lobster dinner. Price depends on weight, and the traditional preparation doesn't call for a master chef. The homely crustaceans are plopped live, yes live, into a pot of boiling water and then served with a stack of napkins, a crock of melted butter for dipping, a bib, and implements for cracking the shell and claws, so you can pick out the succulent, chewy flesh. Elegant, it's not.

Clams are also extremely popular. Soft-shell clams, or 'steamers,' are often served in a bucket. Extract the meat, shuck off the wrinkled membrane from the black neck, wash off any sand by dipping the clam in the 'broth' provided (not for drinking), dip in melted butter and enjoy. Littlenecks and cherrystones, the most common hard-shell clams, are best eaten raw on the half shell with a few drops of lemon juice, tomato sauce or horseradish. But they're also steamed, stuffed and baked. Quahogs (ko-hogs) are huge sea clams. They're usually cut into strips, breaded and deep-fried or used for chowder.

Ah, yes. Chowder, or as locals say, 'chow-dah.' The basic recipe includes clams, clam juice, chunks of potato, milk, cream, flour, butter, onion, celery, salt and pepper. Consistency varies from thin and watery to thick as wallpaper paste. The best chowder is fabulous; the worst will make you swear off the stuff forever.

If wrestling with your meal is not your idea of fine dining, any traditional seafood restaurant worth its sea salt also offers tender broiled scallops, salty-sweet Wellfleet oysters and the ever-dependable cod and scrod (the generic name for any local white-flesh fish, including cod, weighing under 2½lb). But who says you have to go traditional? Boston's Asian, Italian and most other finer restaurants do marvelous things with the same catch.

for dinner; lunch focuses on soups and fancy sandwiches.

King & I *(Map 2, #9; ☎ 617-227-3320; 145 Charles St; lunch specials $6, dinner mains $8-10; open lunch Mon-Sat, dinner daily)* serves ample portions of seafood and tasty pad Thai ($7 to $10). There are plenty of vegetable and tofu options.

The Paramount *(Map 2, #26; ☎ 617-720-1152; 44 Charles St; breakfast $2-10, lunch mains $6-10, dinner mains $7-19)* is a real neighborhood hang-out. Breakfast and lunch are cafeteria-style: pancakes, steak and eggs, meatloaf, lasagna. The place goes slightly upscale at dinner without losing its down-home charm. It has the tastiest chicken piccata in town.

Istanbul Café *(Map 2, #8; ☎ 617-227-3434; 37 Bowdoin St; lunch mains $6-7, dinner mains $14-20)*, a cozy basement dining room, offers the most authentic Turkish food this side of Izmir. Baskets of warm, crusty, Turkish-style pita bread are reason enough to dine here. Roasted meat sandwiches draw crowds at lunchtime. The killer appetizer sampler makes a great meal anytime.

Café Podima *(Map 2, #6; ☎ 617-227-4959; 168 Cambridge St; dishes $5-6.50; open until 11pm)* is a sweet little place with about 40 sandwiches and roll-ups, the most expensive being prosciutto, tomato, fresh mozzarella, roasted vegies and basil. It's a perfect place to take a break without breaking the bank.

Phoenicia *(Map 2, #4; ☎ 617-523-4606; 240 Cambridge St; lunch mains $7, dinner mains $9-15; open 11am-10pm)* serves generous portions of delicious, inexpensive Lebanese food in casual surroundings.

Mid-Range

Artu *(Map 2, #17; ☎ 617-227-9023; 89 Charles St; lunch mains $6-13, dinner mains $12-26; open lunch Tues-Sat & dinner daily)*, a charming storefront trattoria, dishes up simple Italian meals: roasted vegetables, risottos, fresh pastas, calzones and panini (Italian sandwiches).

Figs *(Map 2, #27; ☎ 617-742-3447; 42 Charles St; pizzas & pastas $11-19; open dinner Mon-Fri, noon-10pm Sat & Sun)* excels in

Catch of the Day

Boston is a paradise for seafood lovers; these are the top catches to sample:

- Calamari and linguini at The Daily Catch (p95)
- Fried seafood platter at Barking Crab (p97)
- Clam chowder and boiled lobster at Legal Sea Foods (p97)
- Fried squid at Grand Chau Chow (p100)
- Sushi at Ginza (p100)
- Anything at East Coast Grill (p108)

creative pizzas (with whisper-thin crusts) topped with gourmet ingredients. Although it's pricey, it will feel more like a night out than most pizza joints.

Top End

Beacon Hill Bistro *(Map 2, #28; ☎ 617-723-1133; 25 Charles St; breakfast mains $6-10, lunch mains $9-13, dinner mains $18-21)* manages to be both sophisticated and convivial. The fabulous steak comes with a plateful of crispy frites (french fries). And the reasonably priced wine list contributes to a memorable evening.

Lala Rokh *(Map 2, #22; ☎ 617-720-5511; 97 Mt Vernon St; lunch mains $9-14, dinner mains $14-22; open lunch Mon-Fri, dinner daily)* serves award-winning Persian delicacies featuring aromatic spices and savory herbs. The helpful waitstaff will translate the menu and offer guidance. Try any of the grilled meats or the *morgh*, saffron-seared chicken in a light tomato broth accompanied by basmati rice with cumin, cinnamon, rose petals and barberries ($14).

GOVERNMENT CENTER (MAP 3)

The Faneuil Hall area is busting at the seams with eateries mostly geared to visitors.

Budget

For an enormous variety of take-out eateries under one roof, head to **Faneuil Hall Marketplace** *(Map 3; ☎ 617-338-2323; open 10am-9pm Mon-Sat, noon-6pm Sun, breakfast* *stalls open earlier).* Within the 20 restaurants and 40 food stalls, you'll find chowder, bagels, Indian, Greek, baked goods and ice cream.

Bertucci's *(Map 3, #57; ☎ 617-227-7889; 22 Merchants Row; dishes $8-12; open 11am-10pm)*, a popular place for a sit-down meal of brick-oven pizza ($11 for large cheese, $15 for large 'specialty'), also has salads, pasta dishes and calzones.

Mid-Range

The c. 1826 **Ye Olde Union Oyster House** *(Map 3, #42; ☎ 617-227-2750; 41 Union St; lunch mains $7-15, dinner mains $12-28)* lives up to its venerable status as Boston's most historic raw bar – you can't go wrong with the oysters and a beer. Although the intervening years have been kind to its charm and atmosphere, the menu could use an update.

Marshall House *(Map 3, #47; ☎ 617-523-9396; 15 Union St; dishes $5-16; open 11:30am-11pm, bar open until 2am)* provides a lively, less touristed (but no less atmospheric) alternative to its olde neighbor.

Salty Dog *(Map 3, #52; ☎ 617-742-2094; Quincy Market, Faneuil Hall Marketplace; dishes $8-27; open 11am-11pm)* serves a-cut-above seafood and pub grub. The patio is *the* place to be April through October. The bar stays open until 2am as long as things don't get too rowdy.

Durgin Park *(Map 3, #48; ☎ 617-227-2038; North Market, Faneuil Hall Marketplace; mains $8-36; open 11:30am-9pm)* is known for no-nonsense service, sawdust underfoot and family-style dining. The bill of fare hasn't changed much since 1827: huge slabs of prime rib, fish chowder, chicken potpie, Boston baked beans, and Indian pudding for dessert.

NORTH END (MAP 3)

Italian restaurants dominate this neighborhood, with the city's highest concentration of eateries.

Budget

The legendary **Regina Pizzeria** *(Map 3, #12; ☎ 617-227-0765; 11½ Thatcher St; open 11am-11pm)* has crispy-chewy, thin-crust

Sunday Brunch

Did you party late last night? Join the Bostonians who did, too, for a lazy Sunday meal at these hot eateries:

• Bob the Chef (p101)

• Metropolis Cafe (p102)

• On the Park (p101)

• Zaftigs Eatery (p104)

• Blue Room (p107)

pizza – $16 for a large with two toppings – best consumed with a pitcher of beer (about $10). This no-frills establishment with booths and Formica tables is a North End institution. The waitstaff are famous for their superhuman efficiency and good humor.

Galleria Umberto *(Map 3, #26; ☎ 617-227-5709; 289 Hanover St; pizza slices 85¢; open 11am-2:30pm Mon-Sat)* is a lunchtime legend. The place closes as soon as the generously cut, thick and chewy slices are gone.

Il Panino Express *(Map 3, #25; ☎ 617-720-5720; 266 Hanover St; open 9am-11pm)*, with a self-service counter, has great pasta, monster-sized calzones, and pizza.

Mid-Range

Also known as the calamari café, **The Daily Catch** *(Map 3, #21; ☎ 617-523-8567; 323 Hanover St; mains $9-16; open lunch & dinner daily)* is a tiny storefront with an open kitchen and a line of patrons waiting to get in. Bountiful portions of garlicky, sauteed seafood and linguini are served in the cast-iron skillets in which they were prepared. Get there early, or else.

Rabia's *(Map 3, #30; ☎ 617-227-6637; 73 Salem St; lunch mains $5-20, dinner mains $13-30)* serves the best lunch deal in town. For the 'express lunch,' you choose among seven tasty mains for $5. Eggplant parmigiana with a hefty side of linguini is a favorite.

Cibo *(Map 3, #14; ☎ 617-557-9248; 326 Hanover St; mains $11-18; open daily for dinner, lunch Sun)* is among the many charming, little Italian trattorias in the area – it just happens to be one of the best.

La Piccola Venezia *(Map 3, #31; ☎ 617-523-3888; 263 Hanover St; lunch mains $5-12, dinner mains $9-22)* serves huge portions of old-fashioned, red-sauced dishes: spaghetti and meatballs ($11; less at lunch), tripe, and gnocchi.

Antico Forno *(Map 3, #29; ☎ 617-723-6733; 93 Salem St; lunch mains $6-11, pizza $10-15, dinner mains $16-19)*, a North End Neapolitan, is named for its beehive, wood-burning brick oven. It specializes in pizza; try the 'Vesuvio' (spicy sausage, cherry tomatoes, roasted peppers, mozzarella and ricotta).

Massimino's Cucina Italiana *(Map 3, #3; ☎ 617-523-5959; 207 Endicott St; lunch mains $7-10, dinner mains $11-13)* is off the beaten path, thank goodness. For a little effort, you'll be rewarded with a warm welcome, traditional home cooking, reasonable prices and maybe even a table without too much of a wait.

Pagliuca's *(Map 3, #24; ☎ 617-367-1504; 14 Parmenter St; lunch mains $5-18, dinner mains $8-21)* remains an old-fashioned favorite. There's nothing fancy here, just huge servings of dependable, hearty home-style Italian fare like chicken cacciatore and veal marsala.

Top End

You won't find old-fashioned red sauces at **Marcuccio's** *(Map 3, #15; ☎ 617-723-1807; 125 Salem St; dinner mains $18-28)*. It serves updated Italian fare from an open kitchen in a contemporary, pop art–accented dining room. The menu features risottos, roasted game and robust seafood preparations.

Terramia *(Map 3, #23; ☎ 617-523-3112; 98 Salem St; pasta & rice dinner mains $11-18, seafood & meat dinner mains $17-31)* is an intimate place that showcases the genius of chef-impresario Mario Nocera. The seasonal menu transforms old-world classics into new-world masterpieces. It features the essential beauty of vintage balsamic vinegars, savory mushrooms and rare Italian cheeses.

Prezza *(Map 3, #16; ☎ 617-227-1577; 24 Fleet St; mains $24-32, open dinner Mon-Sat)* is the hottest neighborhood restaurant. Chef Anthony Caturano's amazing cooking features prosciutto-wrapped roasted figs stuffed

Best Lunch Deals

The midday meal is often the best bargain of the day. And at these places, it's even better than usual:

- Istanbul Café (p94)
- Rabia's (p95)
- Chacarero Chilean Cuisine (p97)
- Kashmir (p99)
- Hu Tieu Nam Vang (p100)
- Flour Bakery and Café (p101)
- El Pelon Taqueria (p103)
- Tanjore (p106)

with gorgonzola; roasted trout with onion risotto; and rock shrimp and ravioli with a creamy corn filling. It'll be hard, but save room for dessert!

DOWNTOWN & WATERFRONT (MAP 4)
Budget

South Station Food Court *(Map 4, #62; Atlantic Ave at Summer St)*, within the grandly renovated train terminal, offers fast food from burgers to pizza, but hidden among the usual suspects are a few gems. **Rosie's Bakery** *(Map 4, #62; ☎ 617-439-4684; open 7am-7pm Mon-Fri)* satisfies the most demanding sweet tooth and challenges the most determined dieter. **Boston Coffee Exchange** *(Map 4, #62; open 5am-7:30pm Mon-Fri, 6am-noon Sat)* brews flavorful espresso and cappuccino.

Milk Bottle *(Map 4, #66; ☎ 617-482-3343; 300 Congress St)*, the giant icon near the Children's Museum at Fort Point Channel, is both a landmark and a summer lunchtime favorite. It does a brisk seasonal take-out business.

Corner Mall Food Court *(Map 4, #49; cnr Washington & Summer Sts)*, at Downtown Crossing, is convenient for fast-food take-out if it's raining. It's always crowded and has noisy communal seating.

Mr Dooley's Boston Tavern *(Map 4, #26; ☎ 617-338-5656; 77 Broad St; lunch & dinner dishes $12-16, Sunday breakfast $9)*, one of the few area joints open on weekends, is an Irish-style pub offering 'real' Irish breakfasts on Sunday. Look for imported sausage, black-and-white pudding, homemade brown soda bread, fish and chips, and similar grub. Live Irish music rounds out the weekend scene.

Sultan's Kitchen (*Map 4, #27; ☎ 617-338-7819; 72 Broad St; dishes $7-10; open 11am-5pm Mon-Fri, 11am-3pm Sat*) is a real find. Line up with the crowds at the fast-moving self-service counter, and take your paper plate upstairs to dine. You'll be rewarded with sizable portions of complex and delicately flavored Turkish dishes. Try the sampler plate and the world's best rice pudding.

Milk St Café (*Map 4, #39; ☎ 617-350-7275; Post Office Square; dishes $8-10; open 7am-5pm Mon-Fri*) is pleasant in summer, with tables adjoining a little park. The menu features large (but mediocre) servings of kosher lunch fare such as pasta, salads, soups, sandwiches and pastries.

Cosi Sandwich Shop (*Map 4, #24; ☎ 617-426-7565; 14 Milk St; sandwiches $5-7.50; open 7am-5pm Mon-Fri*) boasts a selection of 20 fillings such as cranberry roasted turkey, tandoori grilled chicken and roasted red pepper. The hearth-baked flat bread is crusty-chewy and delectable.

Jera's Juice Bar (*Map 4, #38; ☎ 617-439-9799; 75-101 Federal St; drinks $3-5; open 7am-5pm Mon-Fri*) blends liquid salads: the 'Big Dig' contains your recommended daily vegie allotment. Mango–passion fruit blend is an excellent antidote for whatever ails you.

Goemon (*Map 4, #10; ☎ 617-367-8670; 189 State St; dishes $6-10; open lunch & dinner Mon-Sat*) specializes in Japanese snacks (sushi, tempura, dumplings) and noodle soups (soba, udon or ramen). The basement dining room, with elegant and soothing ambiance, exceeds most restaurants in this price range. Watch for karaoke on Friday and Saturday nights.

Chacarero Chilean Cuisine (*Map 4, #35; ☎ 617-542-0392; 426 Washington St; sandwiches $5-7; open 11am-6pm Mon-Fri*) makes hefty take-out grilled chicken, beef or vegetarian sandwiches with guacamole and green beans, on fresh crusty rolls. Arrive for an early or late lunch or be prepared to queue up with masses of humanity.

Mid-Range

Barking Crab (*Map 4, #61; ☎ 617-426-2722; 88 Sleeper St; lunch & dinner mains $11-20*), an urban clam shack, offers big servings of delicious fried seafood on paper plates at communal picnic tables on the water's edge. The platters, with fries and coleslaw, are worth every penny.

Intrigue (*Map 4, #42; ☎ 617-856-7744; 50 Rowes Wharf; lunch mains $11-12, dinner mains $11-19; open 7am-9pm Mon-Fri, until later Sat & Sun*), within the Boston Harbor Hotel, is a refined but unpretentious place for a sumptuous breakfast, light meal or dessert and wine. The casually elegant room, complete with harbor view, also serves afternoon tea.

Ben's Café (*Map 4, #15; ☎ 617-227-3370; 45 School St; prix fixe $18 & $25; open lunch Mon-Fri, dinner daily*), the 'bargain basement' of one of Boston's finest restaurants, is located within Maison Robert in the Old City Hall. It offers one of Boston's best culinary deals: the prix fixe menus feature smaller portions of Maison Robert's traditional French fare. Dine on the terrace or in the cozy romantic dining room.

Limbo (*Map 4, #52; ☎ 617-338-0280; 49 Temple Place; dinner mains $19-29*) your way through an entire evening at this hip and happening Ladder District restaurant, jazz lounge and nightclub. The kitchen specializes in stylish presentations of grilled meats and pasta dishes. The food is as snazzy as the patrons.

Top End

Legal Sea Foods (*Map 4, #11; ☎ 617-227-3115; 255 State St; lunch $10-14, dinner mains $15-25*), near the aquarium, has built a local empire on the motto, 'If it's not fresh, it's not Legal.' Servings are generous and the menu is simple: every kind of fish, it seems, broiled, steamed, sautéed, grilled or fried. Try the bluefish pate and the spicy fish and chips at lunch. The clam chowder ($4 to $5) is New England's best. There are also branches near the Theater District (*Map 6, #10; ☎ 617-426-4444; 26 Park Square*); within the Prudential

Center *(Map 5, #53;* ☎ *617-266-6800; 800 Boylston St)*; within the Copley Place shopping mall *(Map 6;* ☎ *617-266-7775)* and in Cambridge's Kendall Square *(Map 9, #53;* ☎ *617-864-3400; 5 Cambridge Center)*. All are open from about noon to 10pm.

Les Zygomates *(Map 4, #70;* ☎ *617-542-5108; 129 South St; lunch mains $8-14, dinner mains $18-28; open lunch Mon-Fri, dinner Mon-Sat)*, in the Leather District, features live jazz most nights, a reasonably priced wine list and a creative French bistro menu. It's a favorite with the cosmopolitan crowd. There's great value in the three-course prix fixe menu ($29).

Trio *(Map 4, #69;* ☎ *617-357-8746; 174 Lincoln St; mains $23-36; open dinner Tues-Sat)*, which doubles as a hot Leather District nightclub, has a lofty, open dining room, with exposed brick and minimalist art work. You'll end up lingering over the small and big plates, which highlight artfully prepared and presented luxe ingredients.

Mantra *(Map 4, #51;* ☎ *617-542-8111; 52 Temple Place; lunch mains $14-17, dinner mains $21-38; open lunch Mon-Fri, dinner Mon-Sat)*, in the Ladder District, is *the* restaurant of the moment. Set in a former bank, the granite and marble dining room is modern, elegant and sleek. Chef Thomas John's

French Indian-inspired preparations are both surprising and special, from complimentary treats that start the meal to sweet bites that end it. The teepee-like hookah den, where patrons retreat for drinks and smokes, is a bit hokey. The rest rooms are a conversation starter (or stopper depending on your point of view); check them out.

Radius *(Map 4, #58;* ☎ *617-426-1234; 8 High St; lunch mains $16-21, dinner mains $25-37; open lunch Mon-Fri, dinner Mon-Sat)*, near South Station, answers the burning question, 'How can a restaurant be so hot and so cool at the same time?' Chef-owner Michael Schlow has created a chic food-lover's paradise. Although pricey at $85 per person, the six-course tasting menu is a culinary showcase. Exceptional wine pairing elevates the experience to even loftier heights (difficult to imagine). You don't have to bust your budget, though: order the vegie tasting plate for $25, or order from the lighter bar menu. Arrive after 7:30pm to avoid the power-suit crowd.

BACK BAY (MAP 5)
Budget
Terrace Food Court *(Map 5, #65; 800 Boylston St)*, a fast-food emporium within the shops at Prudential Center, offers quick,

Where Time Stands Still?

Walk through the front doors of **Jacob Wirth's** *(Map 6, #13;* ☎ *617-338-8586; 31-37 Stuart St)* and **Ye Olde Union Oyster House** *(Map 3, #42;* ☎ *617-227-2750; 41 Union St)* and you might feel like you're in a time warp. Jacob Wirth's, with globe lanterns and loads of brass, probably offers the same German sausage, sauerkraut and ale that it served when it opened in 1868. Ye Olde Union Oyster House has been serving seafood since 1826, though the building predates that by about 100 years. You can dine at the same mahogany bar where Daniel Webster slurped oysters and sipped brandy. In fact, the interior and menu changes at both have been so inconsequential that Ralph Waldo Emerson would probably feel more comfortable than you would here.

The 21st century has arrived, though, at **Locke-Ober** *(Map 4, #47;* ☎ *617-542-1340; 3 Winter Place)*, a Boston Brahmin institution that once seemed impervious to change. Lydia Shire, one of Boston's best-known, trendsetting chefs, is now at the helm. Though the change sent shock waves through the blue-blood set, Shire has tried to soften the blow by refurbishing rather than renovating the elegant, historic dining room, while updating the classic menu, the service, and the atmosphere. Since women were not even admitted to the restaurant until the 1970s, Shire's efforts constitute something of a revolution, albeit a gentle one.

cheap meals. Most eateries are open for lunch and dinner.

Pho Pasteur *(Map 5, #41; ☎ 617-262-8200; 119 Newbury St; dishes $5-12; open 11am-10pm)* is a branch of Boston's favorite Vietnamese restaurant (see Theater District & Chinatown later in this chapter).

Kebab-N-Kurry *(Map 5, #1; ☎ 617-536-9835; 30 Mass Ave; lunch mains $6, dinner mains $13; open lunch Mon-Sat, dinner daily)*, an ever-popular but small basement place, boasts consistently good Indian dishes at consistently good prices.

Café Jaffa *(Map 5, #52; ☎ 617-536-0230; 48 Gloucester St; dishes $4-10)*, is a storefront eatery with large servings and reasonable prices. When was the last time you had authentic Turkish coffee, shwarma or falafel in a place with polished wooden floors and exposed brick?

Trident Booksellers & Cafe *(Map 5, #17; ☎ 617-267-8688; 338 Newbury St; open 9am-midnight)* is the place to head if you think Boston, books and breakfast go together. Shelves are filled with New Age titles, while the menu features down-to-earth salads, sandwiches ($5 to $7), pasta mains ($8 to $12) and desserts; breakfast is served all day. Vegetarians rejoice over the vegan cashew chili.

Mid-Range

Marche Movenpick *(Map 5, #66; ☎ 617-578-9700; 800 Boylston St; open 11:30am-midnight Mon-Fri, 9am-2am Sat & Sun)*, within the shops at Prudential Center, offers an assortment of freshly prepared sushi, stir-fry and rotisserie meats at various food stations, and you can assemble a gourmet meal at cafeteria prices.

Parish Café & Bar *(Map 5, #63; ☎ 617-247-4777; 361 Boylston St; sandwiches $9-12; open 11:30am-2am)* is known for creative sandwiches, each designed by a local celebrity chef. Try Rialto chef Jody Adams' prosciutto and buffalo mozzarella with pesto and a touch of basil oil on grilled white bread – not your average sandwich. Other draws include an outdoor patio, 70 different beers and 20 wines by the glass.

Geoffrey's Café & Bar *(Map 5, #5; ☎ 617-266-1122; 160 Commonwealth Ave; mains $5-12)* dishes up good-sized servings of eclectic home cooking. Look for delicious pasta dishes, hearty sandwiches and creative meat-and-potatoes variations.

Kashmir *(Map 5, #23; ☎ 617-536-1695; 279 Newbury St; lunch mains $16, lunch buffet $9, dinner mains $16-23)*, Boston's finest Indian restaurant, is charming and romantic. The tasty lunch buffet is a bargain, as are the multicourse dinners for two. In fine weather, the sidewalk tables provide a lovely perch.

Casa Romero *(Map 5, #21; ☎ 617-536-4341; 30 Gloucester St; mains $14-28; open dinner)*, hidden down a little alleyway, offers delicious, authentic Mexico City-style cuisine in a lovely courtyard or intimate Talavera-tiled dining room. The enchiladas, verdes or poblanas, are wonderful, as is the *puerco adobado*, roasted pork marinated in sweet oranges and smoked chipotle chile.

Tapeo *(Map 5, #27; ☎ 617-267-4799; 266 Newbury St; tapas $4-8; open lunch Sat & Sun, dinner daily)*, a festive Spanish tapas restaurant, has bodega-style dining rooms and, in fine weather, a patio fronting Newbury St (a nonstop parade). Mains are pricey; order a meal of tapas to keep the tab down.

Top End

Sonsie *(Map 5, #15; ☎ 617-351-2500; 327 Newbury St; mains $9-29; open 7am-midnight)* is perhaps the hippest place to be seen sipping a latte surrounded by Euro-types wearing basic black and dark sunglasses.

Ultimate Dining Experiences

So you have some serious cash to drop on a really memorable meal? With that inexorable combination of cuisine and scene, these places won't disappoint:

- Prezza (p96)
- Mantra (p98)
- Aquitaine (p102)
- Hamersley's Bistro (p102)
- Oleana (p108)

PLACES TO EAT

In warm weather, the French doors are flung open, making the indoor tables seem alfresco. During busy mealtimes, café tables are reserved for diners. Pizza, pasta and other light dishes are available.

THEATER DISTRICT & CHINATOWN (MAP 6)

Theater-goers tend to eat early, so if you're not one of them, plan to dine at these establishments during show time. Chinatown restaurants stay open *very* late by Boston standards.

Budget

Get into the mix at **Mix Bakery** *(Map 6, #18; ☎ 617-357-4050; 36 Beach St; open 7am-7pm)*, which features decadent Western-style cakes as well as a wide variety of traditional Chinese cookies and sweets.

Pho Pasteur *(Map 6, #16; ☎ 617-482-7467; 682 Washington St; open breakfast, lunch & dinner)* serves hearty, hot and cheap meals in a bowl. Most people come for pho (pronounced 'fuh'), the sometimes exotic, always fragrant and flavorful noodle soup ($5.50 for extra large). The Newbury St and Harvard Square locations (see Back Bay earlier in this chapter, and Harvard Square later in this chapter) serve the same great food in more elegant digs.

Hu Tieu Nam Vang *(Map 6, #17; ☎ 617-422-0501; 7 Beach St; open 9am-10pm)* has friendly, helpful staff serving tasty, authentic Vietnamese specialties, from pho to vermicelli dishes. For great value ($6-8), try a hot pot – a crock of steaming rice, vegetables and meat, seafood or tofu in a spicy aromatic sauce. It's enough for two people. There are more than 40 cold drinks and fresh fruit shakes.

Buddha's Delight *(Map 6, #15; ☎ 617-451-2395; 3 Beach St, 2nd floor; lunch specials about $5, dinner $10; open 11am-10pm)* thrills vegetarians with noodle soups, tasty tofu dishes and imitation meat dishes such as soybean 'roast pork.'

Grand Chau Chow *(Map 6, #19; ☎ 617-292-5166; 45 Beach St; lunch $5-6, dinner $8-10; open until 2am)* has excellent seafood specials, ample portions and renowned ginger and black bean sauces. Try the garlicky sauteed pea pod stems and the crispy, chewy, salted fried squid.

City Place Food Court *(Map 6, #11; 10 Park Plaza; open lunch & dinner)*, within the drab State Transportation Building, is great for a rainy day when there's not much change in your pocket. It has a number of fast-food take-out counters and tables.

Mid-Range

At the communal, Japanese-style, cook-it-yourself **Shabu-Zen** *(Map 6, #22; ☎ 617-292-8828; 16 Tyler St; lunch mains $8-13, dinner mains $9-17; open lunch Mon-Fri, dinner Sat & Sun)*, you choose the raw ingredients, skewer and 'swish-swish' (ie, 'shabu-shabu') the meat, tofu, fish or vegies in boiling broth and then dip the morsels in zippy sauces. Sounds complicated, but the staff will help you shabu-shabu your way to culinary nirvana.

Penang *(Map 6, #14; ☎ 617-451-6373; 685 Washington St; mains $8-20; open 11:30am-11:30pm)* serves exotic Malaysian fare in a festive atmosphere (à la Gilligan's Island). Some items are listed with the admonition 'Ask your server for advice before you order!!!' (Test your fortitude with fish heads, pig intestines and chicken feet.) There is plenty on the menu for vegetarians and the less intrepid.

Apollo Grill *(Map 6, #21; ☎ 617-423-3888; 84-86 Harrison Ave; dishes $10-13; open lunch Mon-Fri, dinner 5pm-4am nightly)*, a Japanese-Korean late-night hot spot, features tables with built-in hibachi grills. Tasty appetizers and an extensive sushi menu are a draw, too.

Ginza *(Map 6, #23; ☎ 617-338-2261; 16 Hudson St; lunch mains $8-14, dinner mains $13-20; open lunch daily, dinner 5pm-3:30am Tues-Sat, until 1:30am Sun & Mon)*, a hip Japanese eatery, serves some of the city's best sushi and maki.

SOUTH END (MAP 6)

A bona fide dining destination, the South End satisfies a sophisticated local clientele with gourmet palettes. Depending on the night, neighbors want low-key comfort food or a venue to show off little black dresses and buff bods.

Best Bang for the Buck

No matter the price category, these eateries offer better value than their peers:

• Les Zygomates prix fixe menu (p98)
• Franklin Café (p102)
• Brown Sugar Café (p103)
• Craigie Street Bistrot prix fixe menu (p106)
• B-Side Lounge (p107)

Budget

A pastry lover's paradise, **Flour Bakery and Café** *(Map 6, #80; ☎ 617-267-4300; 1595 Washington St; lunch mains $6; open breakfast until 7pm daily)* offers savory lunchtime sandwiches made with beautiful bread. Look for salads, soups and quiches, too. Service at the sunny storefront gem is cafeteria-style with communal seating.

Delux Café *(Map 6, #44; ☎ 617-338-5258; 100 Chandler St; mains $5-10; open dinner Mon-Sat)* is a place where appearances can be both revealing and deceiving. This place looks like a small, dark bar, and it is; but it serves decidedly upscale, globally inspired food in a friendly, funky-kitschy atmosphere.

Bertucci's *(Map 6, #34; ☎ 617-247-6161; 43 Stanhope St; dishes $8-12; open 11am-10pm)* serves Boston's favorite brick-oven pizza, as well as salads and pasta dishes.

Anchovies *(Map 6, #52; ☎ 617-266-5088; 433 Columbus Ave; dishes $10; open 4pm-2am, kitchen closes 12:45am)*, a favorite neighborhood joint, with a smoky bar in front and a little dining room in back, has meatball subs that rule! The rest of the menu features mix-and-match pastas and sauces, as well as pizzas.

Charlie's Sandwich Shoppe *(Map 6, #51; ☎ 617-536-7669; 429 Columbus Ave; open 6am-2:30pm Mon-Fri, 7:30am-1pm Sat)*, a classic with a few shared tables and the counter, has been serving creative omelets ($6 to $8 with a salad) and breakfast platters ($3.50 to $5 with meat) since 1927. For lunch, turkey hash with two eggs ($6.75), hot pastrami and homemade pies are gobbled by lawyers in suits and laborers in work boots.

Garden of Eden *(Map 6, #59; ☎ 617-247-8377; 571 Tremont St; lunch mains $7-10, dinner mains $10-15; open breakfast, lunch & dinner)*, a comforting café, serves warm and wonderful breakfasts until 2pm, as well as sandwiches, soups, salads and toothsome sweets. Best of all, you can linger over your coffee or wine as long as you want.

Pho Republique *(Map 6, #78; ☎ 617-262-0005; 1415 Washington St; dishes $13-19; open dinner)* serves delicious pho (noodle soup) chock full of vegetables and herbs in a rich savory broth, crispy spring rolls and other beautifully prepared and presented mains.

Mike's City Diner *(Map 6, #81; ☎ 617-267-9393; 1714 Washington St; dishes $7-10; open 6am-3pm)* has service that is warm and old-fashioned (in the positive sense). Although the menu seems homespun (meatloaf and mashed potatoes and gravy, fried chicken, scrambled eggs and ham), the preparation is far from retro.

Tim's Tavern *(Map 6, #41; ☎ 617-437-6898; 329 Columbus Ave; dishes $8-16; open 11am-midnight Mon-Sat)*, another great neighborhood joint serving fab food but cloaked as a divey bar, has arguably the city's best (and biggest and cheapest) burgers. Baby back ribs also draw raves.

Mid-Range

At Boston's best down-home soul food eatery, **Bob the Chef** *(Map 6, #79; ☎ 617-536-6204; 604 Columbus Ave; take-out sandwiches $6, mains $11-14; open lunch & dinner Tues-Sun)*, we're talking barbecue ribs with corn bread, or fried chicken with collard greens or black-eyed peas. Locals love the Sunday jazz brunch, from 10am until 3pm (adult/child $19/14).

Jae's Café & Grill *(Map 6, #67; ☎ 617-421-9405; 520 Columbus Ave; lunch specials $7-9, dinner mains $14-18; open lunch & dinner)* specializes in Korean food but has a full pan-Asian menu. Expect to wait for dinner unless you arrive by 6pm. Although Jae's has other locations around town, they don't measure up to the lively original.

On the Park *(Map 6, #70; ☎ 617-426-0862; 1 Union Park St; mains $15-21, brunch $7-10; open dinner Tues-Sat, brunch Sat &*

Sun), a friendly little neighborhood place that feels like it belongs in New York's Greenwich Village, is bright and funky with lots of local art. The seasonal menu tends towards creative American fare. Weekend brunch, with mimosas, is particularly popular.

Claremont Café (Map 6, #65; ☎ 617-247-9001; 535 Columbus Ave; lunch mains $5-13, dinner mains $12-20; open breakfast, lunch & dinner Tues-Sat, Sun brunch 9am-3pm), a small bistro that draws an artsy cross-section of neighborhood folks, offers generous portions of South American- and Mediterranean-inspired food. Think along the lines of rice dishes, paella and roast chicken. It's very popular for breakfast.

Franklin Café (Map 6, #72; ☎ 617-350-0010; 278 Shawmut Ave; dinner mains $14-17), the South End's most beloved dive, offers up New American comfort food prepared by a gourmet chef. Try the steamed mussels with Pernod, leeks, garlic and white wine, or roasted turkey meatloaf with spiced fig gravy and chive mashed potatoes. The bartender is renowned – have a drink while you wait for a table.

Top End
What's the South End's most popular, chichi restaurant? It's easy to make a case for **Metropolis Cafe** (Map 6, #60; ☎ 617-247-2931; 584 Tremont St; dinner mains $15-22, brunch $10-12; open dinner daily, brunch 9am-3pm Sat & Sun), but since it's tiny, that usually translates into long waits. Ah, but what food! The New American–Mediterranean menu always surprises and delights.

Bomboa (Map 6, #35; ☎ 617-236-6363; 35 Stanhope St; dinner mains $22-28), straddling Back Bay and the South End, sizzles with an exuberant young crowd gathering to sip tropical cocktails on zebra-striped couches or at the sleek bar. The French-Latin menu features dishes like *feijoada,* a Brazilian, smoky-garlicky bean stew, and steak frites served with a spicy *chimichurri* sauce.

Aquitaine (Map 6, #61; ☎ 617-424-8577; 569 Tremont St; Sun brunch $7-15, dinner mains $18-32), *the* neighborhood French bistro and wine bar, serves classic dishes like foie gras, duck confit and coq au vin.

The dining room, soothing and sophisticated with mahogany and warm chocolate tones, has big windows overlooking bustling Tremont St.

Hamersley's Bistro (Map 6, #54; ☎ 617-423-2700; 553 Tremont St; dinner mains $23-37), at the top of every 'best restaurants' list, serves exceptional French-country fare. Chef Gordon Hamersley's specialty is roasted chicken with garlic, parsley and lemon ($24). (Sunday and Monday are Gordon's nights off, though.) The ambiance is urbane and cool, but not too cool.

KENMORE SQUARE & THE FENWAY (MAP 7)
Cheap eats generally rule in this neighborhood.

Budget
With a dozen kinds of bagels and flavors of cream cheese, **Bruegger's Bagel Bakery** (Map 7, #31; ☎ 617-262-7939; 644 Beacon St; open 6am-5pm) will also slap some deli meat and vegies on a bagel if you want a sandwich.

India Quality (Map 7, #33; ☎ 617-267-4499; 484 Comm Ave; lunch mains $7, dinner mains $8-12; open lunch & dinner, closed 3pm-5pm Mon-Fri) serves delicious North Indian cuisine in a pleasant dining room.

The Other Side Cosmic Café (Map 7, #34; ☎ 617-536-9477; 407 Newbury St; sandwiches $6; open 10am-midnight Mon-Sat, noon-midnight Sun) is on the 'other side' of Mass Ave, which few people crossed before this place opened. 'Cosmic' alludes to its funky, Seattle-inspired style. The 1st floor is done in cast iron, while the 2nd floor is softened by mismatched couches and low ceilings. Vegetarian chili, sandwiches, vegie drinks and strong coffee are the order of the day.

Bangkok Cuisine (Map 7, #51; ☎ 617-262-5377; 177A Mass Ave; open lunch & dinner Mon-Sat, dinner only Sun), Boston's first Thai restaurant, is still one of the best. The satay ($4) and pad Thai ($5/8 at lunch/dinner) are very good. When the menu says hot, it means it.

Betty's Wok & Noodle Diner (Map 7, #60; ☎ 617-424-1950; 250 Huntington Ave; lunch & dinner dishes $9-16) appeals to students as

Ice Cream

Regardless of weather, Bostonians never lose their appetite for ice cream.

Steve's *(Map 3, #54; ☎ 617-367-0569; Quincy Market, Faneuil Hall Marketplace)* won fame for 'smush ins', chunks of candy or nuts mixed into the flavor of your choice.

JB Scoops *(Map 4, #62; ☎ 617-443-0500; South Station Food Court)* dishes out traditional regional flavors such as maple walnut and pumpkin pie.

Emack & Bolio's *(Map 5, #20; ☎ 617-247-8772; 290 Newbury St)*, an old-timer on the local gourmet scene, makes the definitive Oreo cookie ice cream (and good nonfat yogurt creations).

At **JP Licks** *(Map 5, #10; ☎ 617-236-1666; 352 Newbury St • Map 7, #4; ☎ 617-738-8252; 311 Harvard St)*, it's a toss-up between white coffee and caramel apple.

Wai Wai *(Map 6, #7; ☎ 617-338-9833; 26 Oxford St)* is Boston's most offbeat choice. Although the tiny basement exudes the aroma of roasting chickens, don't be scared. In addition to quick meals, Wai Wai offers several tropical flavors such as ginger, coconut and banana.

At **Herrell's** *(Map 8, #41; ☎ 617-497-2179; 15 Dunster St • Map 5, #34; ☎ 617-236-0857; 224 Newbury St)*, will it be malted vanilla or chocolate pudding?

Cambridge is lucky to have two branches of **Toscanini's**: near Central Square *(Map 9, #50; ☎ 617-491-5877; 899 Main St)* and in Harvard Square *(Map 8, #45; ☎ 617-354-9350; 1310 Mass Ave)*. Try the gingersnap molasses or Vienna finger cookie.

In Inman Square, **Christina's Ice Cream** *(Map 9, #8; ☎ 617-492-7021; 1255 Cambridge St)* has eclectic flavors such as burnt sugar. The fresh mint is really fresh.

Davis Square's **Denise's Homemade Ice Cream** *(Map 10, #4; ☎ 617-628-2764; 4A College Ave)* serves sorbet, ice cream and yogurt. The flavor of choice is tiramisu.

well as symphony- and theater-goers. Here's the deal: choose noodles or rice, then add some protein (beef or shrimp or chicken), select your own vegies from the salad bar, then add one of seven sauces like Cuban chipotle citrus or kung pao. The large portions are all thrown in a wok and cooked perfectly – and really quickly!

El Pelon Taqueria *(Map 7, #52; ☎ 617-262-9090; 92 Peterborough St; lunch & dinner dishes $4-5)* serves authentic Mexican, including burritos, tamales and huge *tortas* (grilled meat on a toasted roll with black beans, the chef's special limed onions, lettuce and avocado). How do they serve such generous portions of high-quality food at bargain prices? Paper plates and plastic cutlery help.

Taberna de Haro *(Map 7, #21; ☎ 617-277-8272; 999 Beacon St; tapas $6-9; open dinner Mon-Sat)*, an inviting little place serving authentic Spanish tapas and meals, has outdoor seating in warm weather. On a cold blustery evening, order a glass of sherry and enjoy the cozy dining room.

Mid-Range

In addition to bountiful, hearty Brazilian home cooking, **Buteco** *(Map 7, #56; ☎ 617-247-9508; 130 Jersey St; dishes $10-12; open noon-10pm Mon-Fri, 3pm-10pm Sat & Sun)* boasts a relaxed atmosphere. Though the place is justly known for meat dishes, there are a few chicken, fish and vegetarian offerings, too. The weekend dinner special is always *feijoada*, a rich stew of black beans, pork, sausage and dried beef.

Brown Sugar Café *(Map 7, #57; ☎ 617-266-2928; 129 Jersey St; lunch mains $6-8, dinner mains $8-15)* serves beautifully presented, delectable Thai dishes. The mango curry is a revelation: tender sliced chicken simmered in a yellow curry with chunks of ripe mango, tomato, red and green pepper, onion and summer squash. Portions are larger when you take out.

Audubon Circle *(Map 7, #23; ☎ 617-421-1910; 838 Beacon St; lunch mains $5-8, dinner mains $12-14; open 11:30am-1am Mon-Fri, 4pm-1am Sat & Sun)* is a lively place to just hang out or enjoy some of the best burgers and appetizers in town.

Elephant Walk *(Map 7, #22; ☎ 617-247-1500; 900 Beacon St; lunch $7-10, Cambodian dinner mains $12-20, French dinner mains $19-25; open lunch Mon-Sat, dinner Mon-Fri)* is highly regarded for its dual menus of classic French and traditional Cambodian. Many devotees opt for a curry dinner and French dessert.

Ginza *(Map 7, #20; ☎ 617-566-9688; 1002 Beacon St; open lunch & dinner, closed 2:30pm-5pm)* may not be as hip as the Chinatown original, but the sushi is as fresh and it has its own following.

Sorento's *(Map 7, #53; ☎ 617-424-7070; 86 Peterborough St; pizza $10-17, lunch & dinner mains $12-18; also open brunch Sat & Sun)* serves brick-oven pizza and calzones, as well as pasta and seafood dishes.

BROOKLINE (MAP 7)

Take a quick T ride into Coolidge Corner and Brookline Village for an eclectic assortment, including abundant great kosher eateries.

Coolidge Corner

Loaves of triple chocolate, jalapeño corn and sourdough are baked at **Daily Bread** *(Map 7, #15; ☎ 617-277-8810; 1331 Beacon St; open 7am-7pm Mon-Sat, 8am-6pm Sun)*. Calzones, cookies and spinach pies are also available for takeout.

Anna's Taqueria *(Map 7, #10; ☎ 617-739-7300; 1412 Beacon St; dishes $3-5; open 10am-11pm)* sets the standard to which other Beantown burrito bars aspire. Get in line at the no-frills, cafeteria-style counter and hope someone vacates a table.

Rod dee *(Map 7, #9; ☎ 617-738-4977; 1430 Beacon St; dishes $10; open 11:30am-11:30pm)*, a tiny storefront with a take-out counter and a couple of tables, serves fancy restaurant-quality Thai. If you're on a limited budget or don't have time to sit, this is your place.

Bombay Bistro *(Map 7, #14; ☎ 617-734-2879; 1353 Beacon St; lunch mains $6-7, dinner mains $11-15, Sun buffet $10.50)* serves Indian fare in an elegant, understated dining room. Though there is nothing terribly exotic

on the menu, the friendly staff is happy to explain unfamiliar dishes.

Zaftigs Eatery *(Map 7, #3; ☎ 617-975-0075; 335 Harvard St; open 8am-10pm, breakfast served all day)* is a sit-down deli with hearty comfort food – blintzes ($5), noodle kugel ($4), kosher-style hot dogs ($8) and cabbage dinners ($12) – served in a welcoming atmosphere.

Fugakyu *(Map 7, #17; ☎ 617-734-1268; 1280 Beacon St; sushi meals $16-25; open 11:30am-3pm & 5pm-1:30am)* aptly translates as 'house of elegance.' Sleek and upscale, Fugakyu offers a gorgeous array of sushi and sashimi, as well as traditional cooked meals, served by an efficient staff. The sushi bar features a water canal; place your order and then watch as the chef prepares it and sails it to you on a little boat.

Brookline Village

At the tiny self-service storefront, **Bottega Florentina** *(Map 7, #64; ☎ 617-738-5333; 41 Harvard St; dishes $5-11; open 11am-8pm Mon-Sat)*, there are home-cooked Italian meals to eat in or take out.

New England Soup Factory *(Map 7, #72; ☎ 617-739-1899; 2-4 Brookline Place; dishes $5-6; open 10:30am-8pm Mon-Fri, 10:30am-5pm Sat)* has quick wholesome meals. Try the delicious 'triple-strength chicken vegetable' soup; it may be curative. Request a taste before selecting from several soups, all accompanied by crusty-chewy sourdough rolls.

Matt Murphy's Pub *(Map 7, #68; ☎ 617-232-0188; 14 Harvard St; lunch mains $6-8, dinner mains $12-17)* is an ab-fab restaurant hiding in an equally fab bar. Sure it serves pub grub, but the fish is crispy and moist, the chips are hand-cut and the servings are big enough for two. Add well-pulled pints to convivial surroundings and you've got one of the most satisfying places in town.

Village Fish *(Map 7, #66; ☎ 617-566-3474; 22 Harvard St; lunch mains under $10, dinner mains $12-19; open lunch Mon-Fri, dinner daily)* specializes in Italian-style, pan-prepared seafood dishes served with pasta. Favorites include scampi and puttanesca sauce.

Cafés

For a self-proclaimed European-style city, Boston doesn't have a comparably strong café culture. But for an American city, it holds its own.

Caffè Vittoria *(Map 3, #20; ☎ 617-227-7606; 296 Hanover St)*, in the North End, has great old-world charm. Some patrons have been coming here since it opened in the 1930s. To get the full effect, wait for a table in the original dining room, pop a coin in the jukebox and savor your cappuccino with Sinatra.

Caffè dello Sport *(Map 3, #18; ☎ 617-523-5063; 308 Hanover St)*, in the North End, is the primo place for televised sporting events, especially soccer.

Torrefazione Italia Cafe *(Map 5, #44; ☎ 617-424-0951; 85 Newbury St)*, in Back Bay, brews the finest espresso and cappuccino in Beantown. And it's served in style – in lovely ceramic cups and saucers. Set down your shopping bags, order biscotti and linger.

Francesca's *(Map 6, #62; ☎ 617-482-9026; 564 Tremont St)* is a lively South End storefront coffee bar with tables as well as a counter and stools.

Peet's Coffee & Tea *(Map 7, #7; ☎ 617-734-4725; 285 Harvard St)*, bright and spacious in Coolidge Corner, is the first East Coast outpost of the beloved San Francisco Bay Area java emporium. There is another branch in Harvard Square *(Map 8, #53; ☎ 617-492-1844; 100 Mt Auburn St)*.

Au Bon Pain *(Map 8, #42; ☎ 617-497-9797; 1316 Mass Ave)*, in Harvard Square, transcends its popular image as a Frenchified fast-food take-out counter. Students, tourists and locals gather here to read, people-watch and chat. An informal, never-ending tournament takes place at outdoor chess tables.

Café Pamplona *(Map 8; no phone; 12 Bow St)*, located in a cozy unadorned cellar, is the choice of highbrow Harvard Square intellectuals. In addition to espresso, it serves gazpacho, sandwiches and biscotti. The tiny outdoor terrace is delightful in summer.

Tealuxe *(Map 8, #33; ☎ 617-441-0077; Zero Brattle St; open 8am-11pm)*, a tiny Harvard Square storefront with a few tables, is for lovers of steeped leaves. A lucky few can perch by the window sipping extra-bergamot Earl Grey and nibbling coffee cake. There is another location at the corner of Newbury and Clarendon Sts *(Map 5, #43; ☎ 617-927-0400; 108 Newbury St)*.

Beantowne Coffee House *(Map 9, #38; ☎ 617-876-4500; One Kendall Square)* is a cozy and comfortable place to hang with a cup of joe.

1369 Coffee House, in Central Square *(Map 9, #23; ☎ 617-576-4600; 757 Mass Ave)*, and in Inman Square *(Map 9, #3; ☎ 617-576-1369; 1369 Cambridge St)*, is a bohemian place with serious coffee, a laudable selection of tea, a limited snack list and a friendly waitstaff who won't rush you.

Someday Café *(Map 10, #3; ☎ 617-623-3323; 51 Davis Square)*, furnished with well-worn thrift-shop couches, is a slacker joint with boisterous music and board games, espresso and pastries.

Diesel Café *(Map 10, #7; ☎ 617-629-8717; 257 Elm St)*, in Davis Square, serves leaded and unleaded fuel in a friendly, vibrant café with pool tables, booths and comfy chairs. Smoothies, lots of vegetarian snacks and Toscanini's ice cream are also served.

Simon's Coffee House *(Map 10, #29; ☎ 617-497-7766; 1736 Mass Ave)*, between Harvard and Porter Squares, shows classic Hollywood and foreign videos throughout the day. The small café offers light meals, fabulous chocolate cake, coffee drinks and hand-mixed Italian sodas.

PLACES TO EAT

Village Smokehouse *(Map 7, #70; ☎ 617-566-3782; 1 Harvard St; lunch mains $5-9, dinner mains $8-19; open lunch Fri & Sat, dinner daily)* serves Texas-sized portions of Texas-style barbecue. True fans order 'Texas Hawg': beef ribs, brisket, chicken, sausage, and pork baby back ribs ($18).

Café St Petersburg *(Map 7, #71; ☎ 617-277-7100; 236 Washington St; lunch mains $5-7, dinner mains $10-21)* serves Russian food in a charming old-world atmosphere, complete with crystal chandeliers. Look for borscht, steamed sturgeon with potato pancakes and sour cherry blintzes. Top off your evening Russian-style – with a frosty, fruit-flavored vodka.

HARVARD SQUARE (MAP 8)

Head across the Charles for more bustling neighborhoods, many tucked away off the beaten track.

Budget

You're bound to find something fast, filling and cheap at **The Garage** *(Map 8, #56; no phone, 36 John F Kennedy St; open 11am-10pm)*, with a dozen places to eat under one roof, including **Pho Pasteur** *(Map 8, #56; ☎ 617-864-4100; 36 Dunster St)*, another branch of Boston's favorite Vietnamese restaurant (see also Back Bay and Theater District & Chinatown, earlier in this chapter).

Darwin's Ltd *(Map 8, #12; ☎ 617-354-5233; 148 Mt Auburn St; dishes $5-8; open lunch Mon-Fri, dinner Sat & Sun)*, a deli sandwich shop par excellence, serves inventive combinations on fresh-baked bread. There are a few hot dishes such as lasagna and Middle Eastern food, too.

Campo de Fiori *(Map 8, #58; ☎ 617-354-3805; 1350 Mass Ave; dishes $3-6; open 8am-8pm Mon-Fri, 11am-6pm Sat)*, in the Holyoke Center Arcade, specializes in *pane romano*, Roman-style flat bread. Topped with Italian meats, cheeses, vegetables and herbs, it makes a quick snack, or can be ordered sandwich-style with fillings.

Sabra Grill *(Map 8, #68; ☎ 617-868-5777; 20 Eliot St; dishes $6-8; open 10am-10pm)* served fresh and delicious Middle Eastern takeout long before it was trendy. Vegetarians and their contrarians alike will be happy with spinach pie and Greek salad or chicken shwarma and shish kebab.

Bartley's Burger Cottage *(Map 8, #49; ☎ 617-354-6559; 1246 Mass Ave; meals about $10; open 11am-9pm or 10pm Mon-Sat)*, the square's primo burger joint, offers at least 40 burgers. But if none of those suit your fancy, create your own 7oz, juicy masterpiece topped with guacamole or sprouts. Vegie burgers are available too. Bartley's is packed with tables and hungry college students.

Algiers Coffee House *(Map 8, #26; ☎ 617-492-1557; 40 Brattle St; open 8am-midnight)*

has glacial service, but the palatial Middle Eastern decor makes it a comfortable rest spot. Head to the airy 2nd floor and order a falafel sandwich ($7.25), a bowl of lentil soup ($4) or a kebab ($11).

Hi-Rise Pie Co *(Map 8, #9; ☎ 617-492-3003; 56 Brattle St; open 8:30am-5pm Mon-Fri, 9am-5pm Sat, open Sun in summer)*, known for scones and crusty loaves, also has toothsome sandwiches and soups. Outdoor tables are popular in warm weather; indoors is cozy.

Bertucci's *(Map 8, #30; ☎ 617-864-4748; 21 Brattle St; dishes $8-12; open 11am-11pm)* serves brick-oven pizza, as well as salads and pasta dishes.

Mid-Range

A sleek and popular pizza bar, **Cambridge, 1** *(Map 8, #17; ☎ 617-576-1111; 27 Church St; lunch & dinner mains $6-15)* has a simple menu: nine pizzas, five salads and one dessert. The pizzas are exquisite – grilled, crispy and chewy, with seasonal vegies and traditional Italian meats and cheeses. Rosemary potato is a fave. Try to nab a table in the back – the view of the historic Old Burying Ground is lovely.

Tanjore *(Map 8, #67; ☎ 617-868-1900; 13 Eliot St; lunch buffet $8, dinner mains $10-13)*, specializing in regional Indian cooking, serves dishes you won't find elsewhere in Boston. Start with the tasty South Indian dosa (chickpea and lentil crepes served with savory fillings and sauces).

Casablanca *(Map 8, #26; ☎ 617-876-0999; 40 Brattle St; lunch mains $7-13, dinner mains $15-25, bar open until 1am or 2am Mon-Sat)*, inspired by the film, has a romantic atmosphere and modern Mediterranean cuisine. Consider ordering grilled scallops with creamed corn or grilled quail with almond-honey butter and roasted grapes.

Craigie Street Bistrot *(Map 8, #1; ☎ 617-497-5511; 5 Craigie St; mains $17-26; open dinner Wed-Sun)*, a warm and inviting neighborhood gem, offers classic French comfort food such as roasted chicken, stewed plums, and creamy polenta. Chef-owner Tony Maws prepares hearty meals in the tiniest kitchen imaginable. He offers a three-course meal ($29) on Wednesday.

Quintessentially Boston

Whether it be a restaurant dating to the late 1800s, an Irish pub or a college hang-out, these places have Boston (and nowhere else) written all over them:

• Ye Olde Union Oyster House raw bar (p95)
• Durgin Park (p95)
• Regina Pizzeria (p95)
• Matt Murphy's Pub (p104)
• Bartley's Burger Cottage (p106)

Thursday and Sunday (and Friday and Saturday after 9pm).

Top End

Within the Charles Hotel, **Rialto** (Map 8, #60; ☎ 617-661 5050; 1 Bennett St; dinner mains $22-36) is a best-of-the-best. You'll pay handsomely in this understated, Euro-chic elegance, but your meal will be romantic and memorable. Chef Jody Adams' Mediterranean-inspired dishes include Tuscan-style sirloin steak and seared skate in sugar pumpkin puree. The vegetarian main course is always equally creative. Save some money by dining at the bar.

KENDALL SQUARE (MAP 9)

Emma's Pizza (Map 9, #34; ☎ 617-864-8534; 40 Hampshire St; open 11:30am-10pm Tues-Sat) makes crispy thin-crust pies with sauces made from seasonal toppings, fresh herbs and garlic-infused oil. The cheeses are cow, sheep, goat or dairy-free.

Rebecca's (Map 9, #54; ☎ 617-494-6688; 290 Main St; open 7am-4pm Mon-Fri) is known primarily for luscious cakes and tarts; the self-service counter dishes out generous sandwiches, salads, soups and hot mains.

B-Side Lounge (Map 9, #21; ☎ 617-354-0766; 92 Hampshire St; dinner mains $10-17; also open brunch Sat & Sun) is much more than the divey bar it appears to be. Besides being one of the funkiest places for a drink this side of the river, the menu features un-believably good food at reasonable prices. Try the fish taco with mahi-mahi ceviche,

guacamole and chipotle vinaigrette or the signature marinated steak tips with mashed potatoes and fried onions.

Helmand (☎ 617-492-4646; 143 First St; dinner mains $11-18), owned by the family of Afghanistan's head of government Hamid Karzai, serves exceptional Afghan cuisine. Although the menu features lots of grilled meat dishes, vegetarians will be thrilled, too. Try eggplant stuffed with spinach and sauteed with vegies in a spicy tomato and onion sauce, accompanied by a cool yogurt mint sauce, or try anything with pumpkin.

Blue Room (Map 9, #37; ☎ 617-494-9034; One Kendall Square; mains $16-22, Sunday brunch $21) specializes in wood-fired, grilled and artfully presented game, beef and fish. Don't even think about skipping dessert. Though it's difficult to forgo the snazzy dining room, there is outdoor patio seating.

INMAN SQUARE (MAP 9)

City Girl Caffè (Map 9, #13; ☎ 617-864-2809; 204 Hampshire St; mains $7-10; open lunch & dinner Tues-Sun, brunch Sat & Sun) is a casual, friendly eatery with thin-crust pizza, panini, calzones, pasta and salads. Or simply stop by for cappuccino and dessert.

S&S Deli Restaurant (Map 9, #5; ☎ 617-354-0620; 1334 Cambridge St; dishes $7-12; open breakfast, lunch & dinner) has lines forming early on weekends for Belgian waf-fles, pancakes, sandwiches and egg dishes. A neighborhood family institution since 1919.

Ole Mexican Grill (Map 9, #2; ☎ 617-492-4495; 11 Springfield St; dinner mains $14-20; also open brunch 10am-2pm Sun), lively and colorful, serves tasty, innovative Mexican meals hot off the grill. Fresh ingredients are emphasized, and the chef, himself a vegetarian, does not treat vegetables like 2nd-class citizens.

Midwest Grill (Map 9, #11; ☎ 617-354-7536; 1124 Cambridge St; lunch mains $11-17, dinner mains $20), a Brazilian grill house and buffet, welcomes faithful carnivores.

Magnolias Southern Cuisine (Map 9, #10; ☎ 617-576-1971; 1193 Cambridge St; mains $12-23; open dinner Tues-Sat) features Southern regional staples such as pan-fried catfish, jambalaya and pecan pie. The friendly staff

PLACES TO EAT

Just Desserts

In the mood to indulge a sweet tooth? These places will keep your dentist happy.

At **Mike's Pastry** (*Map 3, #19;* ☎ *617-742-305; 300 Hanover St; open 8am-9pm Mon, Wed & Sun, 8am-6pm Tues, 8am-10pm Thur-Sat*), rather than opting for an already-filled pastry shell, order a ricotta cannoli ($2.50), which are filled-to-order.

The Chocolate Bar at **Café Fleuri** (*Map 4, #41;* ☎ *617-451-1900; 250 Franklin St; open 1pm-3pm Sat Sep-May*), in Le Meridien Boston, features 25 mousses, cookies, tarts, gateaux and eclairs at the all-you-can-eat buffet ($23 for adults, $12 for children under 13).

Finale Desserterie (*Map 6, #9;* ☎ *617-423-3184; 1 Columbus Ave; open 11:30am-11pm Mon-Thur, 6pm-11pm Sat, 4pm-11pm Sun*), an elegant yet comfortable dining room, is set up so that you can watch pasty chefs work their magic with creme brulee and chocolate souffle.

The Bristol (*Map 6, #1;* ☎ *617-351-2053; 200 Boylston St*), in the Four Seasons Hotel, serves a fabulously decadent Viennese dessert buffet ($18.50), with live music from 9pm to midnight Friday and Saturday.

LA Burdick Chocolates (*Map 8, #10;* ☎ *617-491-4340; 52D Brattle St; open 8am-11pm Tues-Sat, 9am-10pm Sun & Mon*) only has a handful of tiny tables, but it serves the richest hot chocolate this side of Willy Wonka's Chocolate Factory.

Carberry's Bakery & Coffee House, near Central Square (*Map 9, #24;* ☎ *617-576-3530; 74 Prospect St • Map 10, #18;* ☎ *617-666-2233; 187 Elm St*), boasts excellent pastries and a relaxed, hip atmosphere.

Rosie's Bakery & Dessert Shop (*Map 9, #1;* ☎ *617-491-9488; 243 Hampshire St; open 8am-8pm*) has luscious brownies, tarts and shortbreads.

Tea-Tray in the Sky (*Map 10, #27;* ☎ *617-492-8327; 1796 Mass Ave; open 8am-8:30pm Tues-Thur, 8am-10pm Fri & Sat, 8am-7pm Sun*), a charming dessert and tea shop, boasts over 125 varieties of tea.

and soothing dining room make for a pleasant evening.

Oleana (*Map 9, #14;* ☎ *617-661-0505; 134 Hampshire St; dinner mains $18-26*), owned by resident chef Ana Sortun, is a masterpiece. The Mediterranean- and Middle Eastern-influenced menu features grilled lamb with Turkish spices and fava bean moussaka, as well as grilled sea scallops with basmati-pistachio pilaf. There's a lovely warm-weather patio.

East Coast Grill (*Map 9, #7;* ☎ *617-491-6568; 1271 Cambridge St; dinner mains $14-28; also open brunch Sun*) is Boston's hippest and hoppingest seafood bar and restaurant. Come to eat rather than for quiet conversation. Chef Chris Schlesinger's menu features fresh fish specials and the city's best (and probably priciest) fish and chips. Folks travel miles to belly up to the raw bar. There are always a couple of savory barbecue sandwiches for those with less to spend.

CENTRAL SQUARE (MAP 9)
Budget
Around since the Square's hippie heyday, **Moody's Falafel Palace** (*Map 9, #30;* ☎ *617-864-0827; 25 Central Square; open 10am-midnight*) can't be beaten for a quick bite of tasty wholesome food: tabouli, kebabs and, of course, falafel.

Miracle of Science Bar & Grill (*Map 9, #58;* ☎ *617-868-2866; 321 Mass Ave; dishes $6-10; open 11:30am-1am*) is cool, sleek, and a popular MIT hangout, serving creative burgers, sandwiches, salads and grilled mains.

Mary Chung (*Map 9, #49;* ☎ *617-864-1991; 464 Mass Ave; mains $5-10; open lunch Mon-Fri, dim sum Sat & Sun, dinner daily*), a neighborhood institution, is perhaps the most beloved Mandarin-Szechwan place in Cambridge.

India Pavilion (*Map 9, #29;* ☎ *617-547-7463; 17 Central Square; lunch mains $4.50-6, dinner mains $7-12*) is the oldest Indian restaurant in the Square. The lunchtime buffet (Thursday through Sunday only) is a bargain at $6.

Mid-Range

A tiny storefront, **Baraka Café** (Map 9, #46; ☎ 617-868-3951; 80½ Pearl St; dishes $9-16; open lunch Tues-Sat, dinner Tues-Sun) serves sublime North African–Mediterranean cuisine. Be adventurous – you can't go wrong. The *bedenjal mechoui* ($4), an Algerian appetizer of smoked eggplant and roasted peppers, sounds like a typical Middle Eastern dish, but it's worlds apart in flavor and presentation. Save room for dessert.

Cuchi Cuchi (Map 9, #51; ☎ 617-864-2929; 795 Main St; tapas $7-16; open dinner) features an international tapas menu, encouraging you to sample your way around the globe. The lavishly baroque decor bucks the minimalist design trends omnipresent in Boston's hip eateries. Stained-glass windows, gold-veined mirrors and ornate tiles make the sophisticated, adult clientele feel right at home. And yes, the place is named in honor of Charo.

Green St Grill (Map 9, #39; ☎ 617-876-1655; 280 Green St; mains $14-18; open 3pm-1am, food available 6pm-10pm) is a dive no longer, but a hip and artsy Caribbean bar and grill. True to its roots, though, it still offers spicy, delicious fare and live music nightly. And it continues to attract a vibrant and diverse cross-section of devoted locals.

Central Kitchen (Map 9, #41; ☎ 617-491-5599; 567 Mass Ave; dinner mains $16-23), Central Square's central hangout, serves French bistro dishes in a dark, hip and festive setting. Head to the upstairs lounge, simply referred to as the Enormous Room, to recline on plush couches while you imbibe and munch on snack platters.

ZuZu (Map 9, #45; ☎ 617-864-3278; 474 Mass Ave; dinner mains $12-23), perched between the Middle East Restaurant and its related rock bar, serves sophisticated dishes inspired by Middle Eastern cuisine. Move beyond hummus and falafel to order more exquisite and exotic appetizers (*mazza*). The little dining room, with soft lighting and high ceilings, provides a pleasant backdrop.

Top-End

A 10-table Florentine trattoria, **Centro** (Map 9, #26; ☎ 617-868-2405; 720 Mass Ave; lunch mains $8-11, dinner mains $16-23; open lunch Mon-Fri, dinner daily) serves some the city's best Italian food outside the North End. Since you have to enter the soothing dining room through the adjacent Good Life bar, you might as well have a drink there while you wait for a table.

MASS AVE & PORTER SQUARE (MAP 10)

Cambridge Common (Map 10, #36; ☎ 617-547-1228; 1667 Mass Ave; dishes $7-13; open 11:30am-1am, until 2am Fri & Sat, food available until midnight), a casual neighborhood eatery popular with students, serves meatloaf, burgers, and macaroni and cheese.

Passage to India (Map 10, #23; ☎ 617-497-6113; 1900 Mass Ave; lunch buffet $7, dinner mains $8-12), a neighborhood favorite for reliably good Indian food, is also quiet and comfortable.

Forest Café (Map 10, #35; ☎ 617-661-7810; 1682 Mass Ave; mains $9-15; open lunch Thur-Sat, dinner daily), newly spiffed up without having lost its soul, specializes in upscale authentic cuisine from Mexico's Yucatan region. Classic pork and seafood dishes dominate the menu, which stretches far beyond the usual nachos, tacos and burritos.

Christopher's (Map 10, #20; ☎ 617-876-9180; 1920 Mass Ave; dishes $8-18; open dinner daily, lunch Sat & Sun), known for burgers and microbrews from around the world, also has vegetarian and grain-based dishes.

West Side Lounge (Map 10, #38; ☎ 617-441-5566; 1680 Mass Ave; Sun brunch $7-12, dinner mains $15-21) is not simply a place to see and be seen, but also a great place for a great meal. The New American menu features generous salads, steak and seafood served with flair, and decadent desserts. The hot, hot, hot bar has comfy booths for taking in the scene.

Chez Henri (Map 10, #39; ☎ 617-354-8980; 1 Shepherd St; dinner prix fixe $36, mains $22-27) serves French bistro food with a Cuban accent. It wins raves for delicious down-to-earth food (the bouillabaisse is

PLACES TO EAT

Brewpubs

Microbrews are popular in this college-dominated town. And you can sample some curious and fresh seasonal brews at these fun places.

Commonwealth Pub (Map 3, #22; ☎ 617-523-8383; 138 Portland St; lunch mains $5-16, dinner mains $8-16), which produces over 10 kinds of English-style suds, serves mostly seafood, but you can also get a barbecue chicken sandwich. The basement is comfortably 'clubby,' bands play Thursday through Saturday, and the place is packed when the Bruins and Celtics play nearby. Food is generally served until 10pm; the bar closes at 1am.

Rock Bottom (Map 6, #12; ☎ 617-523-6467; 115 Stuart St • Map 8, #16; ☎ 617-499-2739; 50 Church St) is sophisticated and sleek, and offers seasonal brews and a creative menu from 11am. Though it's often packed with pre- and post-theater crowds, at least the bar serves food until 1am weekdays, 2am weekends.

Boston Beer Works (Map 7, #35; ☎ 617-536-2337; 61 Brookline Ave • Map 3, #5; ☎ 617-896-2337; 112 Canal St), with its exposed tanks and pipes, often has seasonal concoctions such as Boston Red and Blueberry Ale. The appetizers and munchies are pretty good, too. Both venues draw sports fanatics during games. The kitchen serves from 11:30am to 12:45am; the bar closes at 1:30am.

The subterranean **John Harvard's Brew House** (Map 8, #55; ☎ 617-868-3585; 33 Dunster St) smells and feels more like an English pub than the others and has perhaps the best ales and stouts, too. Above-average pub grub is available at lunch ($6 to $8) and dinner ($8 to $17), until 10pm weeknights, 12:30am weekends. Open until 1am weekdays, 2am weekends for drinks.

Cambridge Brewing Co (Map 9, #36; ☎ 617-494-1994; One Kendall Square) has reputable seasonal ales, but beyond the burgers, you'd do better eating elsewhere. This is a convenient place to go after a movie, and it's packed on weekends.

wonderful) and warm, romantic atmosphere. The prix fixe three-course menu is a great deal, but you can also order à la carte.

DAVIS SQUARE (MAP 10)

Picante (Map 10, #15; ☎ 617-628-6394; 217 Elm St; mains $5-7) has serviceable Mexican dishes, plus savory home-style tamales (including vegetarian!).

Mr Crepe (Map 10; ☎ 617-628-1500; 83 Holland St; dishes $8; open lunch & dinner) offers a new twist on fast food. Crepes are folded and wrapped in a foil pouch to take away. Try them savory (with apples and Brie, or with spinach, mushrooms and basil) or sweet (with Nutella, banana and coconut). The name is pretty hokey, but the little place hops. Check out the revolving tinfoil sculpture display – and add your own.

House of Tibet Kitchen (Map 10; ☎ 617-629-7567; 235 Holland Ave; mains $7-9; open dinner Tues-Sun) serves comfort food in a relaxed atmosphere. Popular with locals and college students, the place serves as headquarters for the area's small Tibetan community.

Rosebud Diner (Map 10, #17; ☎ 617-666-6015; 381 Summer St; dishes $6-8; open 8am-midnight), where you can eat real diner food in a real railroad dining car, is loads of fun since the food surpasses the gimmick.

Redbones (Map 10, #12; ☎ 617-628-2200; 55 Chester St; open lunch & dinner), a beloved hole-in-the-wall, receives raves for its great ribs ($11-18), collard greens ($3.50), corn bread (75¢) and sweet potato pie ($4). There are only four menu choices at lunch.

Diva Indian Bistro (Map 10, #11; ☎ 617-629-4963; 246 Elm St; lunch buffet Mon-Fri $8, Sat & Sun $11, dinner mains $12-16) is not your standard Indian restaurant. The decor, service and atmosphere are bright, youthful and festive. Despite the name, the menu is fairly traditional; no fusion pretensions here. You'll find tasty, if standard, renditions of favorites such as saag paneer, lamb korma and tandoori chicken.

Gargoyles on the Square *(Map 10, #14;* ☎ *617-776-5300; 219 Elm St; mains $15-21; open dinner Tues-Sun)*, without the attitude of comparable Boston eateries, serves elegantly prepared and presented New American cuisine. The romantic, candlelit dining room with floor-to-ceiling windows is a haven, overlooking a nightly parade through Davis Square.

CHARLESTOWN (MAP 11)

Sorelle Bakery Café *(Map 11, #5;* ☎ *617-242-2125; 1 Monument Ave; dishes $3-5; open 6:30am-4pm Mon-Fri, 8am-3pm Sat & Sun)* is a tiny place serving coffees, pastries, salads, sandwiches and cold pasta dishes.

Warren Tavern *(Map 11, #4;* ☎ *617-241-8142; 2 Pleasant St; lunch mains $7-13, dinner*

mains $7-21), a c. 1780 neighborhood pub, skillfully chars burgers. The snug, dark quarters are boisterous and congenial, except when the staff is harried and grumpy!

Figs *(Map 11, #6;* ☎ *617-242-2229; 67 Main St; pizzas & pastas $11-19; open dinner)*, the original branch, is just the place to reward yourself with a pizza after climbing the Bunker Hill Monument and strolling the cobblestone streets.

Olives *(Map 11, #10;* ☎ *617-242-1999; 10 City Square; mains $21-31; open dinner Mon-Sat)* has a creative Mediterranean–New American menu prepared from an exposed kitchen. Chef Todd English's original place excels in spit-roasted meats and savory fish preparations. There are two drawbacks though: it's quite noisy and you'll have to wait, unless you arrive very early or very late.

Entertainment

Boston has something for every taste. Whether your idea of a great evening is a boisterous sports bar, a Euro-chic dance club, an Irish music jam, edgy drama, or a rock concert, you'll find it here. Each neighborhood has a distinct vibe but, at the same time, offers a variety of options.

Beacon Hill nightlife centers on relatively quiet bars and cafés on Beacon and Cambridge Sts, while Government Center and Faneuil Hall are home to more lively taverns and rowdy sports bars. The North End and Charlestown are primarily dining destinations, though the cafés are very popular gathering spots after the clubs close. The Downtown 'Ladder District', comprising streets connecting Washington and Tremont Sts, has lots of welcoming bars and nightclubs geared to a range of folks. You could also head to a few swank restaurants and clubs in the Leather District, which, though it sounds racy, is named for the area's former tanneries. Back Bay doesn't have many bars because it has a strong neighborhood group that keeps them out.

The Theater District hosts Broadway blockbuster venues, dinner theater, and nightclubs geared to an older crowd. Adjacent to it, Chinatown's restaurants are the only place to get a beer after 2am. The South End has a few performance venues, spirited bars and chichi cafés, while Kenmore Square and the Fenway are home to sports-themed bars and lots of Landsdowne St nightclubs full of hot and heavy college students. Although Brookline is primarily a dining destination, it boasts a historic art-house cinema and one of the city's friendliest Irish pubs.

Across the river in Cambridge, Harvard Square's street life bustles late into the night. Harvard, Central, Porter, Inman and Kendall Squares are home to tons of coffeehouses, Irish pubs, watering holes and music joints of every stripe. Somerville's Davis Square is a microcosm of all that's fun in Boston: evening foot traffic, relaxed cafés, live music venues, a comedy club and a historic theater.

Best of Boston After Dark

- Irish music at the Black Rose (p113) or Burren (p115)
- Watching a televised game at Boston Beer Works (p113)
- Club-hopping on Landsdowne St (Map 7)
- Salsa and merengue at Sophia's (p119)
- Folk concerts at Club Passim (p117)
- Theater at the American Repertory Theater (p121)
- Street performers in Harvard Square (Map 8)
- Letting go of all inhibitions at Man Ray (p119)
- Live bands at Johnny D's Uptown (p116)

For up-to-the-minute listings, check out the Calendar section of Thursday's *Boston Globe*, Friday's *Boston Herald*, the weekly *Boston Phoenix* or the irreverent magazines *Improper Bostonian* and *Stuff at Night* (free in sidewalk street boxes).

The drinking age for alcoholic beverages is 21, and in most cases you must be 21 to enter a drinking establishment. Some clubs offer '19-plus' nights; check the papers for details.

Much to the chagrin of the lounge lizards and club-hoppers, Boston resolutely retains a puritanical 'early to bed, early to rise' party ethic. Most bars close at 1am, clubs at 2am. The last Red Line trains pass through Park St station at about 12:30am, but other lines vary; a good rule is to be at the nearest T station at about midnight. Otherwise, budget for a cab.

There is a Night Owl service (ie, late night buses) on Friday and Saturday. For more information see Subway in the Getting Around chapter.

All of the establishments and venues listed are located in neighborhoods considered safe by most big-city standards and are within a 10-minute walk of a subway station.

By city ordinance, there is no smoking in Boston bars or restaurants as of May 2003.

The T

Head of the Charles Regatta, Harvard University, Cambridge

Fenway Park, Kenmore Square

Swan boats, Public Garden, Beacon Hill

Trident Booksellers & Cafe, Newbury St, Back Bay

The Coop, Harvard Square, Cambridge

BARS & TAVERNS

Boston is a drinking city. Most of Boston's favorite bars are Irish pubs and taverns, though there are certainly more than a few sports bars with blaring TVs, and swank hotel lounges, as well as a fair number of steadfastly grungy watering holes.

Beacon Hill (Map 2)

Sevens Ale House *(Map 2, #12; ☎ 617-523-9074; 77 Charles St)*, a friendly neighborhood pub, is always crowded. Sit at the bar or in a booth and order a sandwich and beer ($9).

Hill Tavern *(Map 2, #5; ☎ 617-742-6192; 228 Cambridge St)* bustles with a young, professional crowd – workers from the nearby state and federal buildings.

Cheers *(Map 2, #31; ☎ 617-227-9605; 84 Beacon St)*, which inspired the TV sitcom of the same name, remains a fixture on the tourist trail. If there ever was a reason to go here, it's long gone. That said, this authentic English pub was dismantled in England, shipped across the Atlantic and reassembled inside this Beacon Hill townhouse.

Red Hat *(Map 2, #7; ☎ 617-523-2175; 9 Bowdoin St)*, a favorite of Boston politicos, feels more like *Cheers* than its above-mentioned kin.

Government Center & North End (Map 3)

Oyster Bar at Durgin Park *(Map 3, #48; ☎ 617-227-2038; North Market, Faneuil Hall Marketplace)* remains something of a secret. If you want a few oysters or some clam chowder to go with your beer, venture down the narrow stairway and take a seat.

Rack Billiard Club *(Map 3, #45; ☎ 617-725-1051; 24 Clinton St)*, an always hopping upscale pool hall, bar and outdoor café, serves above-average pub grub and has live music. The young professionals who frequent the place come after work in their business duds (a dress code is strictly enforced).

Black Rose *(Map 3, #59; ☎ 617-742-2286; 160 State St)*, an Irish-American pub with a boisterous atmosphere, has live Irish music and well-pulled pints.

Bell in Hand *(Map 3, #38; ☎ 617-227-2098; 45-55 Union St)*, with a tourist-trail location

and plaque proclaiming its status as 'the oldest tavern in the US', could easily descend into kitsch. But the vibe inside is that of your basic neighborhood bar: friendly, unpretentious and popular with a young, after-work crowd.

The Green Dragon *(Map 3, #40; ☎ 617-367-0055; 11 Marshal St)*, sited on yet another historic watering hole, is said to have been frequented by the ever-thirsty patriots. Today, bar-hopping yuppies have far less revolutionary activities on their minds.

Hennessy's *(Map 3, #43; ☎ 617-742-2121; 25 Union St)* makes no claims to have quenched the collective thirst of the Sons of Liberty. Finally! Its pubby atmosphere is cozy and fun, made more so by live Irish music on Saturdays at 4pm.

Fours *(Map 3, #4; ☎ 617-720-4455; 166 Canal St)*, boasting all sports, all the time, is *the* place to begin to appreciate Bostonians' near fanatical obsession with sporting events.

The Grand Canal *(Map 3, #11; ☎ 617-523-1112; 57 Canal St)*, a classy London-style pub, provides a relatively genteel alternative to its boisterous neighbors.

Boston Beer Works *(Map 3, #5; ☎ 617-896-2337; 112 Canal St • Map 7, #35; ☎ 617-536-2337; 61 Brookline Ave)*, Boston's famed beer hall/sports bar, features a revolving list of seasonal microbrews (try the pumpkin pie). There's plenty of room to drink and nosh (the french fries are almost as popular as the brews), watch sporting events and shoot pool.

Irish Embassy *(Map 3, #8; ☎ 617-742-6618; 234 Friend St)*, with a youth hostel upstairs, is a place to meet fellow travelers. However, it's often so loud that you won't be able to hear your new friends' names. There's live music nightly.

Charlestown (Map 11)

Charlestown's **Warren Tavern** *(Map 11, #4; ☎ 617-241-8142; 2 Pleasant St)*, c. 1780, is an atmospheric place for a drink – you can almost see the ghosts of the founding fathers hoisting a pint in the back corner.

Downtown & Waterfront (Map 4)

Littlest Bar *(Map 4, #21; ☎ 617-523-9766; 47 Province St)* really is. No kidding. There's

ENTERTAINMENT

room at the bar for the bartender, you and maybe three kindred spirits. This is a place where nobody can help but know your name.

Emily's *(Map 4, #29; ☎ 617-423-3649; 4850 Winter St)* is a small club, popular with gen-xers who like to lounge on the comfy couches, shoot pool and dance to Top-40 tunes. In spite of velvet curtains, wall mirrors and a strict dress code, it has a mellow vibe, especially on weeknights.

The Good Life *(Map 4, #56; ☎ 617-451-2622; 28 Kingston St)* caters to a nostalgic crowd who think that Sammy, Frank and Dino were the cat's meow. Order from a vast martini menu and start groovin' downstairs to live jazz Thursday through Saturday. When you're on the other side of the river, drop in at its Central Square location *(Map 9, #26; ☎ 617-868-8800; 720 Mass Ave)*.

Silvertone Bar & Grill *(Map 4, #20; ☎ 617-338-7887; 69 Bromfield St)* serves up sultry, piped-in jazz, fine martinis and retro comfort food in basement-level digs. Not the place for a quiet conversation, this place hustles and bustles.

Back Bay (Map 5)

Cottonwood Café *(Map 5, #62; ☎ 617-247-2225; 222 Berkeley St)* serves the best margaritas in Boston.

Barcode *(Map 5, #50; ☎ 617-421-1818; 955 Boylston St)* is what they call the place, but, like 'the musician formerly known as…,' the name is actually a symbol. The neocolonial-accented digs (think bamboo and palm trees) are hopping with a mix of yuppies and local and international university students. The dress code is black, black, and more black. Did we suggest black?

Bukowski Tavern *(Map 5, #51; ☎ 617-437-9999; 50 Dalton St)* is a real Boston bar. What does that mean? It's long on beer (over 100 kinds) and short on poseurs.

Theater District, Chinatown & South End (Map 6)

Rock Bottom *(Map 6, #12; ☎ 617-742-2739; 115 Stuart St)*, part of a national brewpub chain, is a casual place for a pre- or post-theater beer and snack.

Pravda 116 *(Map 6, #3; ☎ 617-482-7799; 116 Boylston St)* serves up pricey vodkas and other cool libations at a long, sleek, icy bar. The back room dance club packs 'em in Wednesday through Saturday after 10pm. Dress code is decidedly Euro chic.

Club Café *(Map 6, #36; ☎ 617-536-0966; 209 Columbus Ave)* has a bar that's a convivial gathering place for gay men and lesbians. Straight folks are always welcome, too.

Clery's Bar & Restaurant *(Map 6, #40; ☎ 617-262-9874; 113 Dartmouth St)*, a fun neighborhood place, gets pretty rowdy on weekends. Simple pub grub is served at lunch and dinner.

Kenmore Square, the Fenway & Brookline (Map 7)

Jillian's Billiard Club *(Map 7, #36; ☎ 617-437-0300; 145 Ipswich St)* has over 50 billiard tables and a dance club, but people also come here to play darts, blackjack, table tennis and virtual reality games. This enormous three-story place has seven bars and a full-service menu.

Atlas Bar & Grille *(Map 7, #41; ☎ 617-437-0300; 3 Landsdowne St)*, with a funky industrial atmosphere once aptly described as 'the Jetsons meet the Copacabana,' is a fun place for a beer – before or after serious club-hopping. Friday and Saturday, a DJ spins recent Top-40 tunes.

Jake Ivory's *(Map 7, #40; ☎ 617-247-1222; 9 Landsdowne St)* features dueling rock and roll pianos and, believe it or not, sing-alongs.

Modern *(Map 7, #42; ☎ 617-536-2100; 36 Landsdowne St)*, with its sleek chrome bar and upholstered seats, is a sophisticated place for a martini.

Linwood Grill *(Map 7, #54; ☎ 617-247-8099; 81 Kilmarnock St)*, at the other end of the spectrum from Modern, is a Fenway mainstay – a true neighborhood place to have a beer (make that a Bud!), chow on barbecue, play darts, pool and pinball, and talk sports. It has live music Wednesday through Saturday.

An Tua Nua *(Map 7, #24; ☎ 617-262-2121; 835 Beacon St)*, a popular Irish pub by day, is transformed into a hopping dance club by night. Whatever the time of day, it's full of university students.

Matt Murphy's Pub *(Map 7, #68; ☎ 617-232-0188; 14 Harvard St)*, a traditional Irish pub in Brookline Village, offers not only a warm and welcoming atmosphere, but also great food. There's always live Irish music Thursday and Saturday; ring ahead for Friday.

Harvard Square (Map 8)
Grafton Street *(Map 8, #51; ☎ 617-497-0400; 1230 Mass Ave)*, though not as authentic as Irish pubs in some of the less touristed neighborhoods, is nevertheless a pleasant place to nurse a pint, especially in summer when the windows overlooking Mass Ave are thrown open.

Hong Kong *(Map 8, #50; ☎ 617-864-5311; 1236 Mass Ave)* is something of an entertainment complex, with a bar wedged above a restaurant and below a dance club. The bar is famed for its killer 'scorpion bowls', which pack a punch and remain a rite of passage for Harvard freshmen.

Shay's Lounge *(Map 8, #70; ☎ 617-864-9161; 58 JFK St)*, primarily a sedate, professorial wine bar, also has tables on the recessed patio. These are hard to come by in fine weather, but they're worth the effort of trying.

Kendall, Inman & Central Squares (Map 9)
Flat Top Johnny's *(Map 9, #35; ☎ 617-494-9565; One Kendall Square)* is a good choice for a relaxing beer and game of billiards. Within Cambridge's high-tech mecca, the place is clean and attracts MIT students and young computer professionals.

Druid *(Map 9, #4; ☎ 617-497-0965; 1357 Cambridge St, Inman Square)*, welcoming and adorned with Celtic artwork, pours proper pints of Guinness and boasts no TV. Traditional Friday Irish jams ('seisiuns') draw a loyal crowd from 6pm to 9:30pm.

Plough & Stars *(Map 9, #16; ☎ 617-441-3455; 912 Mass Ave)*, between Central and Harvard Squares, is a friendly Irish bar with the requisite Guinness and Bass on tap, as well as televised English football matches weekends September through May. Rock and rockabilly bands play most weekends for a $3 cover charge.

Phoenix Landing *(Map 9, #44; ☎ 617-576-6260; 512 Mass Ave, Central Square)*, a social Irish pub with space for talkers in front and dancers in back, offers half-price appetizers from 5pm to 7pm.

Field *(Map 9, #31; ☎ 617-354-7345; 20 Prospect St)* is an unpretentious neighborhood bar where the funky pulse of Central Square is still discernible.

People's Republik *(Map 9, #18; ☎ 617-492-8632; 878 Mass Ave)* feels like some college student's fantasy of what a bar in the Soviet Union or Mao's China should look like. The walls are covered with CCCP posters depicting strong and brave workers. Beer is priced for the thirsty proletariat.

Mass Ave, Porter Square & Davis Square (Map 10)
Temple Bar *(Map 10, #34; ☎ 617-547-5055; 1688 Mass Ave)* has windows that open onto the street and decor reminiscent of the Temple Bar area in Dublin.

Joshua Tree *(Map 10, #8; ☎ 617-623-9910; 256 Elm St, Davis Square)*, a trendy bar-cum-restaurant, has a giant-screen TV for sports action, 27 beers on tap and a DJ or live music Thursday through Saturday.

Burren *(Map 10, #10; ☎ 617-776-6896; 247 Elm St, Davis Square)*, a popular and amiable place oozing Irish atmosphere, features traditional Irish music nightly in the front room and various bands (and an open-mic night) in the back. Try to catch the Tarbox Ramblers, a local country and blues band, on Saturday night.

Under Bones *(Map 10, #12; ☎ 617-628-2200; 55 Chester St, Davis Square)*, the amiable basement bar of the Redbones barbecue joint, specializes in rare brews from Belgium to Boston.

BREWERY TOURS
Mass Bay Brewing Co *(Harpoon Brewery; Map 4, #77; ☎ 617-574-9551; 306 Northern Ave)*, the largest facility in the state, offers free hour-long tours and tastings of its popular Harpoon Ale and India Pale Ale at 1pm and 3pm Friday and Saturday.

Boston Beer Co *(☎ 617-368-5000; 30 Germania St, Jamaica Plain)* produces Samuel

Subway & Street Performers

Boston's streets and T stations have long been a proving ground for talented and enterprising musicians in search of an audience, while aspiring to club gigs and recording contracts. Tracy Chapman, who played in Harvard Square while a Tufts student in the '80s, is the most famous graduate.

Most street performers migrate below ground from November to April rather than risk frostbitten fingers and crowds that can't stand still long enough toss a cold coin. Catch solo acoustic performers at the Red Line at **Park St**; Blue Line at **Government Center**; Blue Line at **State**; Red and Orange Lines at **Downtown Crossing**; Red Line (outbound) at **South Station**; and Red Line (inbound) at **Harvard**.

Outdoor locations include **Faneuil Hall** *(Map 3)*; the pedestrian mall at **Downtown Crossing** *(Map 4)*, which also has fire-and-brimstone orators and anti-fur protesters; and the intersection of Brattle and Mt Auburn Sts near **Harvard Square** *(Map 8)*.

Adams, the only local brew that's achieved international fame. Hour-long tours and tastings are at 2pm Thursday and Friday; noon, 1pm and 2pm on Saturday. Take the T Orange Line to Stony Brook, and then follow signs for two blocks.

LIVE MUSIC

Boston boasts a pretty darn lively alternative rock scene, but then again, plenty of famous folkies got their start at Club Passim. Then again, the jazz scene is fueled by thousands of musicians at Berklee College of Music. All in all, we can thank the tens of thousands of students who migrate through Boston for keeping the music scene hip.

Fleet Boston Pavilion *(Map 4, #76; ☎ 617-728-1600; W www.fleetbostonpavilion.com; 290 Northern Ave)*, a white sail-like summertime tent with sweeping harbor views, hosts nationally known pop, rock and jazz performers. Shuttle buses run from South Station before and after shows.

Rock

Plenty of nationally known alternative and rock bands got their start in Boston-area clubs; in fact, there are more than 5000 bands registered here. Unless otherwise noted, cover charges vary from $5 to $15, depending on the act's fame quotient.

Orpheum Theater *(Map 4, #30; ☎ 617-679-0810; 1 Hamilton Place)*, an intimate but slightly worn venue for rock concerts, hosts the likes of Phish and Beck. Since the hall has great acoustics, it comes as no surprise that the New England Conservatory began here and the Boston Symphony Orchestra first played here in 1881. One theory has it that the term 'Brahmin' originated here, too: many proper Bostonians stormed out during one Brahms premier and those who stayed to hear the wild new symphony were dubbed 'Brahmins.'

TT the Bear's *(Map 9, #48; ☎ 617-492-0082; 10 Brookline St, Central Square)* has been an intimate die-hard live rock joint since the mid-1970s.

Middle East *(Map 9, #45; ☎ 617-354-8238; 472 Mass Ave, Central Square)* usually has three different gigs (from belly dancing to rockabilly to ska) going simultaneously. There's always a free jazz show in the 'corner.' The Middle East also serves pretty good (and well-priced) food until midnight or 1am.

Lizard Lounge *(Map 10, #36; ☎ 617-547-0759; 1667 Mass Ave)*, between Harvard and Porter Squares, features live original music nightly. Casual dress is cool in this intimate, basement-level place.

Toad *(Map 10, #21; ☎ 617-497-4950; 1920 Mass Ave, Porter Square; no cover)* is a tiny, ultra-casual place where local bands perform funk, R&B, rock and soul nightly.

Johnny D's Uptown *(Map 10, #1; ☎ 617-776-2004; 17 Holland St, Davis Square)*, one of the city's best and most eclectic venues, features a different musical style nightly. Sunday night salsa and blues jams (and Monday night bluegrass) are popular; Sunday jazz brunches are mellow.

Paradise *(☎ 617-562-8800; 967-969 Comm Ave; tickets $10-30)*, a small club known for eclectic musical tastes, hosts live rock bands nightly. Ride the T Green Line,

'B' branch to Pleasant St, the sixth stop after Kenmore Square.

Jazz

TK's Jazz Cafe *(Map 3, #51; ☎ 617-227-7579, 617-854-7677 schedule; Quincy Market Building, North St)*, a popular restaurant and bar, maintains its own laid-back vibe amid bustling Quincy Market. There is music seven days a week; a jazz pianist throughout the day, duets during dinner, and ensembles in the late evening. There is sometimes a cover to hear nationally known acts.

Wally's Café *(Map 6, #74; ☎ 617-424-1408; 427 Mass Ave; no cover)*, gritty and storied, is the last survivor of the jazz clubs that once enlivened this neighborhood. There is music 365 days a year. Monday is blues; Tuesday and Wednesday are jazz–funk fusion; Thursday is Latin jazz; Friday and Saturday are traditional; and Sunday sees afternoon jam sessions and evening jazz–funk.

Berklee Performance Center *(Map 7; ☎ 617-266-7455, 617-747-2261 box office; 136 Mass Ave)* hosts jazz concerts by Berklee College of Music's renowned faculty and exceptional students during the school year. The center also hosts big-name performers at big-buck prices.

Regattabar *(Map 8, #60; ☎ 617-661-5000, 617-876-7777 tickets; 1 Bennett St; tickets $10-26)*, on the 3rd floor of the Charles Hotel, is an upscale yacht-club sort of place that books internationally known groups Tuesday through Saturday. If a show is sold out, a limited number of general seating tickets go on sale one hour before show time.

Ryles *(Map 9, #12; ☎ 617-876-9330; 212 Hampshire St, Inman Square; open Sun brunch & from 8pm Tues-Sun)* boasts two floors of local and national recording acts in an intimate dining setting. You'll hear jazz, world music, R&B and blues. Swing lessons are offered on Saturday night ($12). There's a Sunday jazz brunch, where the music is free.

Blues

House of Blues *(Map 8, #65; ☎ 617-491-2583, 617-497-2229 tickets; 96 Winthrop St)*, in Harvard Square, was opened by 'Blues Brother' Dan Aykroyd in 1992 and has since become a major force on the national blues scene. The music begins at 9pm or 10pm; tickets cost $6 to $30. The all-you-can-eat-and-listen-to Sunday gospel brunch ($28, or $13 for just the food) is a downright religious experience for some. Reservations are required.

Cantab Lounge *(Map 9, #25; ☎ 617-354-2685; 738 Mass Ave)* is grungy, dark and laid-back, in keeping with the longtime tradition of pre-rehab Central Square. It remains a well-established bluegrass, blues and oldies venue where students hang with locals and listen to live music nightly. The big draws, Little Joe Cook and the Thrillers, take the stage Thursday through Saturday.

Folk

Although clubs occasionally book folk acts, two Cambridge places are devoted to folkies.

Club Passim *(Map 8, #19; ☎ 617-492-7679, 617-492-5300; 47 Palmer St)*, in Harvard Square, is a small but venerable club nationally known for supporting the early careers of singer-songwriters Jackson Browne, Tracy Chapman and Patty Larkin. Tuesday is open-mic night. Passim also serves lunch and dinner daily in an alcohol-free environment.

Nameless Coffeehouse *(Map 8, #21; ☎ 617-864-1630; 3 Church St; open fall-spring; suggested donation $3-4)*, in Harvard Square within the First Parish Church (Unitarian Universalist), is a low-key place that sponsors acoustic singer-songwriters on most Saturday nights.

Somerville Theatre *(Map 10, #2; ☎ 617-625-5700; 55 Davis Square)*, a refurbished classic venue, stages concerts.

DANCE CLUBS

The thriving club scene, which has gone upscale in recent years, is fueled by a constant infusion of thousands of students. Clubs are fairly stable, although the nightly lineup often changes. Check the *Boston Phoenix* or *Improper Bostonian* for up-to-the-minute information. The clubs along Lansdowne St and in the Fenway (near Kenmore Square) cater to an international university crowd. Those in the Theater District are favored by young professionals; Man Ray, in Cambridge, defies generalization.

ENTERTAINMENT

Gay & Lesbian Venues

Many straight clubs feature gay and lesbian nights. Check Bay Windows or talk to the folks at We Think the World of You (see the boxed text 'Booklover's Paradise' in the Shopping chapter).

Chaps/Vapor *(Map 6, #25; ☎ 617-695-9500; 100 Warrenton St)*, one of the most popular bars and dance clubs, has something for everyone. Tuesday is 'Groove' night with house music; Wednesday features Latin music; Friday is techno and house; and Saturday ends with serious dance music; and Sunday tea dances start at 7pm. Male go-go dancers light up Friday through Sunday.

Jacques *(Map 6, #29; ☎ 617-426-8902; 79 Broadway St)* features drag queen cabaret. Shows nightly; cover $4 to $6.

A mixed crowd gathers at the **Club Café** *(Map 6, #36; ☎ 617-536-0966; 209 Columbus Ave)* bar and restaurant. Thursday is girls' night, in the front anyway. Sunday brunch is always packed.

Fritz *(Map 6, #45; ☎ 617-482-4428; 26 Chandler St)*, a casual watering hole with a nice atmosphere, is mostly men, but women certainly aren't turned away.

Avalon *(Map 7, #37; ☎ 617-262-2424; 15 Lansdowne St)* has blistering house music on Sunday. Monday is anything but 'Static,' as it's called, when the transgendered community, gays and drag queens converge at Axis (Map 7, #38; % 617-262-2437; 13 Lansdowne St). Just about anything goes.

Ramrod *(Map 7, #47; ☎ 617-266-2986; 1254 Boylston St)* is a traditional leather bar, while downstairs at **Machine** *(☎ 617-536-1950)*, it's a hot, high-tech dance club.

Thursday is reserved for the boys at **Man Ray** *(Map 9, #47; ☎ 617-864-0400; 21 Brookline St)* in Central Square.

Most clubs reward those who arrive before 11pm with no waiting in line or lower cover charges. The downside: early birds may be dancing by themselves. Cover charges vary widely, from free (if you arrive early) to $15, but the average is more like $10 on weekends. Many clubs have dress codes. While you may be admitted wearing jeans – as long as they're not frayed nor accompanied by a T-shirt, sneakers and a baseball cap – most clubbers are decked out in their version of their finest. You may feel out of place unless you, too, are wearing something that suggests you've got enough dough to pay your bar tab.

Theater District, Chinatown & South End (Map 6)

Big Easy *(Map 6, #4; ☎ 617-351-7000; 1 Boylston Place; open Tues & Thur-Sat)*, appealing to a slightly older crowd, is decked out in New Orleans Mardi Gras style. Eclectic cover bands play on weekends, and a DJ spins Latin and international on Tuesday. You can watch from the 2nd-floor balcony if you prefer.

La Boom *(Map 6; ☎ 617-542-3689; 25 Boylston Place; open Fri & Sat)* spins Top-40, dance and house music.

Roxy *(Map 6, #31; ☎ 617-338-7699; 279 Tremont St; open Thur-Sat)*, a restored ballroom in the Tremont House, plays Latin on Friday and techno on Saturday. No jeans, sneakers or T-shirts.

Venu *(Map 6, #25; ☎ 617-338-8061; 100 Warrenton St; open Tues & Thur-Sat)* is super-chic. To signal your status as an insider, don your favorite Armani knockoff and arrive fashionably late for DJ-spun tunes.

Matrix *(Map 6, #31; ☎ 617-542-4077; 275 Tremont St; open Fri & Sat)* plays high energy house and trance music on one side and '70s, '80s and '90s Top-40 and hip-hop on the other.

Aria *(Map 6, #27; ☎ 617-338-7080; 246 Tremont St; open Tues-Sat)*, plush and Parisian-themed, attracts a fashionable crowd and plays either house music or hip-hop and R&B. Reservations and 'proper dress' required.

Kenmore Square, the Fenway & Brookline (Map 7)

Avalon *(Map 7, #37; ☎ 617-262-2424; 15 Lansdowne St; open Mon & Thur-Sat)*, Boston's premier dance club, sports four lounges, a balcony and great sound and lighting systems. Some of the world's best DJs fly in to spin. The club also features techno and trance music on Saturday.

Axis *(Map 7, #38; ☎ 617-262-2437; 13 Lansdowne St; open Thur-Sat)*, with two dance floors, has a predominantly punk, subterranean feel with progressive house music.

The smaller **Bill's Bar** *(Map 7, #39; ☎ 617-421-9678; 5½ Lansdowne St; open daily)* is packed with BU students. A house DJ spins alternative music nightly; sometimes Bill's has bands, too.

Sophia's *(Map 7, #45; ☎ 617-351-7001; 1270 Boylston St; open Wed-Sun)*, popular with the Euro-glamour set, is a Latin club with hardwood floors, exposed brick and a rooftop terrace. In the winter, a tent keeps the roof hot (as if the music didn't).

Kendall, Inman & Central Squares (Map 9)

Man Ray *(Map 9, #47; ☎ 617-864-0400; 21 Brookline St; open Wed-Sat)*, in Central Square, is the area's most 'underground' club. Man Ray encourages creative attire; you won't find the Gucci crowd here. Fetishwear is suggested on Friday; when in doubt wear black rather than flannel. Every night, though, is for exhibitionists; dress to impress, express or distress. Man Ray has a varied lineup of industrial rock, high-energy dance tunes or campy, classic disco trash and '80s new wave.

CINEMA

Art and foreign film culture is alive and well in Boston and Cambridge. Tickets cost about $8.

Loews Boston Common *(Map 4, #54; ☎ 617-423-3499; cnr of Tremont & Avery Sts)* features snazzy digs and 18 big screens smack in the middle of town.

Coolidge Corner Theatre *(Map 7, #5; ☎ 617-734-2500; 290 Harvard St)*, the area's only not-for-profit movie house, shows documentaries, foreign films and first-run movies. (One screen is enormous!)

Museum of Fine Arts, Boston *(Map 7; ☎ 617-369-3306 information, 617-369-3770 tickets; 465 Huntington Ave)* screens a wide variety of films – silent, avant-garde and local – in the Remis Auditorium.

Free Outdoor Fun

Shakespeare on the Common *(Map 2, #40; ☎ 617-423-7600)*, at the Parkman Bandstand on Boston Common, is fast becoming a summer tradition. Because of meager funding, they're able to produce only one play for two weeks in early August. Catch 'em if you can.

Hatch Memorial Shell *(Map 2; ☎ 617-727-9547)*, on the Charles River Esplanade, hosts rock, jazz and classical performances from late June to mid-September. Check the newspaper for midweek evening shows and midday weekend shows. There are public rest rooms and an inexpensive snack bar here. 'Free (family-oriented) Friday Flicks' are shown at dusk in July and August. You'll be sitting on the lawn, so bring a blanket and picnic.

The summer concert series at **City Hall Plaza** *(Map 3; ☎ 617-635-4505)* has been going strong for 30 years. At 7pm Wednesday from June through August, the program features oldies and big bands, as well as local musicians and ethnic dance troupes. This is where you'll find the mayor as well as hundreds of seniors, who come from all over Greater Boston to kick up their heels.

During the summer, the city sponsors free concerts at **Copley Square** *(Map 5; ☎ 617-635-4505)*. At lunchtime on Thursday in June and September, it's classical, and at 5:30pm on Thursday in July and August, it's mellow jazz.

Boston Park Rangers *(☎ 617-635-7383)* offers hordes of informative walking tours year-round.

Harvard Film Archive & Film Study Library
(Map 8, #22; ☎ 617-495-4700; 24 Quincy St)
is reason enough for film buffs to come to
Boston. It screens at least two films daily at
the Carpenter Center for the Visual Arts, and
directors and actors are frequently on hand to
talk about their work.

Brattle St Theatre (Map 8, #26; ☎ 617-876-
6837; 40 Brattle St), a no-frills 1890 repertory
theater, is a film lover's 'cinema paradiso'. It
regularly shows film noir, independent films
and directors' series. You can often catch a
classic double feature for $8.

Sony/Loews Cinema Harvard Square
(Map 8, #20; ☎ 617-864-4580; 10 Church St)
screens first-run Hollywood and some independent and foreign films. Costumes and
audience participation are encouraged at the
cult classic, *Rocky Horror Picture Show*,
shown at midnight Saturday.

Kendall Square Cinema (Map 9;
☎ 617-494-9800; One Kendall Square), a
classy venue, has good-sized screens, comfy
seats, neo–Art Deco decor and an espresso
machine that can churn out a cup of java
every 10 seconds.

Somerville Theatre (Map 10, #2; ☎ 617-
625-5700; 55 Davis Square), another refurbished classic venue, offers second-run
films.

THEATER

Boston is a 'try-out' city for pre-Broadway
shows. The producers work out the kinks
here and if it plays to good reviews, off to
Broadway it goes. Boston also gets touring
Broadway shows. More adventurous shows
are staged by very good university groups.
Many smaller companies live on long-
running shows with a Boston bent.

Commercial Theater Venues

Wang Center (Map 6; ☎ 617-482-9393; 270
Tremont St) is opulent and enormous, and
hosts the Boston Ballet, extravagant music,
dance events and occasional movies. Many
seats, though, are so high and far from the
stage that they cause nosebleeds.

Shubert Theatre (Map 6; ☎ 617-482-
9393; 265 Tremont St) hosts the Boston
Lyric Opera and smaller ballet productions.

Buying Tickets

Bostix (Map 3, #56; ☎ 617-723-5181;
Ⓦ www.bostix.org; Faneuil Hall • Map 5, #57;
☎ 617-723-5181; Copley Square) sells half-
price tickets to select same-day performances
beginning at 11am; cash only. (You can buy
full-price advance tickets here, too.) Both
kiosks are open 10am to 6pm Tuesday through
Saturday, 11am to 4pm Sunday; the Copley
Square kiosk is also open Monday.

Hub Ticket Agency (Map 6, #26; ☎ 617-426-
8340) is located in a trailer at the corner of
Tremont and Stuart Sts.

Ticketmaster has a cash-only counter at
Tower Records (Map 7, #46; ☎ 617-247-5900;
1249 Boylston St) in the Fenway.

Harvard Box Office (Map 8, #57; ☎ 617-
496-2222; 1350 Mass Ave), in the Holyoke
Center Arcade in Harvard Square, sells tickets
to Harvard University events and venues.

Out-of-Town Ticket Agency (☎ 617-247-
1300, 800-442-1854) is a telephone service
with impatient operators, so before dialing,
know what you want or suffer.

Colonial Theatre (Map 6; ☎ 617-426-
9366, 617-931-2787 tickets; 106 Boylston St)
and **Wilbur Theater** (Map 6; ☎ 617-426-9366,
617-931-2787 tickets; 246 Tremont St)
receive pre- and post-Broadway touring
companies.

Emerson Majestic Theatre (Map 6;
☎ 617-824-8000; 219 Tremont St) is a restored
beaux arts beauty.

Boston Center for the Arts (BCA; Map 6;
☎ 617-426-7700; 539 Tremont St), with three
distinctive performance spaces, hosts unusual productions. The resident companies,
Speakeasy and Theater Offensive, which
produces gay- and lesbian-themed works,
guarantee that there's rarely a dull moment
at the BCA.

University Companies

Huntington Theatre Co (Map 7; ☎ 617-266-
0800; 264 Huntington Ave; tickets $12-67),
Boston University's highly regarded company, performs modern and classical plays

in the Greek revival Boston University theater. Half-price student 'rush' tickets are available for $12 two hours prior to curtain for every performance.

American Repertory Theater (Map 8, #8; ☎ 617-547-8300; 64 Brattle St; tickets $24-57), referred to as the A-R-T, is prestigious and stages new plays and experimental interpretations of classics in Harvard University's Loeb Drama Center. Every Monday morning 50 tickets are set aside for the following Saturday's (less expensive) matinee. You literally pay what you can. Student rush tickets are sold 30 minutes prior to curtain for $12.

Hasty Pudding Theatricals (Map 8, #59; ☎ 617-495-5205; 12 Holyoke St) is home to the Harvard undergraduate dramatic society, founded in 1795 (see the boxed text 'Hasty Pudding Awards' in the Things to See & Do chapter).

Smaller Companies

Mobius (Map 4, #72; ☎ 617-542-7416; 354 Congress St, 5th floor), an artist-run center for experimental work, presents some kind of art-in-progress every other weekend. Tickets are sometimes free, but usually about $5 to $18.

Charles Playhouse (Map 6; 74 Warrenton St), with two stages, has presented **Shear Madness** (☎ 617-426-5225; tickets $34), a comical whodunit murder mystery with audience participation, nightly since 1980. It holds the record for America's longest-running play. **Blue Man Group** (☎ 617-426-6912; tickets Tues-Sun $43 & $53) occupies the other stage with a mixed-media performance art piece that pokes fun at the arts community.

Joey & Maria's Comedy Wedding at the **Tremont House** (Map 6, #31; ☎ 800-733-5639; 275 Tremont St; tickets Fri/Sat $45/49), a long-running show that spoofs Italian-American nuptials, plays on Friday and Saturday at 7:30pm. Tickets include an Italian buffet and admission to Matrix nightclub.

COMEDY CLUBS

Bostonians are serious about comedy, sorta. If you feel like laughing, you have options.

Comedy Connection (Map 3, #53; ☎ 617-248-9700; Quincy Market, Faneuil Hall Marketplace; tickets $12 and up), on the 2nd floor above the food court, is one of the city's oldest and biggest comedy venues. Tickets are cheaper midweek.

Improv Asylum (Map 3, #34; ☎ 617-263-6887; 216 Hanover St; shows Wed-Sat $15-20) showcases some edgy performance art that's a cross between theater and comedy.

Nick's Comedy Stop (Map 6, #25; ☎ 617-482-0930; 100 Warrenton St; shows Thur-Sat $10-15) features local and national jokesters.

Improv Boston (Map 9, #9; ☎ 617-576-1253; 1253 Cambridge St; Wed, Thur & Sun $5, Fri & Sat $12), at the **Improv Boston Theater**, is a well-respected long-running troupe that makes things up it goes along.

Jimmy Tingle's Off Broadway (Map 10, #9; ☎ 617-591-1616; 255 Elm St; shows Wed-Sun $20), a new Davis Square club featuring homegrown and nationally known funny man Tingle, also hosts other comedians. Raised in Cambridge, Jimmy's humor is laced with serious social and political commentary.

READINGS & LECTURES

With so many illustrious bookstores and such a literate populace, it's no surprise that publishers send distinguished authors to give readings here. You'll find them at **Barnes & Noble** and **Borders** near Downtown Crossing, **Wordsworth** in Harvard Square, and **Brookline Booksmith** in Coolidge Corner (see the boxed text 'Booklover's Paradise' in the Shopping chapter).

Grolier Poetry Book Shop (Map 8, #48; ☎ 617-547-4648; 6 Plympton St), in Harvard Square, sponsors regular readings at various Harvard Square locations.

Third Rail (Map 9, #25; ☎ 617-354-2685; 738 Mass Ave), at the Cantab Lounge (Central Square), hosts Wednesday night poetry readings and slams.

Ford Hall Forum (☎ 617-373-5800), the oldest continuing public lecture series in the country (begun in 1908), sponsors lively and spirited dialogues on topical world events. Venerable speakers have included Martin Luther King Jr, Maya Angelou, Winston Churchill, Gloria Steinem, Al Gore and MacArthur Genius Award recipient John Bonifaz. Lectures are held in the fall, winter

ENTERTAINMENT

BSO & the Boston Pops

The preeminent **Boston Symphony Orchestra** (☎ 617-266-1492; W www.bso.org; 301 Mass Ave) performs at **Symphony Hall** (Map 7), a National Historic Landmark. Fortunately, the ambitious programs of the world-renowned orchestra match the near-perfect acoustics. Designed by McKim, Mead & White in 1900, the hall was the world's first designed according to acoustic principles; it's still one of the top three. Every aspect was designed to not trap or muffle music: seats are upholstered in leather; floors are hardwood oak; balconies are shallow; and the stage angles in so that the music is projected forward. Group tours are offered by appointment, but individuals can latch onto them.

Symphony Hall is also home to the Boston Pops. Thanks to its 'Evening at Pops' public television series and an ambitious world touring schedule, the Pops is America's most well-known orchestra. Youthful and exuberant conductor Keith Lockhart leads an upbeat repertoire of Broadway show tunes and popular classical music (hence the name 'Pops') from May to mid-July, and again for most of December.

The Pops' free 4th of July concert at the **Hatch Memorial Shell** (Map 2) is a Boston tradition. Diehards pack a day's worth of provisions and diversions and arrive as early as 4am to lay their blanket on the lawn and wait until the evening musical program of rousing patriotic marches and Tchaikovsky's *1812 Overture*. The exhilarating, nationally televised spectacle is complete with a choreographed fireworks display.

The BSO performs Tuesday and Thursday through Saturday, from late September to late April. BSO tickets cost $27 to $80, Pops tickets are slightly less. For BSO same-day discounted rush tickets (one per person; you don't have to be a student), line up at the Cohen box office at 5pm on Tuesday or Thursday for the 8pm show, at 9am Friday for the 2pm show.

and spring at Old South Meeting House and Northeastern University.

BALLET

Boston doesn't have a history of supporting innovative dance groups, perhaps because the Boston Ballet is so safe.

The highly regarded **Boston Ballet** (Map 6; ☎ 617-695-6950 information; tickets $15-82) performs classical and modern works (and the wildly popular year-end *Nutcracker*) at the Wang. Students can get rush tickets for $12.50 the day of the performance.

CHAMBER MUSIC

Chamber music thrives mostly in churches, with one notable exception.

New England Conservatory of Music (NEC; Map 7; ☎ 617-585-1122 concert line, 617-536-2412 box office; Jordan Hall, 30 Gainsborough St; admission free) hosts professional and student chamber and orchestral concerts in the acoustically superlative hall. Founded in 1867, the NEC is the country's oldest music school. Eben Jordan, of Jordan

Marsh department store fame, contributed his money in 1904 to help build the intimate hall.

Emmanuel Church (Map 5, #48; ☎ 617-536-3356; 15 Newbury St) offers scads of great concerts, many of which carry a moderate fee. Most Sunday services (which begin at 10am) end with a Bach cantata. Call the church's concert line.

Many churches offer free concerts in reverential surroundings. Check out **Old West Church** (Map 3; ☎ 617-227-5088; 131 Cambridge St) for 8pm Tuesday summertime concerts; **King's Chapel** (Map 4; ☎ 617-227-2155; 58 Tremont St) for year-round concerts at 12:15pm Tuesday; **Cathedral Church of St Paul** (Map 4; ☎ 617-482-4826; 138 Tremont St) for classical concerts at 12:15pm Wednesday, October to May; and **Trinity Church** (Map 5; ☎ 617-536-0944; 206 Clarendon St) for organ recitals at 12:15pm Friday, September to June.

SPECTATOR SPORTS

Boston is a big sports town, and emotions run high during each sporting season. Be warned that simply asking a local, 'Hey, what do you think of the Sox this season?' could start an impassioned conversation.

Boston University *(Map 7; ☎ 617-353-3838)*, **Boston College** *(☎ 617-552-3000)* and **Harvard University** *(Map 8; ☎ 617-495-2211)* have tough hockey and football teams and spirited, loyal fans. In April, look for the annual Bean Pot Tournament, college hockey's local rivalry.

Catch the **New England Revolution** *(☎ 877-438-7387)*, the region's pro soccer team, from mid-April to early October in suburban Foxboro.

The **Boston Red Sox** play baseball in **Fenway Park** *(Map 7; ☎ 617-267-1700 tickets; W www.redsox.com; 4 Yawkey Way; bleacher seats $20, regular tickets $27-70)*, the nation's oldest ballpark, built in 1912, and certainly one of the most storied (see the boxed text 'Fenway Park' in the Things to See & Do chapter). The season runs from early April to late September or into October if the Sox make it into postseason. Sit with the 'common fan' in outfield bleacher seats.

Games generally start at 1:05pm and 7:05pm.

The **Boston Celtics** *(☎ 617-523-3030 information, 617-931-2000 tickets; W www.celtics .com; tickets $10–95)* play basketball from late October through April at the cavernous **Fleet Center** *(Map 3; 150 Causeway St)*.

The **Boston Bruins** *(☎ 617-624-1900 information, 617-931-2222 tickets; W www.boston bruins.com; tickets $25-85)* play hockey in the **Fleet Center** *(Map 3; 150 Causeway St)* from mid-October to mid-April. You can buy Bruins and Celtics tickets in person at the box office, at the western end of the Fleet Center.

The **New England Patriots** *(☎ 508-543-8200, 800-543-1776; W www.patriots.com)* play football in the spanking new, state-of-the-art **Gillette Stadium** *(Route 1, Foxboro)* about 50 minutes south of Boston. Tickets start at $50, if you can get them. The season runs from late August to late December. There are direct trains ($8 round trip) and buses ($8 round trip) between South Station and the stadium; contact the **MBTA** *(☎ 617-222-3200)* for exact times.

Shopping

You can go to the Gap anywhere; instead, seek out Boston's offbeat shops and boutiques. Stores are generally open Monday through Saturday from 9am or 10am until 6pm or 7pm, unless otherwise noted. Most are also open on Sunday from noon to 5pm.

WHAT TO BUY
Antiques

Antiques are pricey, but you can always window-shop on Charles and River Sts on Beacon Hill.

At **Boston Antique Co-op I & II** *(Map 2; ☎ 617-227-9810, 617-227-9811; 119 Charles St)* dealers specialize in arts and crafts, silver, early 17th- and 18th-century textiles, and personal trinkets.

Eugene Galleries *(Map 2, #19; ☎ 617-227-3062; 76 Charles St)* has a remarkable selection of antique Boston prints and maps.

The **Nostalgia Factory** *(Map 3, #13; ☎ 617-720-2211; 51 N Margin St)* has authentic Hollywood movie posters, out-of-print magazines and political collectibles.

Cambridge Antique Market *(Map 9; ☎ 617-868-9655; 201 McGrath-O'Brien Hwy)* has a little something of everything in its five stories – furniture, glass, clothing, pottery and jewelry.

Art & Crafts

While Newbury St has the most expensive and dense concentration of galleries (see Newbury St under Where to Shop later in this chapter), a few others allow you to support local artists without losing your shirt. Poke around the **Leather District** *(Map 4)*, bounded by Atlantic Ave and Lincoln, Kneeland and Essex Sts, and on **Harrison Ave** *(Map 6)* in the South End for avant-garde galleries.

Fort Point Arts Community Gallery *(Map 4, #73; ☎ 617-423-4299; 300 Summer St)*, where there's always something interesting on display, is the focal point for Boston's cutting edge arts community.

Society of Arts & Crafts *(Map 5, #38; ☎ 617-266-1810; 175 Newbury St)*, a

prestigious nonprofit operation, was founded in 1897. The downtown branch has high-quality weaving, leather, ceramics, furniture and other handcrafted items.

The gift shop at the historic **Women's Education & Industrial Union** *(Map 5, #64; ☎ 617-536-5651; 356 Boylston St)* features handcrafted gifts, from quilts and toys to books and stationery.

Bromfield Art Gallery *(Map 6, #73; ☎ 617-451-3605; 27 Thayer St)*, the city's oldest cooperative, is also one of the more accessible, affordable and reputable galleries.

Space 12 Gallery *(Map 6, #76; ☎ 617-423-9760; 12 Union Park St)*, the exhibition space and home of art dealer Gregory Shea, shows the work of international artists. He also hosts readings and performance art.

Qingping Gallery and Teahouse *(Map 6, #64; ☎ 617-482-9988; 231 Shawmut Ave)* is hard to categorize – there's no place like it in Boston. Primarily an art gallery, it's also a purveyor of fine and rare teas from China, as well as a soothing gathering spot for people interested in Chinese culture and politics. Owner Wu Jianxin presides over an old-fashioned salon with occasional book readings, lectures and discussions.

Stone's Throw Gallery *(Map 7, #12; ☎ 617-731-3773; 1389 Beacon St, Coolidge Corner)* has earthy ceramics and textiles for the home.

Harvard Collections *(Map 8, #43; ☎ 617-496-0700; 1350 Mass Ave)* has fine reproductions and original works inspired by the immense holdings of the university's museums, from African masks and carvings to Roman glass jewelry.

Cambridge Artists' Cooperative *(Map 8, #15; ☎ 617-868-4434; 59A Church St)*, where craftspeople double as sales staff, displays the work of over 150 artists, with prices ranging from $5 to $1000.

Clothing & Accessories

New Clothing Forget Austin and Albuquerque! **Helen's Leather** *(Map 2, #16; ☎ 617-742-2077; 110 Charles St)* has cowboy boots (sizes up to 15), along with gorgeous jackets.

The Original Levi's Store *(Map 5; ☎ 617-375-9010; 800 Boylston St)*, which sells only the real thing, is located within the Shops at Prudential Center.

Stylish simplicity and casual comfort reign at these Harvard Square boutiques: **Clothware** *(Map 8, #11; ☎ 617-661-6441, 52 Brattle St)*, **Jasmine/Sola** *(Map 8, #25; ☎ 617-354-6043; 37 Brattle St)* and **Tess** *(Map 8, #32; ☎ 617-864-8377; 20 Brattle St)*. Between Harvard and Porter Squares, look for **Dakini** *(Map 10, #33; ☎ 617-864-7661; 1704 Mass Ave)*.

Thrift Stores & Outlets Ritzy neighborhoods have ritzy closets that trickle down to ritzy castoffs, and when proceeds benefit local charitable institutions, everyone's in the mood to give.

Beacon Hill Thrift Shop *(Map 2, #29; ☎ 617-742-2323; 15 Charles St; open Tues & Thur)*, given its tony location, feels more like an estate sale than a bargain bin.

Transitions *(Map 6, #82; ☎ 617-536-8999; 1736 Washington St)* is a treasure trove of clothing, costume jewelry, furnishings and odds and ends. Who knows what you might find? Profits go to a local homeless shelter.

The Discovery Shop *(Map 7, #69; ☎ 617-277-9499; 300 Washington St, Brookline Village)* has a decent selection of gently worn clothing for women of all sizes. Benefits flow to the American Cancer Society.

Beth Israel Hospital Thrift Shop *(Map 7, #65; ☎ 617-566-7016; 25 Harvard St, Brookline Village; open Tues-Sat)* isn't cheap but the stuff is still a bargain. The friendly place has high-quality goods: clothes, housewares

and overstock from Boston boutiques. Proceeds go to special hospital projects.

Morgan Memorial Goodwill *(Map 9, #43; ☎ 617-868-6330; 520 Mass Ave • Map 10, #13; ☎ 617-628-3618; 230 Elm St)* has outposts in Davis Square and Central Square. There's nothing fancy here, just lots of cheap stuff.

Shoes In a tiny shoebox of a store, **Nahas Shoes** *(Map 2, #21; ☎ 617-723-6176; 65 Charles St)* has a solid selection of fashionable and comfortable shoes at reasonable prices.

DSW Shoe Warehouse *(Map 4, #34; ☎ 617-556-0052; 385 Washington St)* is truly an emporium of bargain-priced shoes. The dizzying array of men's, women's, and children's shoes are enough to wear out even the most dedicated shoe shopper. Check out the deeply discounted racks in the back of the store.

Footpaths *(Map 4, #7; ☎ 617-338-6008; 489 Washington St)* emphasizes attractive, casual comfort.

Simons Shoes *(Map 7, #6; ☎ 617-277-8980; 282 Harvard St, Coolidge Corner)* provides relief for weary feet.

Jasmine/Sola and **Sola Men** *(Map 8, #25; ☎ 617-354-6043; 37 Brattle St)* have funky shoes for both sexes. Caution: six-inch platforms and cobblestone streets don't mix!

Vintage In addition to rentals, **Boston Costume** *(Map 6, #28; ☎ 617-482-1632; 69 Kneeland St)* has fishnet stockings and feather boas. Why? You might consider picking something up before heading to Fetish Friday at Man Ray (see Dance Clubs in the Entertainment chapter).

Clothes Encounters *(Map 7, #11; ☎ 617-277-3031; 1394 Beacon St)*, near Coolidge Corner, has a fine selection.

Second Time Around *(Map 8, #63; ☎ 617-491-7185; 8 Eliot St)* and **Oona's Experienced Clothing** *(Map 8, #52; ☎ 617-491-2654; 1210 Mass Ave)* are in Harvard Square.

Great Eastern Trading Co *(Map 9, #27; ☎ 617-354-5279; 49 River St)* offers high-quality goods and costume jewelry in Central Square.

Garment District *(Map 9, #33; ☎ 617-876-5230; 200 Broadway)* is near Kendall Square. If your memories of the '60s and

'70s have faded like an old pair of jeans, the Garment District, with its huge collection of psychedelic clothing, will bring them back with a vengeance.

Dollar-a-Pound Plus *(Map 9, #33;* ☎ *617-876-5230)*, downstairs, is a flea market gone berserk with special merchandise and pricing methods. Piles of mostly nondescript used clothing are dumped on the warehouse floor and folks wade through, looking for their needle in the haystack. Upon checkout, your pile is weighed and you pay 'by the pound' – usually $1.50, but on Friday it's even less (they gotta get rid of this stuff). There are also books, records, cassettes and kitchen supplies, all individually priced to move. Hours are irregular; call ahead.

Food & Drink

Two Beacon Hill shops have fancy selections of cheese, deli meats, freshly baked bread and pastries, fruit and vegetables: **Savenor's** *(Map 2, #3;* ☎ *617-723-6328; 160 Charles St)* and **DeLuca's Market** *(Map 2, #30;* ☎ *617-523-4343; 11 Charles St)*.

South End Formaggio *(Map 6, #71;* ☎ *617-350-6996; 268 Shawmut Ave)* carries a cornucopia of rare imported and speciality foods. Consult the knowledgeable staff at the cheese counter.

Trader Joe's *(Map 7, #16;* ☎ *617-278-9997; 1317 Beacon St)*, in Brookline's Coolidge Corner, imports treats from around the globe, then repackages and sells them under its brand name.

Cardullo's *(Map 8, #34;* ☎ *617-491-8888; 6 Brattle St)* carries an impressive assortment of imported treats.

Although you can certainly find decent fruit and vegies in grocery stores, two Cambridge stores in Central Square really stand out. **Harvest Co-Op** *(Map 9, #40;* ☎ *617-661-1580; 581 Mass Ave)* and **Bread & Circus** *(Map 9, #19;* ☎ *617-492-0070; 115 Prospect St)* offer organic produce and lots of healthy prepared foods. There's another Bread & Circus *(Map 7, #59;* ☎ *617-375-1010; 15 Westland Ave)* just off Mass Ave. While you're there, check out the community bulletin boards for neighborhood events.

For Every Body

Two apothecaries in Harvard Square will appeal to your senses.

Harnetts *(Map 8, #14;* ☎ *617-491-4747; 47 Brattle St)* carries a vast array of lotions, potions, herbs and aromatic oils. If not downright curative, a visit here will at least be therapeutic.

Colonial Drug *(Map 8, #13;* ☎ *617-864-2222; 49 Brattle St)*, a delightfully quaint establishment that produces hundreds of scents, is best known as a perfumery although it stocks standard drugstore products.

Music

Boston has two music superstores, each with two locations: **HMV** *(Map 4, #48;* ☎ *617-357-8444; 24 Winter St, Downtown Crossing • Map 8, #27;* ☎ *617-868-9696; 1 Brattle St)*; and **Tower Records** *(Map 7, #46; 617-247-5900; 1249 Boylston St • Map 8, #54; 617-876-3377; 95 Mt Auburn St; open until midnight)*.

Looney Tunes *(Map 7, #48;* ☎ *617-247-2238; 1106 Boylston St)*, **Cheapo Records** *(Map 9, #32;* ☎ *617-354-4455; 645 Mass Ave, Central Square)* and **Disc Diggers** *(Map 10, #6;* ☎ *617-776-7560; 401 Highland Ave, Davis Square)* are the best of the best as far as used CD and record stores go. With thousands of college students passing through annually, such places abound.

Skippy White's Records *(Map 9, #42;* ☎ *617-491-3345; 538 Mass Ave, Central Square)* has the definitive selection of rap, reggae, soul, R&B, funk and gospel.

Sandy's Music *(Map 9, #17;* ☎ *617-491-2812; 896A Mass Ave)*, near Central Square, specializes in new and used folk and Celtic recordings.

Outdoor Gear & Travel Accessories

Hilton's Tent City *(Map 3, #7;* ☎ *617-227-9242; 272 Friend St)* is dusty and musty, but boasts four floors of tents (set up to test out). They have all the camping accessories, equipment and clothing you'll ever need – at the lowest prices around.

Sherman's *(Map 4, #31;* ☎ *617-742-4400; 42 Bromfield St)* or upscale **Willowbee & Kent** *(Map 5, #60;* ☎ *617-437-6700; 519 Boylston St)*

Farmers Markets

Touch the produce and you risk the wrath of pushcart vendors at Haymarket (Map 3). No one else in the city matches their prices on ripe-and-ready fruit and vegetables. Not strictly a farmers market, the vendors buy wholesale and sell by the pound. They don't take kindly to those buying a peach here, a banana there. The bustling spectacle takes place every Friday and Saturday, with the best bargains on Saturday afternoon.

Most neighborhoods have a seasonal farmers market from mid-May to late November. In addition to just-picked fruit and local vegetables, you might find Vermont farmstead and artisanal cheese, crusty loaves and tempting fruit tarts, all fresh, fresh, fresh. Locations (% 617-626-1700) include:

City Hall Plaza (Map 3)	Monday and Wednesday, 11am to 6pm
Downtown Crossing (Map 4)	Washington and Summer Sts, almost daily, 9am to 5pm
Copley Square (Map 5)	Tuesday and Friday, 11 am to 6 pm, to late October
Coolidge Corner (Map 7)	parking lot at Center and Beacon Sts, Thursday, 1:30 pm to dusk, to late October
Charles Hotel courtyard (Map 8)	Sunday, 10am to 3pm
Central Square (Map 9)	parking lot 5 at Bishop Allen Dr, Monday, noon to 6 pm
Cambridgeport (Map 9)	Memorial Dr at Magazine St, Saturday, 10:30 am to 3:30 pm
Davis Square (Map 10)	parking lot at Day and Herbert Sts, Wednesday, noon to 6 pm

have everything from suitcases to passport pouches.

Eastern Mountain Sports *(EMS; ☎ 617-254-4250; 1041 Comm Ave)* is another good source for hiking and camping gear, books and maps. If you can't find it at Hilton's, you'll find it here. Ride the T Green Line, 'B' branch to Babcock.

WHERE TO SHOP
Beacon Hill (Map 2)
While lovely Charles St has an ever-increasing number of intriguing shops, it remains true to its blue-blood roots with quite a few high-priced antique shops.

Government Center & North End (Map 3)
Faneuil Hall Marketplace *(Quincy Market; Map 3; ☎ 617-338-2323; open until 9pm Mon-Sat, until 6pm Sun)* is perhaps the most popular shopping area. Supposedly, upwards of 15 million people visit annually, and it wouldn't surprise us. The five buildings are filled with 100-plus tourist-oriented shops, pushcart vendors and national chain stores. Finding the few funky shops here is as easy as finding needles in a haystack. Yes, it's expensive and crowded, especially on the weekends, but it can be fun, too. There are lots

of fast-food outlets, bars, street performers and outdoor benches to rest your weary feet.

The North is mostly filled with speciality grocers (see the North End walking tour in the America's Walking City chapter).

Downtown & Waterfront (Map 4)
Downtown Crossing, an outdoor pedestrian mall, has practical shops geared to everyday needs. There are two flagship department stores, **Filene's** *(Map 4; ☎ 617-357-2100; 426 Washington St)* and **Macy's** *(Map 4; ☎ 617-357-3000; 450 Washington St)*, as well as smaller outlets for clothing, jewelry, shoes, books and electronics. The area is enlivened by street musicians, fast-food and souvenir pushcart vendors, a few outdoor cafés and benches for people-watching.

Back Bay (Map 5)
In addition to Newbury St, two huge, luxe indoor malls might entice you to part with your cash. **Copley Place** *(Map 5; ☎ 617-369-5000; 100 Huntington Ave)* encompasses two hotels, a first-run cineplex, glass walkways, restaurants and dozens of very elegant shops.

The Shops at Prudential Center *(Map 5; ☎ 617-267-1002; 800 Boylston St)*, with about 75 stores and eateries within an atrium-like

SHOPPING

SHOPPING

One-of-a-Kind Shops

These shops defy categorization, carrying interesting stuff not found elsewhere.

Charles St Supply (Map 2, #25; ☎ 617-367-9046; 54 Charles St) has cheap lawn chairs for Esplanade concerts.

Black Ink (Map 2, #15; ☎ 617-723-3883; 101 Charles St) specializes in 'unexpected necessities' such as rubber stamps of antique engravings and trinkets made from recycled detritus.

Marika's (Map 2, #14; ☎ 617-523-4520; 130 Charles St), opened by owner Matthew Raisz's Hungarian grandmother over 50 years ago, is a treasure trove of fine – and finely chosen – collectibles.

London Harness Company (Map 4, #36; ☎ 617-542-9234; 60 Franklin St) specializes in beautifully crafted leather goods and fine gifts for folks you'd like to impress with your good taste.

Windsor Button (Map 4, #50; ☎ 617-482-4969; 35 Temple Place), an institution since 1936, has the most extensive button collection you're likely to encounter. If you've lost a button and despaired of ever finding one to match, try here.

As a change of pace from quickie postcards, these shops will inspire you to thoughtful prose or poetry. Look for a wide selection of pens, speciality papers, notebooks and cards at **Bromfield Pen Shop** (Map 4, #32; ☎ 617-482-9053; 5 Bromfield St) and **Paper Source** (Map 10, #25; ☎ 617-497-1077; 1810 Mass Ave), near Porter Square.

Jack's Joke Shop (Map 6, #6; ☎ 617-426-9640; 38 Boylston St) will help you find your sense of humor if you've lost it.

South End kitsch, from Barbies in drag to feather boas, is the raison d'être of **Bang** (Map 6, #42; ☎ 617-292-9911; 59½ Clarendon St).

Fresh Eggs (Map 6, #43; ☎ 617-247-8150; 58 Clarendon St) features 'everything for your nest'.

Aunt Sadie's (Map 6, #77; ☎ 617-357-7117; 18 Union Park St), a fragrant boutique known mainly for candles, also features hand-crafted bags (some made of grass) and distinctive glass and tableware.

Pod (Map 7, #67; ☎ 617-739-3802; 313 Washington St, Brookline Village), befitting a tiny shop, has gifts celebrating the art of minimalism.

MDF (Map 8, #31; ☎ 617-491-2789; 19 Brattle St), short for Modern Design Furnishings, sells small eclectic domestic accessories.

Urban Outfitters (Map 8, #40; ☎ 617-864-0070; 11 JFK St) specializes in grunge-chic for the home and body.

Learningsmith (Map 8, #28; ☎ 617-661-6008; 25 Brattle St), with mind-stretching gifts, suggests that fun and games can be educational.

Abodeon (Map 10, #31; ☎ 617-497-0137; 1731 Mass Ave), between Harvard and Porter Squares, is where '60s kitsch meets '90s retro. Austin Powers wannabes can find Lucite dining chairs, cocktail shaker sets and old Rat Pack records.

Nomad (Map 10, #28; ☎ 617-497-6677; 1741 Mass Ave), between Harvard and Porter Squares, has brightly painted furniture, glassware, rugs and clothing from around the world and around the corner.

Joie de Vivre (Map 10, #26; ☎ 617-864-8188; 1792 Mass Ave), with a nod and a wink, has lighthearted and hip gifts sure to inspire a smile. It's between Harvard and Porter Squares.

Pluto (Map 10, #16; ☎ 617-666-2005; 215 Elm St, Davis Square), equal parts postmodern gallery and store, has description-defying assortments of whimsical housewares and fashion accessories.

---

space, boasts one of the few urban grocery stores, **Star Market**, on the ground level.

Newbury St Boston's premier shopping street, Newbury St (ⓦ www.newbury-st.com) is lined with chic boutiques, cafés and art galleries running the gamut from stodgy to funky. Second only to New York's Fifth Ave in price-per-square-foot, these eight high-rent blocks have some seriously tempting places to lighten your wallet. It's heaven for both Boston's 'old money' elite and international trust-fund students using dad's gold card. For the rest of the world, it's great for strolling, window-shopping and people-watching.

Start at Newbury St and Mass Ave, where you'll find the hipper stores. Walking east, internationally inspired craft shops give way to designer boutiques. By the time you reach Berkeley St you'll question whether or not you're dressed appropriately to even walk down the street, let alone to enter stores. Assume a pose that says, 'Of course I have a Swiss bank account, doesn't everyone?'

Between Mass Ave and Hereford St look for **Urban Outfitters** (Map 5, #7; ☎ 617-236-0088, 361 Newbury St), which stocks the latest in urban-grunge and industrial-chic clothing and housewares.

Virgin Records (Map 5, #8; ☎ 617-247-5900; 360 Newbury St), a pilgrimage site for music mavens, has the city's largest tune selection.

Beadworks (Map 5, #9; ☎ 617-247-7227; 167 Newbury St) has all the components for making your own jewelry.

Patagonia (Map 5, #11; ☎ 617-424-1776; 346 Newbury St) carries the finest outdoor fleecewear.

Jasmine (Map 5, #11; ☎ 617-867-4636; 344 Newbury St) is the first stop for youthful women's clothing.

Sola (Map 5, #14; ☎ 617-437-8465; 329 Newbury St) carries stylish women's shoes at affordable prices.

Condom World (Map 5, #16; ☎ 617-267-7233; 332 Newbury St) has throw-away goods. Don't ask, don't tell.

Newbury Comics (Map 5, #16; ☎ 617-236-4930; 332 Newbury St) sells used and new alternative rock CDs and records, as well as comic books.

Between Hereford and Gloucester Sts, look for **Smash City Records** (Map 5, #17; ☎ 617-536-0216; 304 Newbury St), a good used CD and record outpost.

John Fluevog (Map 5, #18; ☎ 617-266-1079; 302 Newbury St) has shoes which are more fun to look at than comfortable to walk in.

Kakadu (Map 5, #19; ☎ 617-437-6666; 291 Newbury St), an Israeli gallery, features colorful handcrafted home accessories.

Filene's Basement

The granddaddy of Boston bargain stores, Filene's Basement (Map 4; ☎ 617-542-2011; 426 Washington St) carries overstocked and irregular items at everyday low prices. But that's just the beginning. Items are automatically marked down the longer they remain in the store. With a little luck and lots of determination, you could find a $300 designer jacket for $30. In reality, though, the chances of finding something perfect (meaning well-made, undamaged, in your size and in a color other than fire-engine red) are pretty slim.

The annual wedding gown sale is a madhouse. Anxious brides-to-be in bodysuits line up before dawn and stampede in when the doors open. Each then grabs every dress she can put her hands on, regardless of size or style. As mothers and friends guard the stashes, hundreds of women try on dress after dress – in the aisles! Feuds break out over dresses left unattended. Those left standing after the melee usually depart with a designer gown at a fraction of the retail price.

Even on a normal day, the place looks like a tornado hit it within an hour of opening. Patience and good humor are prerequisites for this unique place; don't miss it.

Michael Price Gallery (MPG; Map 5, #22; ☎ 617-437-1596; 285 Newbury St) showcases art that's about as edgy as Newbury St can handle.

Between Gloucester and Fairfield Sts, you'll find **India Antiques** (Map 5, #24; ☎ 617-266-6539; 279 Newbury St), where you can get a henna tattoo along with Indian antiques and music.

Zoe (Map 5, #24; ☎ 617-375-9135; 279 Newbury St) is the place for decorating a Soho loft (or just fantasizing about it).

Shambala Tibet (Map 5, #25; ☎ 617-437-0436; 270 Newbury St) showcases Himalayan jewelry, music, textiles and artifacts.

Gargoyles, Grotesques & Chimera (Map 5, #30; ☎ 617-536-2362; 262 Newbury St) is a dimly lit showroom that feels like the crypt of a medieval cathedral.

Matsu (Map 5, #29; ☎ 617-266-9707; 259 Newbury St) sells exquisite clothing and gifts inspired by a Japanese Zen aesthetic.

DeLuca's (Map 5, #32; ☎ 617-262-5990 239 Newbury St) is a purveyor of gourmet groceries.

Between Fairfield and Exeter Sts, look for the **Closet Upstairs** (Map 5, #33; ☎ 617-267-5757; 223 Newbury St), a bit musty and dingy, but packed with retro second-hand clothing.

Emporio Armani (Map 5, #35; ☎ 617-262-7300; 210 Newbury St) is a hip-hop outpost of Italian fashion.

The Hempfest (Map 5, #36; ☎ 617-421-9944; 207 Newbury St) sells products made from hemp, the botanical cousin of marijuana, including items to wear, items to furnish one's home and even items to eat.

Niketown (Map 5, #37; ☎ 617-267-3400; 200 Newbury St), as much a destination as a store, is a palatial footwear emporium dedicated to the proliferation of consumer-oriented American sports culture.

Between Exeter and Dartmouth Sts, there are two contemporary used-clothing shops, **Closet** (Map 5, #38; ☎ 617-536-1919; 175 Newbury St), and **Second Time Around** (Map 5, #39; ☎ 617-247-3504; 176 Newbury St), which are gold mines of barely worn designer clothing.

Between Dartmouth and Clarendon Sts, pop into **Kelly Barrette Fine Art** (Map 5, #40; ☎ 617-266-2475; 129 Newbury St), which features emerging artists and contemporary masters.

riccardi (Map 5, #42; ☎ 617-266-3158; 116 Newbury St) is the place to shop with the Euro-chic hipsters before hitting the clubs.

Between Clarendon and Berkeley Sts, you'll find **Gallery NAGA** (Map 5, #45; ☎ 617-267-9060; 67 Newbury St), which exhibits fine art and crafts by well-known artists as well as up-and-comers.

Louis, Boston (Map 5, #61; ☎ 617-262-6100; 234 Berkeley St) caters to discriminating men and women, though not equally; there are three floors of high-end apparel for men, one for women.

A number of fine galleries congregate on the last block, from Berkeley to Arlington Sts. They're worth a look even if you can't afford to buy. Check out **Robert Klein Gallery** (Map 5, #46; ☎ 617-267-7997; 38 Newbury St) for photography and **Alpha Gallery** (Map 5, #47; ☎ 617-536-4465; 14 Newbury St) for 20th-century American and European paintings and sculptures.

Barbara Krakow Gallery (Map 5, #49; ☎ 617-262-4490; 10 Newbury St), perhaps the most highly respected Newbury St gallery, provides an elegant venue for contemporary artists.

South End (Map 6)

A neighborhood deep in the throes of gentrification, the South End boasts lots of ever-changing speciality stores along Tremont St. But there are also an increasing number of them along lower Washington St, Shawmut Ave, and Columbus Ave.

Brookline (Map 7)

Most stores in Brookline Village and Coolidge Corner are fun, small, unique and individually owned.

Cambridge (Map 8, 9 & 10)

Harvard Square (Map 8) has upwards of 150 shops within a few blocks. Although the area used to boast an avant-garde sensibility and dozens of independent stores, most of the funkier shops have been replaced by chains. Nevertheless, there's still a bustling street life with musicians and performance artists.

Cambridgeside Galleria (Map 9; ☎ 617-621-8666; 100 Cambridgeside Place), near Kendall Square in East Cambridge just beyond the Science Museum, has about 100 speciality shops and department stores within the three-story mall.

Inman Square (Map 9) has become a magnet for establishments priced-out of their old Central Square digs. Since it's a bit off the beaten path, Inman may be able to retain its beatnik charm.

Central Square (Map 9), long considered the edgy-funky heart of Cambridge, is in the midst of a gentrified makeover. A few unique shops remain, but old-time shopkeepers lament that their future is cloudy.

Booklover's Paradise

Boston and Cambridge are a booklover's paradise. The Harvard Square Visitors Information Booth hands out a free brochure of Harvard Square's more than 30 bookstores, and the Yellow Pages lists over 100. Here are a few worth searching out.

For guidebooks and maps, travel to **Rand McNally Map & Travel Store** (Map 3, #58; ☎ 617-720-1125; 84 State St).

The Brattle Book Shop (Map 4, #53; ☎ 617-542-0210; 9 West St) is a treasure crammed with out-of-print, rare and first-edition books.

The outstanding **Globe Corner Bookstore** (Map 8, #18; ☎ 617-497-6277; 28 Church St) specializes in travel guides and literature, and carries hundreds of speciality and topographical maps.

Borders (Map 4, #19; ☎ 617-557-7188; 10-24 School St) has more than 200,000 titles and a café for when you tire.

The popularity of **Spenser's Mystery Books** (Map 5, #33; ☎ 617-262-0880; 223 Newbury St) is no mystery.

Trident Booksellers & Cafe (Map 5, #12; ☎ 617-267-8688; 338 Newbury St) specializes in New Age.

We Think the World of You (Map 6, #63; ☎ 617-574-5000; 540 Tremont St) features gay and lesbian titles.

Lucy Parsons Center (Map 6, #66; ☎ 617-267-6272; 549 Columbus Ave) stocks 'literature of liberation', including titles on radical environmentalism, radical social thought and anarchy.

The three-story **Barnes & Noble** at Boston University (Map 7, #30; ☎ 617-267-8484; 660 Beacon St) is one of New England's biggest.

Schoenhof's Foreign Books (Map 8, #66; ☎ 617-547-8855; 76A Mt Auburn St), near Harvard Square, has foreign-language books and dictionaries.

Nearby is one of the most famous poetry bookstores in the US: the **Grolier Poetry Book Shop** (Map 8, #48; ☎ 617-547-4648; 6 Plympton St).

Harvard Book Store (Map 8, #47; ☎ 617-661-1515; 1256 Mass Ave) is considered the Square's premiere intellectual bookstore.

Within a block of each other are the original **Wordsworth** (Map 8, #29; ☎ 617-354-5201; 30 Brattle St) and **Curious George Goes to Wordsworth** (Map 8, #37; ☎ 617-498-0062; 1 JFK St), specializing in children's books.

You don't have to be a student to shop at 'the Coop' (rhymes with snoop). The **Harvard Cooperative Society** (Map 8, #35; ☎ 617-499-2000; 1400 Mass Ave) in Harvard Square, carries three floors of books and music and everything emblazoned with the crimson logo.

In Davis Square, **McIntyre & Moore Booksellers** (Map 10, #9; ☎ 617-629-4840; 255 Elm St) offers friendly environs for used-book browsers and buyers.

Brookline Booksmith (Map 7, #8; ☎ 617-566-6660; 279 Harvard St), in Coolidge Corner, is among the best independent bookstores in the US. Period.

The inviting **Albatross Books** (Map 7, #63; ☎ 617-739-2665; 45 Harvard St) in Brookline Village sells rare and used volumes.

Somerville's **Davis Square** (Map 10) has a number of trendy shops, cafés and bars. They've joined the popular Somerville Theatre and a couple of die-hard neighborhood diners to make this a great place to hang out.

The bohemian spirit of Harvard Square is making its way up Mass Ave toward Porter Square. Numerous unique boutiques on this stretch of **Mass Ave** (Map 10) afford a more creative shopping alternative.

Porter Exchange (Map 10, #24; 1815 Mass Ave), just south of Porter Square, is known locally as Little Tokyo. This mall contains Japanese eateries (including a Japanese bakery at the center of the atrium) and a few clothing, cosmetics and gift shops.

Excursions

Part of what makes Boston one of the USA's most livable cities is its easy access to the countryside. To the west, the colonial towns of Lexington and Concord have attractive historic centers. The north shore, including Salem, Marblehead and Gloucester, has rich maritime history.

On the south shore lies Plymouth, where the Pilgrims landed in 1627; today, much of the town is devoted to Pilgrim history. Cape Cod is New England's premier beach playground, accessible by bus and boat, but more convenient by car.

LEXINGTON & CONCORD

Lexington, about 18 miles northwest of Boston, has a colonial village green and plenty of history. On April 18, 1775, Paul Revere, William Dawes and Samuel Prescott set out on their midnight ride from Boston to Lexington and Concord to warn that the British were coming.

Colonial Concord, dignified and beautiful, has a rich literary history. In the 19th century, Concord was home to essayist, preacher and poet Ralph Waldo Emerson (1803–82); essayist and naturalist Henry David Thoreau (1817–62); short-story writer and novelist Nathaniel Hawthorne (1804–64); and novelist and children's book author Louisa May Alcott (1832–88). Concord also has scenic roads for bicycling and the placid Concord River for canoeing. On April 19, 1775, direct from Lexington Green, the British were defeated at North Bridge, a battle that Ralph Waldo Emerson called 'the shot heard round the world' (see Shot Heard Round the World in the Facts about Boston chapter). It's a nice place to paddle. Concord is also famous for its grapes: n 1850, resident Ephraim Bull began commercial table grape agriculture in the USA. And for years, the Welch's company was headquartered on Main St.

Information

The Lexington **chamber of commerce** (☎ 781-862-1450; 1875 Mass Ave; open

Beyond Beantown's Borders

Feeling the need to escape the confines of Boston to gain a richer appreciation of the region? Head to these highlights within an hour (or three) of Boston:

• Sense the colonial and literary ghosts of Lexington and Concord

• Transcend your circumstances at Walden Pond

• Fall under Salem's spell

• Swim at Gloucester's Wingaersheek Beach

• Marvel at Plymouth's *Mayflower II*

• Go cruisin' in Provincetown

9am-5pm daily in summer, 10am-4pm in winter) maintains a visitors center opposite Battle Green (formerly known just as Lexington Green), next to Buckman Tavern. Exhibits recall the 1775 events.

In Concord, when the **chamber of commerce information booth** (☎ 978-369-3120; Heywood St; open daily June–mid-Oct, Sat & Sun mid-Apr–May) isn't open, head to the chamber's **main office** in Wright Tavern (see Concord Walking Tour later in this chapter).

The **Minuteman National Historical Park** (☎ 978-369-6993; open 9am-5pm daily mid-May–Oct, 9am-4pm daily Nov–mid-May) has a visitors center off Rte 2A.

Lexington Green & Around

The **Lexington minuteman statue** guards the southeastern end of **Battle Green**, commemorating the bravery of the militia who met the British here. The green is tranquil, shaded by tall trees and surrounded by dignified churches and stately houses. Behind the church that towers over the green is **Ye Olde Burying Ground**, with tombstones dating back to 1690.

Lexington Historical Society (☎ 781-862-1703; 1332 Mass Ave; 1 house adult/child

BOSTON EXCURSIONS

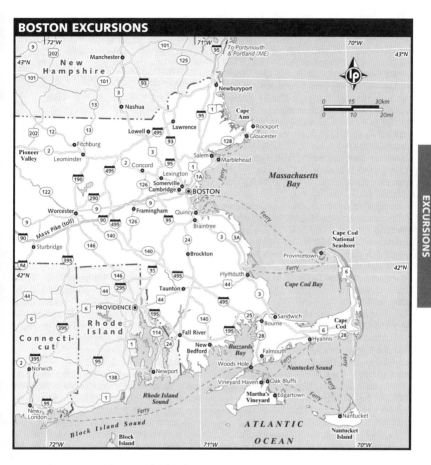

6-16 yrs $5/3, 3 houses $12/7) maintains three houses which are open April through October. Facing the green and built in 1709, **Buckman Tavern** *(☎ 781-862-5598; 1 Bedford St)*, where the minutemen spent tense hours anticipating the redcoats' arrival, is now a worthy museum of colonial life. **Munroe Tavern** *(☎ 781-674-9238; 1332 Mass Ave)*, built in 1695 about seven blocks southeast of the green, was a British command post and field infirmary, and is now furnished with battle mementos and artefacts from President Washington's 1789 visit. Built in 1698, **Hancock Clark House** *(☎ 781-861-0928; 36

Hancock St) contains furnishings and portraits of leaders of the Hancock and Clark families.

Concord Walking Tour

From Monument Square, head southeast on Lexington Rd to **Wright Tavern**, one of the first places British troops searched for rebel arms on April 19, 1775. At the opposite end of the square is the 1716 **Colonial Inn**. Then walk 15 minutes north along Monument St to the **Old Manse** *(☎ 978-369-3909; guided tours adult/senior/student/child $7/6/6/5; open 10am-5pm Mon-Sat & noon-5pm Sun mid-Apr–Oct)*, built in 1769, owned by the

Emerson-Ripley family for 169 years and now filled with Emerson family furnishings. (Newly married Hawthorne and his wife lived here from 1842 to 1845.)

Just north and west is the **Old North Bridge**, site of the first Revolutionary War battle. Across the bridge is Daniel Chester French's statue the **Minute Man**, on the way up the hill to the **Buttrick Mansion**, the park's North Bridge Visitors Center. Retrace your steps, stop at **Sleepy Hollow Cemetery** and visit **Authors' Ridge**, where lie Emerson, Thoreau and his family, the Alcotts, Hawthorne and his wife, and Ephraim Bull.

From Monument Square, head southeast for five minutes to the **House of Ralph Waldo Emerson** (☎ 978-369-2236; 28 Cambridge Turnpike; adult/child $7/5; open 10am-4:30pm Thur-Sat & 2pm-4:30pm Sun mid-Apr–Oct), which contains many original 19th-century furnishings. Emerson hosted his renowned circle of friends here from 1835 until his death in 1882.

A bit east is the **Concord Museum** (☎ 978-369-9609; 200 Lexington Rd; adult/senior/child/family $7/6/3/16; open 9am-5pm Mon-Sat & noon-5pm Sun Apr-Dec, 11am-4pm Mon-Sat & 1pm-4pm Sun Jan-Mar). It contains a lantern hung in Boston's Old North Church as a signal to Revere, Dawes and Prescott; furnishings from Emerson's study; and the world's largest collection of Thoreau artefacts.

Continue east down Lexington Rd to Louisa May Alcott's home, **Orchard House** (☎ 978-369-4118; 399 Lexington Rd; adult/senior/child/family $8/7/5/20; open 10am-4:30pm Mon-Sat & 1pm-4:30pm Sun Apr-Oct, 11am-3pm Mon-Fri, 10am-4.30pm Sat & 1pm-4.30pm Sun Nov-Mar). Alcott lived here for 20 years and wrote *Little Women* here in 1868. The house and furnishings are open to view; you must take a guided tour.

Down the way is the **Wayside** (☎ 978-369-6975; 455 Lexington Rd; adult/child $4/ free; open Thur-Tues 9:30pm-5:30pm mid-Apr–Oct), where Louisa May Alcott also lived and which she described in *Little Women*. (Nathaniel Hawthorne lived here at one time, too.)

Walden Pond

Thoreau put the naturalist beliefs of Transcendentalism – that God 'transcended' all things – into practice when he built himself a rustic cabin here, several miles from town. His 1854 memoir of his time there (from 1845 to 1847), *Walden, or Life in the Woods*, praised nature and disapproved of the stresses of civilized life.

The glacial Walden Pond is about 3 miles south of Concord's Monument Square along Walden St (MA 126) south of MA 2. Now a state park with a summer parking fee, there's a swimming beach, facilities and a footpath around the pond. The site of Thoreau's cabin is on the northeast side, marked by a cairn and signs.

Canoeing

South Bridge Boat House (☎ 978-369-9438; 496-502 MA 62, Concord), west of Monument Square on the Sudbury River, rents canoes and kayaks for cruising the Concord, Sudbury and Assabet Rivers from April until the first snowfall. Rates are $10 hourly, $40 daily on weekends, with weekday and student discounts.

Places to Stay & Eat

Lexington In the center of Lexington's business district is the motel **Battle Green Inn** (☎ 781-862-6100, 800-343-0235; 1720 Mass Ave; doubles $79-99).

More than a dozen eateries lie within a five-minute walk of Battle Green. Look for **Via Lago Gourmet Foods** (☎ 781-861-6174; 1845 Mass Ave; open Mon-Sat), with pricey sandwiches, soups and salads.

Bertucci's (☎ 781-860-9000; 1777 Mass Ave; open lunch & dinner daily), right in the center of town, serves pizza, pasta, salad and light meals.

Lemon Grass Thai Cuisine (☎ 781-862-3530; 1710 Mass Ave; open lunch & dinner daily) has meal-in-a-bowl soups with noodles ($7) and other delicious Thai dishes for only slightly more.

Dabin (☎ 781-860-0171; 10 Muzzey St; open lunch Mon-Sat, dinner daily), a half-block south of Mass Ave, is a good spot for sushi.

Concord At MA 2 near the Concord rotary (traffic circle) is **Best Western Concord Motel** (☎ 978-369-6100, 800-528-1234; 740 Elm St; doubles with light breakfast $109-124).

The 1716 **Colonial Inn** (☎ 978-369-9200; 48 Monument Square; doubles in original building $55-225, in Prescott wing $135-179) has 16 guest rooms in its atmospheric main building and 33 in the modern Prescott wing. The inn's dining room, tavern and front porch are a center of town social life.

Cheese Shop (☎ 978-369-5778; 29 Walden St; open Tues-Sat) is the place to visit for a huge sandwich or picnic supplies.

Walden Grill (☎ 978-371-2233; 24 Walden St; open daily), a tavern-like place, has sandwiches ($6) at lunch and traditional New England fare at dinner ($18 to $23).

Chang An (☎ 978-369-5288; 10 Concord Crossing; lunch $8-10, dinner $10-18; open daily) has the best Chinese cuisine in town.

Getting There & Away
To reach Lexington from Boston or Cambridge, take MA 2 west to exit 54 (Waltham St) or exit 53 (Spring St). From Lexington to Concord, follow the signs from Battle Green to Concord and Battle Rd, the route taken by the British troops on April 19, 1775. If you're coming to Concord directly from Boston, it's about 20 miles driving west on MA 2.

MBTA (☎ 617-222-3200, 800-392-6100; w www.mbta.com) bus Nos 62 (Bedford VA Hospital) and 76 (Hanscom Field) run from the Alewife Red Line T terminus through Lexington center hourly on weekdays, less frequently on Saturday, with no Sunday service. Trains run between North Station and Concord and West Concord Stations on the Fitchburg/South Acton line. The 40-minute ride costs $4, half-price for children age five to 11 (under five free).

The Minuteman Commuter Bikeway runs 14 miles from the Alewife Red Line stop in Cambridge to Lexington and Concord. You can rent bikes from **Ata Cyles** (☎ 617-354-0907; 1773 Mass Ave), in Cambridge between Harvard and Porter Squares (also on the Red Line).

SALEM
The famous Salem witch trials of 1692 have obscured this beautiful city's true claim to fame: its glorious maritime history.

Salem Common, Derby Wharf and Essex St Mall, a pedestrian way through historic Salem, are all walkable. The train station is a five-minute walk from Essex St Mall. The 1.7-mile Heritage Trail connects Salem's major historic sites; follow the red line on the sidewalk.

Try the **chamber of commerce visitors center** (☎ 987-744-0004; w www.salem-chamber.org; 63 Wharf St; open 9am-5pm Mon-Fri) or the **National Park Service (NPS) visitors center** (☎ 978-740-1650; 2 New Liberty St; open 9am-5pm daily).

Things to See & Do
America's oldest private museum in continuous operation, the extensive **Peabody Essex Museum** (☎ 978-745-1876, 800-745-4054; Essex St Mall; open 10am-5pm Mon-Sat, noon-5pm Sun, closed Mon Nov-May) is one of the best museums in New England. It showcases art, artefacts and curiosities brought back from the Far East by ships out of Salem. Put this on your list of things to do.

Old-house lovers should also seek out **Chestnut St**, among the country's most architecturally lovely streets.

The tragic events of 1692 have spawned many witch-related attractions, the most authentic of which is the **Witch House** (☎ 978-744-0180; 310½ Essex St; adult/senior/child $6/5/3; open 10am-4:30pm daily mid-Mar–June & Sept-Nov, 10am-6pm daily July & Aug). Examinations of persons accused of witchcraft were held in this magistrate's home.

Salem Witch Museum (☎ 978-744-1692; 19½ Washington Square N; adult/senior/child 6-14 yrs $6.50/6/4.50; open 10am-5pm daily Sept-June, 10am-7pm daily July & Aug) contains dioramas, exhibits and audiovisual shows and has costumed interpretive staff.

Witch Dungeon Museum (☎ 978-741-3570; 16 Lynde St; adult/senior/child $6/5/4; open 10am-5pm daily Apr-Nov) re-creates a witch trial.

House of the Seven Gables (☎ 978-744-0991; 54 Turner St; adult/senior/child 6-17 yrs

$10/9/6; open 10am-5pm daily Apr-Dec, 10am-5pm Mon-Sat & noon-5pm Sun Jan-Mar), Salem's best historic house, was made famous in Nathaniel Hawthorne's novel *The House of the Seven Gables* (1851), which portrays the gloomy Puritan atmosphere of early New England.

Custom House *(adult/child 6-16 yrs $5/3 for tours)* on Derby Wharf is the centerpiece of the **Salem Maritime National Historic Site** *(☎ 978-740-1660)*, but first go to the **Central Wharf Visitors Center** *(open 9am-6pm in summer, 9am-5pm in winter)*.

Places to Stay & Eat

Winter Island Maritime Park *(☎ 978-745-9430; 50 Winter Island Rd; tent sites $20, RV sites $25-35; open May-Oct)* has 15 tent and 30 RV spots.

Clipper Ship Inn *(☎ 978-745-8022; 40 Bridge St/MA 1A; doubles $70-185)* has 60 motel rooms.

Coach House Inn *(☎ 978-744-4092, 800-688-8689; 284 Lafayette St; doubles $95-155)*, built in 1870 and about a mile south of town, has 11 antique-filled rooms (most with private bathroom).

Stephen Daniels House *(☎ 978-744-5709; 1 Daniels St; singles $95, doubles $115-145)* must be Salem's oldest lodging, with parts dating from before the witch trials. Prices are higher at Halloween.

Red's Sandwich Shop *(☎ 978-745-3527; 15 Central St; open lunch daily)*, in the 1698 London Coffee House building, has (guess what?) sandwiches.

Front St Coffeehouse *(☎ 978-740-6697; 20 Front St; open 7am-7pm daily)* is the coolest place for espresso and scones. Sandwiches are served 11am to 4pm.

Museum Place Mall *(2 East India Square)* has breakfast and quickie lunch places, including **Thai Place** *(☎ 978-741-8008; open lunch & dinner daily)*, where a big plate of pad Thai costs $7.

In a Pig's Eye *(☎ 978-741-4436; 148 Derby St; open lunch daily, dinner Mon-Sat)* has an eclectic menu, including salads, vegetarian dishes and pasta for less than $14. Monday and Tuesday are Mexican nights, and there's live entertainment most evenings.

Getting There & Away

MBTA Commuter Rail *(☎ 617-222-3200, 800-392-6100; w www.mbta.com)* trains run frequently from Boston's North Station to Salem. When the station is open, buy tickets before boarding or pay a $2 surcharge. MBTA bus Nos 450 and 455 from Boston's Haymarket Square (near North Station) take longer than the train and cost no less.

Salem lies 20 miles northeast of Boston, a 35-minute drive if it's not rush hour. From Boston, follow US 1 north across the Mystic River (Tobin) Bridge and bear right onto MA 16 toward Revere Beach, then follow MA 1A (Shore Rd) to Salem. MA 1A becomes Lafayette St in Salem and takes you right to Essex St Mall and the common.

MARBLEHEAD

First settled in 1629, Marblehead's Old Town is a picturesque maritime village with narrow, many one-way, winding streets and brightly painted colonial and early-American houses. Parking is a problem in summer, so park inland and explore on foot. Washington, State and Mugford Sts intersect at Old Town House, the nearest thing Marblehead has to a main square. Heading southeast along Washington and State Sts brings you to the State St Landing, the town's main dock. Marblehead Neck is a wooded island east of the town center. It's connected to the mainland by the Ocean Ave causeway.

The **chamber of commerce information booth** *(☎ 781-639-8469; w www.marble headchamber.org; cnr Pleasant, Spring & Essex Sts)* offers a walking tour brochure and map. Off-season, try the chamber's **office** *(☎ 781-631-2868; 62 Pleasant St; open 9am-5pm Mon-Fri)*, in the Masonic Lodge.

Things to See & Do

Old Town is perfect for strolling, café-sitting, window-shopping, photo-snapping and picnicking. A block west of State St Landing, Crocker Park has excellent harbor views and picnic possibilities. Access to Marblehead Neck's **Audubon Bird Sanctuary** *(Ocean Ave)* is on the southwest side via Risley Rd.

The patriotic painting *The Spirit of '76* (1876) in **Abbott Hall** *(☎ 781-631-0000;*

admission free; open 8am-5pm Mon-Fri Nov-May) depicts three Revolutionary War figures – a drummer, a fife player and a flag bearer. Hours are extended from June to October.

The Georgian **Jeremiah Lee Mansion** (☎ 781-631-1069; adult/senior/student/child under 10 $5/4/4/free; open 10am-4pm Tues-Sat & 1pm-4pm Sun mid-June–Oct), near Hooper and Washington Sts, houses period furnishings and collections of toys and children's furniture, folk art and nautical and military artefacts.

Across the street, the historic 1728 **King Hooper Mansion** (☎ 781-631-2608; 8 Hooper St; admission free; open 10am-4pm Tues-Sat, 1pm-5pm Sun) houses the Marblehead Arts Association and holds four floors of changing exhibits.

Places to Stay & Eat

Marblehead has two dozen B&Bs; they're small, so reservations are essential.

A Lady Winette Cottage (☎ 781-631-8579; 3 Corinthian Lane; doubles $100-120) is a Victorian cottage with two rooms sharing a bathroom.

The three-room **Bishops B&B** (☎ 781-631-4954; 10 Harding Lane; doubles $85-160) is right on the water.

Harbor Light Inn (☎ 781-631-2186; 58 Washington St; doubles $125-275) is Marblehead's 'big' hostelry, with 21 rooms and a heated pool. Half the rooms have fireplaces and five have Jacuzzis.

The Landing (☎ 781-631-1878; 81 Front St; lunch $10-18, dinner $20-40; open daily), near State St Landing, is a pubby place with a long menu and indoor and outdoor dining.

Driftwood Café (☎ 781-631-1145; 63 Front St; dishes $3-7; open breakfast & lunch daily), across from the Landing, is an inexpensive Marblehead fixture.

Crosby's Market (☎ 781-631-1741; 118 Washington St; open 7am-9pm daily) is a large, upscale market with an extensive deli section.

Getting There & Away

From Salem, follow MA 114 southeast for 4 miles to Marblehead, where it becomes Pleasant St.

From Boston, take **MBTA** (☎ 617-222-3200, 800-392-6100; W www.mbta.com) bus No 441 or 442 from Haymarket Square (near North Station) or bus No 448 or 449 from Downtown Crossing or South Station.

CAPE ANN

North of Boston, Cape Ann offers fishing, art galleries and quintessential New England quaintness. The region makes for a relaxing day trip or longer sojourn out of the city.

Gloucester & Around

Incorporated in 1623 by fisherfolk, until the early 1990s Gloucester made its living at fishing. In the mid-1990s, when most of the once-rich fishing grounds were closed due to overfishing, about 20,000 anglers found themselves out of work.

Washington St runs from Grant Circle (a traffic circle/rotary on MA 128) to St Peter's Square, a brick plaza overlooking the sea. Rogers St, the waterfront road, goes east from the plaza; Main St, the business and shopping thoroughfare, is one block inland. East Gloucester, with the Rocky Neck artists' colony, is on the southeastern side of Gloucester Harbor.

The Cape Ann **chamber of commerce** (☎ 978-283-1601, 800-321-0133; W www.capeannvacations.com; 33 Commercial St) is just south of St Peter's Square. In summer, a **visitors information office** is open in Stage Fort Park, on the west side of the Annisquam River. Pick up its fine walking tour map of the Maritime Trail or follow signs posted around town.

Things to See & Do Cape Ann's natural beauty, in particular the narrow peninsula of Rocky Neck, has attracted artists for at least a century. Follow Main St east and south around the northeastern end of Gloucester Harbor to East Gloucester. Turn onto Rocky Neck Ave, park in the lot on the right and walk five minutes to the galleries and restaurants.

Hammond Castle Museum (☎ 978-283-7673; Hesperus Ave, Magnolia; tours adult/senior/student/child $6.50/5.50/5.50/4.50; open 10am-5pm daily), the eccentric castle-home of collector Dr Hammond, epitomizes

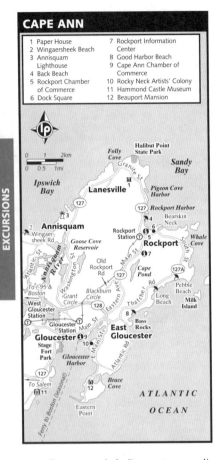

CAPE ANN

1 Paper House
2 Wingaersheek Beach
3 Annisquam Lighthouse
4 Back Beach
5 Rockport Chamber of Commerce
6 Dock Square
7 Rockport Information Center
8 Good Harbor Beach
9 Cape Ann Chamber of Commerce
10 Rocky Neck Artists' Colony
11 Hammond Castle Museum
12 Beauport Mansion

many European periods: Romanesque, medieval, Gothic and Renaissance.

A lavish 'summer cottage,' **Beauport Mansion** (☎ 978-283-0800; 75 Eastern Point Blvd, East Gloucester; adult/senior/child $10/9/5; open 10am-4pm Mon-Fri mid-May–mid-Sept, 10am-4pm Sat & Sun mid-Sept–mid-Oct) is a wildly eclectic but artistically surprising place.

The best and most popular beach is **Wingaersheek Beach** (admission per car Mon-Fri $10, Sat & Sun $15), on Ipswich Bay, with a view of the **Annisquam lighthouse**. Take the Concord St exit from MA

128 and head north several miles. Another big beach is **Good Harbor Beach**, east of East Gloucester off MA 127A on the way to Rockport. Arrive early on hot days and weekends.

Places to Stay & Eat There are 250 sites on 50 wooded acres at **Cape Ann Campsite** (☎ 978-283-8683; 80 Atlantic St, Gloucester; sites without/with electricity $22/32).

Follow Eastern Point Ave until it becomes Atlantic Rd to find several sea-view motels, most of which are closed mid-November to mid-April. Room rates vary widely, from $95 to $280. Look for **Ocean View Resort & Inn** (☎ 978-283-6200, 800-315-7557; 171 Atlantic Rd); **Atlantis Motor Inn** (☎ 978-283-0014; 125 Atlantic Rd); and **Bass Rocks Ocean Inn** (☎ 978-283-7600, 800-528-1234; 107 Atlantic Rd). As for B&Bs, try **Gray Manor** (☎ 978-283-5409; 14 Atlantic Rd), close to Good Harbor Beach.

There are plenty of dining options downtown. **Virgilio's Italian Bakery** (☎ 978-283-5295; 29 Main St; open lunch daily) is a place to grab pizza ($1.50), picnic supplies and cookies. **Blackburn Tavern** (☎ 978-282-1919; 2 Main St; mains $9-13; open lunch & dinner daily), at Washington St, is an upscale tavern with sandwiches ($6), main courses and, of course, drinks.

The Gull (☎ 978-281-6060; 75 Essex Ave/MA 133; dishes $10-24; open dinner mid-May–mid-Oct), a bright and upbeat place overlooking a marina, has excellent seafood. Try the lobster rolls, grilled tuna or a full-fledged clambake.

In the Rocky Neck section of town, head to **The Studio** (☎ 978-283-4123; 51 Rocky Neck Ave; dinner mains $17-21; open lunch & dinner seasonally), overlooking Smith's Cove, for any kind of seafood.

Getting There & Away Trains operated by **MBTA Commuter Rail** (☎ 617-222-3200, 800-392-6100; w www.mbta.com) run from Boston's North Station to Gloucester (one hour, $4.50).

AC Cruise Line (☎ 617-261-6633; 290 Northern Ave) sails from Boston's Seaport District to Gloucester once each Saturday and

Sunday from late May to early September. The ferry trip allows for a three-hour visit to Gloucester. Round-trip tickets cost $23 for adults, $18 for seniors and children.

Rockport & Around

A century ago, Winslow Homer and other acclaimed artists came here to paint fisherfolk who wrested a hard living from the sea. Today, Rockport is supported by tourists who come to watch artists.

The center of town is Dock Square, at the beginning of Bearskin Neck. Most everything is within a 10-minute walk of it. The train station is less than a 15-minute walk west of Dock Square. Parking is difficult on summer weekends. Park at one of the lots on MA 127 from Gloucester and take the shuttle bus.

The **chamber of commerce** (☎ 978-546-6575, 888-726-3922; **w** www.rockportusa.com; 3 Pier Ave; open 9am-5pm Mon-Sat in summer, 10am-4pm Mon-Fri in winter) is just off Main St, uphill from Dock Square. The **Rockport Information Center** (open in summer) is on MA 127 as you enter Rockport from Gloucester.

Note that Rockport is 'dry,' with no alcohol for sale in stores or restaurants.

Things to See & Do Rockport is a walking town. Start at Dock Square and wander along Bearskin Neck, finally emerging at the breakwater overlooking Rockport Harbor and Sandy Bay. The **red fishing shack** decorated with colorful buoys is 'Motif No 1.' Artists have been painting and photographing it for so long that it well deserves its tongue-in-cheek name. Then follow Main St west and north from Dock Square to reach **Back Beach** on Sandy Bay, the nearest beach to the town center. For excellent views, walk 10 minutes southeast from Dock Square along Mt Pleasant St, then east along Atlantic Ave or Heywood Ave to the public footpath marked **'Way to the Headlands.'**

Only a few miles north of Dock Square along MA 127 is **Halibut Point State Park** (☎ 978-546-2997; parking $2; open daily). A 10-minute walk brings you to abandoned granite quarries and a granite foreshore

perfect for picnicking, sunbathing, reading or painting.

Inland from Pigeon Cove is the **Paper House** (☎ 978-546-2629; 52 Pigeon Hill St; admission by donation; open 10am-5pm daily Apr-Oct), a curiosity that was begun in 1922 and finished 20 years and 100,000 newspapers later. Made of folded, rolled and pasted papers, some walls are 215 layers thick. The furnishings – even a grandfather clock and a piano – are wrapped in newspapers, too.

Places to Stay & Eat Founded in 1906 by the National League of Working Women, **Rockport Lodge** (☎ 978-546-2090; 61 South St; singles/doubles/triples per person with 2 meals $50/45/40, beds without meals $35) offers beds to women only. Linen is provided, but bring your own towels.

Lantana House (☎ 978-546-3535, 800-291-3535; 22 Broadway; doubles $80-95), conveniently located, has some of the least-expensive rooms.

Sally Webster Inn (☎ 978-546-9251, 877-546-9251; 34 Mt Pleasant St; doubles $95-120), a handsome Federal colonial built in 1832, offers rooms with private bathroom.

Addison Choate Inn (☎ 978-546-7543, 800-245-7543; 49 Broadway; doubles $115-175), a lovely Greek revival place, is among the more charming and historic inns.

Bearskin Neck is crowded with ice-cream shops, cafés and eateries. You'll pass several places good for a bowl of chowder, fish and chips, or cheap lobster.

Roy Moore Lobster Co (☎ 978-546-6696; open 11am-8pm mid-Apr–mid-Oct; dishes $3-16) has the Neck's cheapest lobster-in-the-rough.

Roy Moore's Fish Shack Restaurant (☎ 978-546-6667; open 11am-8pm daily Apr-Oct, 11am-8pm Fri-Sun Nov & Dec; mains $4-18), upstairs next-door to Roy Moore Lobster Co, is more refined and has fairly low prices given its ocean-view dining.

Brackett's (☎ 978-546-2797; 25 Main St; dishes $8-20; open lunch & dinner Wed-Sun mid-Apr–mid-Oct), a cozy little pubby place with water views, specializes in rich seafood casseroles.

My Place by the Sea (☎ 978-546-9667; 68 Bearskin Neck; lunch $5-12, dinner $20-29; open daily June-Sept; open irregular days Apr, May, Oct & Nov) has panoramic bay views, indoor and outdoor seating and an interesting menu. Lunch is good value, and the New American dinners are very good.

Helmut's Strudel (☎ 978-546-2824; 69 Bearskin Neck; open seasonally), almost near the outer end, serves strudels, croissants, pastries, cider and coffee.

Woodman's (☎ 978-768-6057; 121 Main St/MA 133; mains $7-25; open lunch & dinner seasonally), in neighboring Essex, is renowned for heavenly clams (fried, raw, stewed). If you have a car and don't stop at this roadhouse, you'll never forgive yourself.

Getting There & Around Rockport is the terminal for **MBTA Commuter Rail** (☎ 617-222-3200, 800-392-6100; ⓦ www.mbta.com) trains on the Rockport line. The trip from Boston takes about two hours, costs $5 for adults and leaves from North Station.

If you're driving, MA 127 makes two loops around Cape Ann, both passing through Rockport. From Boston it takes one hour to drive the 40 miles to Rockport; from Gloucester it's 7 miles (about 15 minutes); from Salem it takes about 40 minutes to cover the 23 miles.

The **Cape Ann Transportation Authority** (CATA; ☎ 978-283-7916) operates bus routes around Cape Ann that are both scenic and useful. Most fares are less than $1.

NEWBURYPORT

Architecturally, this town is lost in time. Among the five largest towns in America at the outset of the Revolution in 1775, Newburyport (35 miles north of Boston) prospered as a shipping port and center for silversmiths. Today the center is a model for historic preservation and gentrification. It's also gateway to Plum Island, a national wildlife refuge.

All major roads (MA 113, US1 and US 1A) lead into the center of the historic district, around the junction of Water and State Sts. The **Greater Newburyport Chamber of Commerce** (☎ 978-462-6680; ⓦ www.new buryportchamber.org; 38R Merrimac St; open 9am-5pm Mon-Fri, 10am-4pm Sat, noon-4pm Sun) is quite helpful.

Things to See & Do

Custom House Maritime Museum (☎ 978-462-8681; 25 Water St; adult/child $5/4; open 9am-5pm Tues-Sat, 1pm-4pm Sun) will give you a good idea of the town's rich maritime history as a major shipbuilding center and seaport.

Parker River National Wildlife Refuge (☎ 978-465-5753; Plum Island; car/bike/pedestrian $5/2/2; open sunrise-sunset daily), with 9 miles of sandy beaches and over 4500 acres to explore, is an excellent place to watch birds (over 800 species live here), swim and escape the general bustle of Boston.

Places to Stay & Eat

The Garrison Inn (☎ 978-499-8500; 11 Brown Square; doubles $130-210), a boutique hotel with 24 1st-class rooms, has been a hostelry since it opened in the early 1900s.

The Clark Currier Inn (☎ 978-465-8363; 45 Green St; doubles mid-May–Dec $125-185, off-season $95-145), a genteel Federal mansion built in 1803, has eight period guest rooms, but in warm weather you can hang out at the lush fish pond and gazebo.

The Grog (☎ 978-465-8008; 13 Middle St; dishes $7-16; open lunch & dinner daily) rules with Mexican dishes served in a pubby atmosphere. After 9pm Wednesday through Sunday, rock and roll bands play popular covers for a 20-something crowd.

The Rockfish (☎ 978-465-6601; 35 State St; dishes $6-17; open lunch & dinner daily), a great place for people-watching as it features large street-side open windows, has spicy rockfish cakes and cold brews downstairs. Head upstairs for inventive fusion cuisine.

Getting There & Away

Take the **MBTA Commuter Rail** (☎ 617-222-3200, 800-392-6100; ⓦ www.mbta.com) train from North Station to Newburyport. The fare is $5 and there are 10 weekday trains, six on weekends. If you're driving, take I-95 north to exit 57 and follow the signs to downtown. There are free parking lots at Green and Merrimac Sts.

PLYMOUTH & AROUND

'America's home town' is synonymous with the Pilgrims who stepped ashore in 1620, seeking a place to practise their religion without interference from government. Plymouth Rock – a weathered ball of granite – can be seen in a minute, but the symbol is elucidated in nearby museums and exhibits.

'The rock' is within walking distance of most museums and restaurants. Main St, the main commercial street, is a block inland.

The town's visitors center is **Destination Plymouth** (☎ 508-747-7533; W www.visit -plymouth.com; 170 Water St; open 9am-5pm Apr-Nov, 9am-8pm late May–early Sept).

Things to See & Do

If Plymouth Rock, open to view all the time for free, tells little about the Pilgrims, **Mayflower II** (☎ 508-746-1622; adult/child $8/6; open 9am-5pm daily Apr–late Nov), a re-creation of the small ship in which they made the fateful voyage, speaks volumes. With all the provisions, animals and seed needed to establish a colony, 102 people lived on this tiny vessel for 66 days, subsisting on moldy biscuits, rancid butter and brackish water. Discounted combination tickets (adult/child $22/14) include Plimoth Plantation.

A mile south of Plymouth Rock, **Plimoth Plantation** (☎ 508-746-1622; MA 3A; adult/ child $20/12; open 9am-5pm daily Apr–late Nov) is an authentic re-creation of settlements from 1627. Everything in the village – costumes, implements, vocabulary, artistry, recipes and crops – has been painstakingly researched and accurately reproduced. Hobbamock's (Wampanoag) Homesite replicates Native American community life during the same period.

Pilgrim Hall Museum (☎ 508-746-1620; 75 Court St; adult/senior/child/family $5/4.50/ 3/15; open 9:30am-4:30pm daily Feb-Dec) displays artefacts that the Pilgrims and their Wampanoag neighbors used daily.

Plymouth National Wax Museum (☎ 508-746-6468; 16 Carver St; adult/child $6/2.75; open 9am-5pm daily Nov, Mar & Apr, 9am-7pm May-Oct) has life-sized wax figures – 180 in 26 scenes – that recount the Pilgrims' progress from England to America.

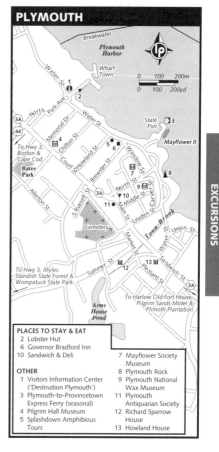

PLYMOUTH

PLACES TO STAY & EAT
2 Lobster Hut
6 Governor Bradford Inn
10 Sandwich & Deli

OTHER
1 Visitors Information Center ('Destination Plymouth')
3 Plymouth-to-Provincetown Express Ferry (seasonal)
4 Pilgrim Hall Museum
5 Splashdown Amphibious Tours
7 Mayflower Society Museum
8 Plymouth Rock
9 Plymouth National Wax Museum
11 Plymouth Antiquarian Society
12 Richard Sparrow House
13 Howland House

Richard Sparrow House (☎ 508-747-1240; 42 Summer St; adult/child $2/1; open 10am-5pm Thur-Tues Apr–late Dec), built in 1640 by an original settler, is the oldest house in Plymouth.

The 1667 **Howland House** (☎ 508-746-9590; 33 Sandwich St; adult/senior/child $4/ 3/2; open 10am-4:30pm daily late May–mid-Oct) began as the residence for a family that came over on the *Mayflower*.

Mayflower Society Museum (☎ 508-746-2590; 4 Winslow St; open 10am-4pm Fri-Sun June & early Sept–mid-Oct, 10am-4pm daily July-early Sept) dates from 1754 and shows how wealthy Plymouth became in just over a century.

Plymouth Antiquarian Society *(☎ 508-746-0012)* maintains three **historic houses** *(adult/child 1 house $4/2, 3 houses $6/2; open 10am-3pm Mon-Fri July & Aug, occasionally in fall)*. Stop in first at the 1677 **Harlow Old Fort House** *(119 Sandwich St)*, which shows how second-generation Plymouth colonists lived.

Splashdown Amphibious Tours *(☎ 508-747-7658; Harbor Place; adult $17, child $3-10; operates; daily mid-May–Sept, Sat & Sun mid-Apr–mid-May & Oct)* utilizes authentic WWII vehicles to transport visitors on narrated trips around town and the harbor.

Places to Stay & Eat

Myles Standish State Forest *(☎ 508-866-2526, 877-422-6762 for reservations; camping late May–mid-Oct, park open year-round; sites $12)*, about 6 miles south of Plymouth, boasts 16,000 acres, 450 camp sites,16 miles of biking and hiking trails and 16 ponds (two with beaches). Take MA 3 exit 5 or MA 58 to South Carver.

Wompatuck State Park *(☎ 781-749-7160, 877-422-6762 for reservations; open late May–early Sept; sites $12)*, off MA 228, Hingham, is 30 miles north of Plymouth. The 2900-acre park has 260 camp sites, 12 miles of paved biking trails, and even more mountain-biking trails and hiking trails.

Governor Bradford Inn *(☎ 508-746-6200, 800-332-1620; 98 Water St; doubles in season $93-130, Sept-May $59-79)* is conveniently located; some of its 94 rooms have sea views.

Pilgrim Sands Motel *(☎ 508-747-0900, 800-729-7263; 150 Warren Ave; doubles mid-June–mid-Oct $130-170, off-season $80-140)* is just across from Plimoth Plantation.

Fast-food shops line Water St opposite the *Mayflower II*. For better food at lower prices, walk a block inland to Main St to **Sandwich & Deli** *(☎ 508-746-7773; 65 Main St; dishes $4-6; open breakfast & lunch daily)*. It has clam chowder, sandwiches and other quick lunches.

Lobster Hut *(☎ 508-746-2270; dishes $6-18; open lunch & dinner daily)*, at Town Wharf, has indoor and outdoor seating, a sea view, and big plates of reasonably priced fried clams and tasty fish and chips.

Getting There & Away

Plymouth is 40 miles south of Boston via US 3; if it's not rush hour, the drive takes less than an hour.

Frequent **Plymouth & Brockton** *(P&B; ☎ 508-746-0378, 508-746-4795 for Plymouth station; w www.p-b.com)* buses connect Boston and Plymouth in 60 minutes. For those on foot, though, the P&B terminal is inconveniently located at the visitors center, exit 5 off US 3.

Trains depart Boston's **South Station** *(☎ 617-222-3200, 800-392-6100; w www .mbta.com)* for Cordage Park, where **GATRA** *(☎ 508-747-1819)* buses connect to Plymouth Center. One-way tickets on the 'liberty link' cost 75¢.

The **Plymouth-to-Provincetown Express Ferry** *(☎ 508-747-2400, 800-242-2469; adult/ senior/child/bike round-trip $30/25/20/3; operates daily mid-June–early Sept)*, departing from State Pier, takes 90 minutes. It departs at 10am and returns from Provincetown at 4:30pm, which means you have five hours in Provincetown.

CAPE COD

'The Cape' is arguably New England's favorite summer destination, and it's driven by tourism. Beaches cover much of its 400-mile shoreline, and there's real beauty in the outer Cape's dune-studded landscapes, its tall sea grass and its colonial towns. Although you can see parts of the Cape in a day trip, if you have three or four days it's all the better.

Orientation & Information

The Sagamore and Bourne Bridges span the Cape Cod Canal, linking the Cape to the mainland. Use the Sagamore Bridge for Rte 6A, Hyannis, the Outer Cape and Provincetown.

MA 28, which heads south from the Bourne Bridge to Falmouth, runs along the southern shore past Hyannis and into Chatham, heading north to Orleans. Between Falmouth and Chatham, MA 28 is congested with strip malls, fast-food joints and motels.

US 6, also called the Mid-Cape Hwy, an inland highway from the canal to Orleans and on to Provincetown, is the only through street.

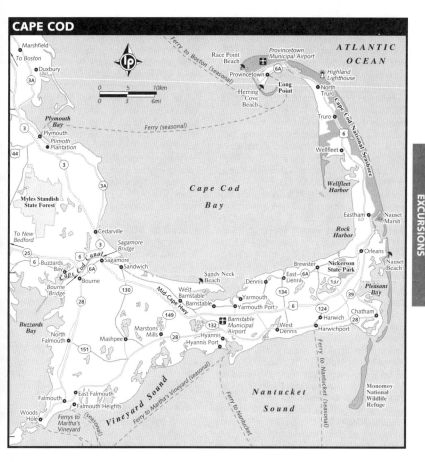

The alternative is MA 6A, a scenic two-lane road between Sandwich and Orleans.

The paved **Cape Cod Rail Trail**, great for bicycling and in-line skating, follows an abandoned flat railroad bed for 26 miles from Dennis to Wellfleet. Park at Nickerson State Park or the trailhead on Rte 134 in South Dennis, south of US 6. You can rent wheels at both places.

Cape-wide information can be found at the **Massachusetts Tourist Information Center** (☎ 508-746-1150; open 8:45am-5pm daily year-round, until 8pm summer), in Plymouth at exit 5 off MA 3.

Once on Cape Cod, stop at the Cape Cod **chamber of commerce** (☎ 508-862-0700, 800-332-2732; W www.capecodchamber.com), just off US 6 at exit 6 in Hyannis.

Route 6A

If you have time, you won't regret taking this scenic byway rather than the inland US 6. A historical commission tightly restricts building, keeping the former 'King's Highway' safe from the clutter that plagues MA 28.

Sandwich, founded in 1637, is one of the Cape's most attractive towns. The quaint village center boasts a duck pond and **Dexter Grist Mill** (near Main and River Sts); fine historic houses, including the c. 1675 **Hoxie House** (☎ 508-888-1173; 18 Water St); the famous **Sandwich Glass Museum** (☎ 508-888-0251; 129 Main St), chronicling the town's glass-making heyday from 1825 to 1888; and a renowned horticultural park, **Heritage Museums & Gardens** (☎ 508-888-3300), with indoor collections of Americana.

Each side of the **Cape Cod Canal** has a well-maintained bike trail. In Sandwich, you can rent bicycles at **Sandwich Cycles** (☎ 508-833-2453; 40 MA 6A).

Through **Barnstable**, MA 6A continues as a tranquil, winding route dotted with antique stores, art galleries, craft shops and pricey B&Bs. The **West Parish Meeting House** (☎ 508-362-8624), Rte 149 between US 6 and MA 6A, dates from 1717. Barnstable's best attraction is **Sandy Neck Beach**, off MA 6A, a 6-mile stretch of barrier beach with a 9-mile (round-trip) trail through dunes and salt marshes. Parking is $10.

In **Yarmouth**, the **Winslow Crocker House** (☎ 508-362-4385; 250 MA 6A) is a lovely Georgian house filled with antiques dating from the 17th century. The **Captain Bangs Hallet House** (☎ 508-362-3021), off MA 6A, was once home to a prosperous sea captain. The historic **Hallet's** (☎ 508-362-3362; 139 MA 6A) began as an apothecary in 1889 and still boasts its original soda fountain. **Grey's Beach** (also known as Bass Hole Beach), off Centre St from MA 6A, has a dramatic boardwalk that stretches over a tidal marsh.

Continuing along MA 6A, **Dennis** boasts the **Cape Museum of Fine Arts** (☎ 508-385-4477; MA 6A), representing Cape artists working in a variety of media.

From **Scargo Tower** (take MA 6A to Old Bass River Rd to Scargo Hill Rd), you can see to Provincetown on a clear day. **Chapin Memorial Beach**, off MA 6A, is a long, dune-backed beach. As with all bayside beaches, at low tide you can walk for a mile onto the tidal flats. Parking is $10.

Cape Playhouse (☎ 508-385-3838, 508-385-3911; 820 MA 6A) is one of the Cape's best summer theaters. Next door, the **Cape Cinema** (☎ 508-385-2503) shows foreign, art and independent films.

In **Brewster**, stop at the **Cape Cod Museum of Natural History** (☎ 508-896-3867; MA 6A). The museum offers walking trails, plus canoe, kayak and seal-watching trips.

The 2000-acre **Nickerson State Park** (admission free) boasts eight ponds, trails for bicycling and walking, picnic sites and sandy beaches. You can rent all sorts of boats on Flax Pond within the park.

From mid-April to early May, thousands of herring migrate from the ocean to fresh water in order to spawn at the picturesque **Stony Brook Grist Mill & Herring Run**, at Setucket and Stony Brook Rds (both off MA 6A).

Places to Stay With the exception of a couple of camping grounds, MA 6A is lined with places that were once sea captains' houses and have now been converted into romantic B&Bs.

Shawme Crowell State Forest (☎ 508-888-0351, 877-422-6762 for reservations; camp sites $10-12; open year-round), off Rte 130 from MA 6A, in Sandwich, has 285 wooded sites on 3000 acres.

Nickerson State Park (☎ 508-896-3491, 877-422-6762 for reservations; 3488 MA 6A, Brewster; camp sites $12-15; open May-Oct) has the Cape's best camp sites. Period. There are 420 wooded sites, some with pond views. Most sites are rented first-come, first-served. Don't get your hopes up in the summer, though.

Spring Garden Motel (☎ 508-888-0710, 800-303-1751; 578 MA 6A; doubles July-Aug $95-135, off-season $79-119), about 5 miles east of Sandwich, has eight rooms overlooking a tranquil salt marsh, and two apartments.

Wedgewood Inn (☎ 508-362-5157; 83 MA 6A, Yarmouthport; doubles June-Oct $135-205, off-season $115-165) is a lovely place with nine spacious rooms filled with antiques, oriental carpets and fireplaces.

Isaiah Hall B&B Inn (☎ 508-385-9928, 800-736-0160; 152 Whig St; doubles $105-155, suites $185; open mid-Apr–mid-Oct), off MA 6A in Dennis, offers 10 nice rooms, and very nice innkeepers. Prices are a little lower off-season.

Legal Sea Foods, Long Wharf, waterfront district

Sonsie, Newbury St, Back Bay

JON DAVISON

Provincetown waterfront, Cape Cod

KIM GRANT

RICHARD CUMMINS

WITCH MUSEUM

Cranberry harvest, Cape Cod

Salem Witch Museum, Salem

Places to Eat For an authentic English afternoon tea ($10), try **Dunbar Tea Shop** (☎ 508-833-2485; 1 Water St, Sandwich; open lunch daily). It also offers a ploughman's lunch ($9), soup, quiche and Scottish shortbread at lunchtime.

Mill Way Fish & Lobster Market (☎ 508-362-2760; Barnstable Harbor; dishes $5-10; open lunch Apr-Aug) has excellent fish sandwiches and fried seafood.

Inaho (☎ 508-362-5522; 157 MA 6A, Yarmouthport; dinner $12-23; open daily) offers fabulous sushi, traditional bento boxes, tempura and more wonderfully exotic dishes.

Contrast Bistro and Espresso Bar (☎ 508-385-9100; 605 MA 6A, Dennis; lunch $7-9, dinner $10-22; open almost daily), a modern bistro with lively art, serves large portions of frittatas and grilled chicken sandwiches. Daily specials are always a good bet.

Brewster Fish House (☎ 508 896 7867; 2208 MA 6A; lunch $8-13, dinner mains $15-26; open Apr-Nov), a modest-looking roadside place, serves simple but deceptively creative seafood. And everyone appreciates its consistency; you'll wait unless you're in line by 6pm.

Hyannis

The commercial and transportation hub of Cape Cod, Hyannis is highly trafficked. The waterfront and Main St areas have been rejuvenated, and it's a pleasant place to wait for a bus. From US 6, take Rte 132 south (exit 6) to the airport traffic circle/rotary to Barnstable Rd to Main St.

The Hyannis area **chamber of commerce** (☎ 508-362-5230, 800-449-6647; 1481 Rte 132; open 9am-4:30pm Mon-Sat year-round & 10am-2pm Sun late May-early Sept) is about a mile south of US 6.

Places to Eat Open morning until late at night, **Prodigal Son** (☎ 508-771-1337; 10 Ocean St; dishes $6-8) is a laid-back coffeehouse with a limited but sufficient selection of lunch and dinner plates and a fine selection of microbrews and wine.

Spiritus (☎ 508-775-2955; 500 Main St; sandwiches $6; open daily), a popular, funky hang-out, serves strong coffee, pizza by the slice and filling sandwiches.

La Petite France (☎ 508-771-4445; 349 Main St; dishes $5-10; open lunch Apr-Dec) has onion soup, Mediterranean salads, clam chowder, and sandwiches made with baguettes and home-roasted meats.

RooBar City Bistro (☎ 508-778-6515; 586 Main St; mains $15-25; open dinner daily) is the coolest, hippest place in the area. The New American fusion cuisine rocks, as does the late-night bar scene.

Getting There & Away The downtown **Plymouth & Brockton** (☎ 508-746-0378; Center & Main Sts) bus connects Boston to Hyannis and points east, to Provincetown. There are about 30 daily buses from Boston to Hyannis ($14 one-way) and six daily buses from Hyannis to Provincetown ($9 one-way).

Hyannis is one of the few places on Cape Cod where you can rent a car. **Hertz** (☎ 800-654-3131) and **National** (☎ 800-227-7368) are at Barnstable Municipal Airport; **Trek** (☎ 508-771-2459) is two blocks away.

Hyannis is 79 miles (1½ hours) from Boston and 50 miles (1¼ hours) from Provincetown.

Orleans

There are two major reasons to play in Orleans: Pleasant Bay and Nauset Beach. Stop in at **Goose Hummock Outdoor Center** (☎ 508-255-2620; off MA 6A, Town Cove) to be set up with kayak rentals, advice and tours for paddling around this tranquil marsh and bay. Or head to the 9-mile-long barrier beach in East Orleans; take Main St to Beach Rd and follow it to the end. Body surfing is great on this Atlantic Ocean beach. Parking costs $10 mid-June to early September and $5 on weekends a month before and after that.

Hot Chocolate Sparrow (☎ 508-240-2230; Old Colony Way; open daily), behind CVS off Rte 6A, has excellent espresso and snacks. For outdoor seafood, head to **Kadee's Lobster & Clam Bar** (☎ 508-255-6184; 212 Main St; lunch $6-14, dinner $10-18; open mid-May– early Sept) after a day at the beach.

Chatham

Chatham is the most patrician Cape town. It's pricey, but it's worth a drive around. On Shore Rd, stop at the **Fish Pier** (where fishers unload the daily catch every afternoon) and **Chatham Light** overlooking the dramatic Lighthouse Beach. If you have a few hours to spare, take a **seal-watching trip** out to remote Monomoy Island or catch a launch out to equally remote South Beach with the **Beachcomber** (☎ 508-945-5265). Boats depart from the Fish Pier.

Before heading out, pick up some chicken or berry pies (or both) from **Marion's Pie Shop** (☎ 508-432-9439; pies $3-7; open 7am-6pm Apr-Dec).

Outer Cape

Eastham, Wellfleet and **Truro** are the most seasonal, and quietest, towns on the Cape, even in summer. Eastham is perhaps best known for a less than amicable 1620 'encounter' between the Pilgrims and Native Americans. Wellfleet's lure includes its art galleries, fine beaches and famous oysters. Sleepy Truro has good camping and beaches.

Everything of interest is on or just off US 6, the only highway from Eastham to Provincetown. Beyond North Truro, MA 6A veers off US 6 and is filled with motels as it heads into Provincetown. Wellfleet is best explored by foot or bike. Main and Commercial Sts run more or less parallel to each other in the center of town. Continue west along either road to scenic Chequessett Neck Rd.

The **Cape Cod National Seashore** (**CCNS**), which includes the entire eastern shoreline from Chatham to Provincetown, is known for its pristine, seemingly endless beaches, dunes, nature trails, ponds, salt marshes and forests.

Things to See & Do In Eastham, at the **Salt Pond Visitors Center** (☎ 508-255-3421; open 9am-4:30pm daily year-round, until 5pm Mar-Oct), off US 6, there are excellent exhibits and films about the Cape's geology and history. Check the daily list of ranger- and naturalist-led walks and talks, usually free.

Also in Eastham, east of US 6 atop Fort Hill, a mid-19th-century sea captain's house, **Edward Penniman House** (☎ 508-255-3421), has been restored by the NPS. Opening times vary considerably; ask at the Salt Pond Visitors Center. Nearby, a lovely 1½-mile (round-trip) walking trail skirts the marsh and heads inland through a red maple swamp. A **bike trail** from the Salt Pond Visitors Center to Coast Guard Beach takes you across a salt marsh and through an archetypal forest. Rent bikes across from the visitors center at **Little Capistrano Bike Shop** (☎ 508-255-6515).

In Wellfleet, Audubon's 1000-acre **Wellfleet Bay Wildlife Sanctuary** (☎ 508-349-2615), west off US 6, boasts walking trails that crisscross tidal creeks, salt marshes and a bay beach. The 8-mile **Great Island Trail**, off Chequessett Neck Rd, requires four hours, sunscreen, water and a bit of stamina to walk over soft sand. The lack of human presence more than compensates for the effort. The **Cape Cod Rail Trail** (see Cape Cod Orientation & Information earlier in this chapter) ends at LeCount Hollow Rd, a couple of miles from two good beaches. You can rent bikes at the **Idle Times Bike Shop** (☎ 508-255-8281; open mid-June–mid-Sept).

In North Truro, **Highland Light**, also known as Cape Cod Light, is east of US 6. It replaced the Cape's first lighthouse, built here in 1798. Adjacent is the Cape's oldest public golf course. And adjacent to that, the **Highland House Museum** (☎ 508-487-3397), once a summer hotel, is now a local museum.

A 4-mile **bike path** runs from Head of the Meadow Beach in Truro, past the Pilgrim Heights Area, to the end of Highhead Rd.

Beaches In Eastham, **Coast Guard Beach**, east of the visitors center, is backed by tall dune grasses. Facilities include rest rooms, showers and changing rooms. Just north, **Nauset Light Beach** is also great. Parking at both is $10 daily mid-June to early September.

In Wellfleet, **Marconi Beach**, off US 6, is a narrow ocean beach backed by high dunes; facilities include showers. Parking is $10.

In Truro, **Head of the Meadow Beach**, east off US 6, is a wide, dune-backed beach with changing rooms. The bayside **Corn Hill Beach**, off US 6, is lovely for a relaxing walk or for windsurfing. Parking at both is $10.

Places to Stay There are 50 beds in eight cabins at **Hostelling International, Mid-Cape** (☎ 508-255-2785, 800-909-4776 for reservations in-season; **W** www.usahostels .org; 75 Goody Hallet Drive, Eastham; beds members/nonmembers $19/22; open mid-May–mid-Sept). Reservations are essential in summer. From US 6 and the Orleans traffic circle/rotary, follow Harbor Rd to Bridge Rd to Goody Hallet Drive.

Hostelling International, Truro (☎ 508-349-3889, 800-909-4776 for reservations in-season; **W** www.usahostels.org; N Pamet Rd, Truro; beds members/nonmembers $22-24/25-27; open mid-June–early Sept) is a former Coast Guard station just five minutes from the beach with 42 beds.

North Truro Camping Area (☎ 508-487-1847; Highland Rd, Truro; sites for 2 people $20; open year-round) reserves about 100 of its 350 mostly wooded sites for tents.

Maurice's Campground (☎ 508-349-2029; US 6, Wellfleet; sites for 2 people $25; open mid-May–mid-Oct), on the rail trail, reserves a quarter of its 180 sites for tents. It also has cottages ($500 weekly) and cabins ($75 nightly).

Overlook Inn (☎ 508-255-1886; US 6, Eastham; doubles June-Oct $95-200, off-season $95-105), on the rail trail, across from the Salt Pond Visitors Center, offers 11 antique-filled rooms and charming common rooms. Rates include full breakfast.

Blue Gateways (☎ 508-349-7530; 252 Main St, Wellfleet; doubles late May-Sept $120-130, off-season $100-110) has three homey guest rooms.

Places to Eat Deli meats and salads rolled up in pita bread are served at **Box Lunch** (☎ 508-349-2178; 50 Briar Lane, Wellfleet; sandwiches $5-7; open daily).

Lighthouse (☎ 508-349-3681; 317 Main St, Wellfleet; dishes $4-10; open breakfast, lunch & dinner) doesn't do anything fancy. But it is open year-round, with decent food at decent prices and Guinness on tap.

Moby Dick's (☎ 508-349-9795; US 6, Wellfleet; dishes $6-25; open lunch & dinner daily early May–early Oct), a self-service place with indoor picnic tables and great clam chowder, is the best fried- fish joint on the Outer Cape. Bring your own beer or wine.

Jams, Inc (☎ 508-349-1616; Truro; open late May-early Sept), off US 6, has fancy picnic foods such as rotisserie chicken and salmon pâte.

Village Café (☎ 508-487-5800; 4 Highland Rd, Truro; dishes $4-7; open mid-May–Oct) is an informal little place that offers bagels, hearty sandwiches and soup.

Adrian's (☎ 508-487-4360; US 6, North Truro; breakfast $3-8, dinner $8-23; open dinner mid-May–mid-Oct, breakfast Sat & Sun spring & fall, daily in summer), overlooking the dunes and ocean, offers popular breakfast huevos rancheros and frittatas. An Italian menu with brick-oven pizzas reigns at dinner.

Entertainment Off Ocean View Dr, **Beachcomber** (☎ 508-349-6055; Cahoon Hollow Beach, Wellfleet; open daily May-Sept, until 1am in summer) is an indoor-outdoor, all-in-one restaurant, bar and beachside nightclub.

Duck Creeke Tavern Room (☎ 508-349-7369; 70 Main St, Wellfleet; open daily May–mid-Oct) is a fine, cozy place to listen to live jazz, folk and Latin music. While you're here you can also nosh on good burgers, pizza and upscale but light bistro fare.

Wellfleet Drive-In (☎ 508-349-7176, 800-696-3532; US 6) shows double features at dusk late April through September.

Getting There & Around On its way from Boston and Hyannis to Provincetown, the **Plymouth & Brockton** (☎ 508-746-0378, **W** www.p-b.com) bus stops at the following points: across from Eastham Town Hall (US 6); at D&D Market in South Wellfleet (US 6) and the town hall in Wellfleet center (off US 6); and at Jam's in Truro center and Dutra's Market in North Truro (both just off US 6).

Provincetown

Provincetown is the Cape's liveliest resort town and New England's gay mecca. Painters

EXCURSIONS

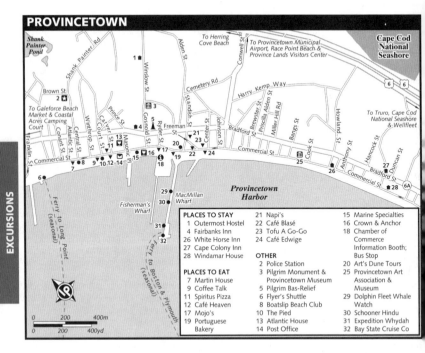

PROVINCETOWN

PLACES TO STAY	OTHER
1 Outermost Hostel	21 Napi's
4 Fairbanks Inn	22 Café Blasé
26 White Horse Inn	23 Tofu A Go-Go
27 Cape Colony Inn	24 Café Edwige
28 Windamar House	

PLACES TO STAY
1 Outermost Hostel
4 Fairbanks Inn
26 White Horse Inn
27 Cape Colony Inn
28 Windamar House

PLACES TO EAT
7 Martin House
9 Coffee Talk
11 Spiritus Pizza
12 Café Heaven
17 Mojo's
19 Portuguese Bakery

21 Napi's
22 Café Blasé
23 Tofu A Go-Go
24 Café Edwige

OTHER
2 Police Station
3 Pilgrim Monument & Provincetown Museum
5 Pilgrim Bas-Relief
6 Flyer's Shuttle
8 Boatslip Beach Club
10 The Pied
13 Atlantic House
14 Post Office

15 Marine Specialties
16 Crown & Anchor
18 Chamber of Commerce Information Booth; Bus Stop
20 Art's Dune Tours
25 Provincetown Art Association & Museum
29 Dolphin Fleet Whale Watch
30 Schooner Hindu
31 Expedition Whydah
32 Bay State Cruise Co

and writers, Portuguese-American anglers and solitude seekers and their families make up this tolerant, year-round community of 3500. The outpost also has long stretches of pristine beach, dramatic sand dunes, contemporary art and one-of-a-kind shops and boutiques. 'P-town,' as it's known to outsiders but never to locals, is jam-packed from late June to early September as its seasonal population swells to 40,000. Because of special events, it's also crowded on weekends through October.

Commercial St is the town's main drag. About 3 miles long, the one-way street functions as the town's boardwalk. There are plenty of public parking lots.

The **police station** (☎ 508-487-1212; 26 Shank Painter Rd) and a **post office** (☎ 800-275-8777; 211 Commercial St) are easily reached.

The **chamber of commerce information booth** (☎ 508-487-3424; 307 Commercial St, MacMillan Wharf; W www.ptownchamber

.com; open 9:30am-4:30pm daily May-Oct, 10am-4pm Nov-April) has lots of good information.

Things to See Provincetown began attracting artists in the early 1900s, and by the 1920s, there was a fashionable art colony. The town remains a vital center of the American arts scene with more than 20 galleries. Pick up a Provincetown Gallery Guide for the current crop.

Provincetown Art Association & Museum (☎ 508-487-1750; 460 Commercial St; open 12pm-5pm daily May-Sept, until 8pm or 10pm Fri & Sat late July–Sept, Sat & Sun Oct-April) one of the country's foremost small museums was organized in 1914.

The Pilgrims first set foot on American soil in 1620 at Provincetown, at the western end of Commercial St. After failing to find adequate supplies, they forged on to Plymouth. The **Pilgrim Bas-Relief**, behind the Provincetown Town Hall, commemorates the

Mayflower Compact, a predecessor to the US Constitution.

Pilgrim Monument & Provincetown Museum (☎ 508-487-1310, 800-247-1620; *High Pole Hill Rd; adult/child $6/3; open 9am-5pm daily Apr–Nov*) affords great views, while the museum portrays the Pilgrims' early challenges and the lives of later whaling captains.

Expedition Whydah (☎ 508-487-8899; 16 *MacMillan Wharf; adult/child $8/6; open 9am-5pm daily Apr–mid-Oct, 9am-5pm Sat & Sun mid-Oct–Dec*) boasts the only authenticated collection of pirate artefacts anywhere in the world. The ship just happened to sink in waters near Marconi Beach (see Beaches under Outer Cape earlier in this chapter).

Activities Off US 6, **Race Point Beach** has pounding surf and high dunes stretching as far as the eye can see. Parking costs $10 for cars, for $3 bicycles. **Herring Cove Beach**, at the end of US 6, has calmer water and more spectacular sunsets. **Long Point Beach** is reached via a water shuttle or a two-hour walk along the stone jetty at the western end of Commercial St.

There are 7 miles of paved **bike trails** within the Cape Cod National Seashore (CCNS). Rent bicycles at **Galeforce Beach Market** (☎ 508-487-4849; 144 *Bradford St Extensions*) on the edge of town ($3 to $4 hourly, $14 to $19 daily).

Province Lands Visitors Center (☎ 508-487-1256; *open 9am-5pm daily early May–late Oct*), at the end of Race Point Rd, has dozens of scheduled nature-oriented programs.

Flyer's Shuttle (☎ 508-487-0898; 131A *Commercial St*) ferries sunbathers to remote Long Point mid-May to early October ($8/12 one-way/round trip).

Organized Tours To explore the dunes within the CCNS try **Art's Dune Tours** (☎ 508-487-1950; *cnr Commercial & Standish Sts*) which offers hour-long, narrated, 4WD dune tours from mid-April to mid-November. Rides cost $12 to $16 per person.

Willie Air Tours (☎ 508-487-0240; *Race Point Rd*), at the airport, offers spectacular trips for $60 for one person, or $105 for three.

The traditional **Schooner Hindu** (☎ 508-487-3000) departs from MacMillan Wharf mid-May to mid-October for two-hour bay sails. Adults pay $10 to $16, children $7.

Of the half-dozen companies that offer 3½-hour whale-watching trips, **Dolphin Fleet Whale Watch** (☎ 508-349-1900, 800-826-9300; *MacMillan Wharf; adult $20-22, child $19; operates mid-Apr–Oct*) is the best, with onboard naturalists.

Places to Stay On the edge of town, **Coastal Acres Camping Court** (☎ 508-487-1700; *West Vine St Extension; sites $25; open Apr-Nov*) has wooded sites for tents and trailers.

Outermost Hostel (☎ 508-487-4378; 26-28 *Winslow St; beds $19*), a privately run hostel, has five grungy cabins housing six grungy bunks each. Common space includes a kitchen and living room; barbecues and picnic tables are handy.

Cape Colony Inn (☎ 508-487-1755; 280 *Bradford St; doubles late June–early Sept $103-116, off-season $69-73; open June-Oct*) has 54 simple rooms. Two-room suites cost a bit more, but they're a good deal for four people.

Provincetown has a hundred delightful small inns and guesthouses. In summer, most are booked well in advance. If you can't make advance reservations, arrive early and ask the chamber of commerce for help.

Windamar House (☎ 508-487-0599; 568 *Commercial St; doubles June-Aug $75-150, off-season $65-110; open Apr-Dec*) has six lovely rooms and two even-better apartments.

White Horse Inn (☎ 508-487-1790; 500 *Commercial St; singles mid-June–Aug $60, doubles $80-90, apartments $125-140*) rents 12 simple rooms, each decorated with local art, most with shared bathroom. There's a three-night minimum stay for the six bungalow-style apartments.

The 14-room **Fairbanks Inn** (☎ 508-487-0386; 90 *Bradford St; doubles mid-June–mid-Sept $119-289, off-season $65-175*), a gracious, historic, 18th-century hostelry, has been upgraded with fine amenities.

Places to Eat Without a doubt, the place to go for a late-night slice is **Spiritus Pizza**

(☎ 508-487-2808; 190 Commercial St; open 11:30am-2am Apr–mid-Nov). Its strong coffee and pastries will jump-start you into the next morning.

Coffee Talk (☎ 508-487-3780; 205-209 Commercial St; open daily May–mid-Oct) makes exotic protein and fruit drinks, and, of course, juice for java junkies.

Portuguese Bakery (☎ 508-487-1803; 299 Commercial St; open daily Apr-Oct) serves Provincetown's favorite snack, a big hunk of hot, sugar-dusted fried dough.

Mojo's (☎ 508-487-3140; Ryder St; dishes $3-13; open 11am-5pm daily mid-May–mid-Oct), at MacMillan Wharf, is a classic fried-fish shack.

Café Blasé (☎ 508-487-9465; 328 Commercial St; dishes $10-20; open 9am-midnight daily late May–mid-Sept), where the principal activity is dishing people sauntering by, offers good crabmeat sandwiches, Caesar salads and garden burgers.

Café Heaven (☎ 508-487-9639; 199 Commercial St; breakfast & lunch $5-8; open Apr-Nov, dinner in summer only) is light and airy but small and crowded. It's a value-oriented, three-meal-a-day place for omelets, cold salads and dinnertime create-your-own-pasta dishes ($10 to $18).

Tofu A Go-Go (☎ 508-487-6237; 336 Commercial St; lunch $7-10, dinner under $14; open Apr-Oct) boasts a wide vegetarian menu, a traditional Japanese macrobiotic menu and a vegie burger with upwards of 28 ingredients.

Napi's (☎ 508-487-1145; 7 Freeman St; lunch $6-13, dinner mains $18-26; open lunch in summer, dinner year-round), an institution, serves an eclectic line-up including organic salads and Portuguese linguica.

Café Edwige (☎ 508-487-2008; 333 Commercial St; breakfast $5-10, dinner mains $18-24; open mid-May–mid-Oct), the most popular breakfast place, offers frittatas, tofu casserole, broiled flounder, and fruit pancakes. At night, the cuisine ratchets up a notch, with diverse Thai and international offerings.

Martin House (☎ 508-487-1327; 157 Commercial St; mains $16-33, prix fixe $50-85; open daily), in a rustic 18th-century dwelling

Gay & Lesbian Hang-outs

Always look for posted playbills around town to see what's current, especially at **Esther's** and **Vixen** (women), and **Chaser's** and **Post Office Cabaret** (mixed).

Boatslip Beach Club (☎ 508-487-1669; 161 Commercial St), known for its popular afternoon tea dances (3:30pm to 6:30pm), also rents pool chairs for watching all the hard bods.

The Pied (☎ 508-487-1527; 193A Commercial St), a longtime waterfront women's bar, hosts 'post-tea' parties at 6:30pm.

Atlantic House (A-House; ☎ 508-487-3821; 4 Masonic Place) features three men's bars – leather, disco and an intimate bar with a fireplace. Some say the A-House is responsible for year-round tourism.

Crown & Anchor (☎ 508-487-1430; 247 Commercial St), open year-round, draws a leather-and-Levi's crowd as well as a disco-and-drag crowd. Its cabaret acts, filled to the rafters with queens, are the cat's meow.

with lots of fireplaces, is well suited to year-round dining and splurging. An innovative menu leaves room for desserts such as bread pudding and raspberry crumble.

Shopping Commercial St, lined with creative speciality shops, sells everything from leather implements of torture to artsy T-shirts, from sculpture to handcrafted jewelry. As you wander, don't miss **Marine Specialties** (☎ 508-487-1730; 235 Commercial St), a cavernous store filled with surplus army and navy stuff, camping and outdoor gear and random odd items.

Getting There & Away Daily year-round flights are provided by **Cape Air** (☎ 508-487-0241, 800-352-0714) from Boston to Provincetown's municipal airport, about 4 miles from town and reached via taxi.

From mid-May to mid-October, the **Bay State Cruise Co** (☎ 617-748-1428; w www.baystatecruisecompany.com; 200 Seaport Blvd, Boston) operates ferries to Provincetown. The *Provincetown II* takes three hours and costs $30 round trip (same day); $21 for children age 4 to 12. If you're intent on shaving an hour off that time, it will cost you: tickets aboard the *Provincetown Express* cost $49/75 one-way/round trip, regardless of age. The *Provincetown II* operates on Saturday and Sunday mid-May to late June and early September to mid-October (daily in summer).

The **Plymouth & Brockton** (☎ *508-778-9767;* **w** *www.p-b.com)* bus, which stops at the chamber of commerce, operates five times daily (3½ hours; $27 one-way) between Provincetown and Boston.

If you're driving, it takes about 2½ hours (assuming you don't get bogged down in the traffic exodus) to traverse the 128 miles to Provincetown.

LONELY PLANET

ON THE ROAD

Travel Guides explore cities, regions and countries, and supply information on transport, restaurants and accommodation, covering all budgets. They come with reliable, easy-to-use maps, practical advice, cultural and historical facts and a rundown on attractions both on and off the beaten track. There are over 200 titles in this classic series, covering nearly every country in the world.

 Lonely Planet Upgrades extend the shelf life of existing travel guides by detailing any changes that may affect travel in a region since a book has been published. Upgrades can be downloaded for free from **www.lonelyplanet.com/upgrades**

For travellers with more time than money, **Shoestring** guides offer dependable, first-hand information with hundreds of detailed maps, plus insider tips for stretching money as far as possible. Covering entire continents in most cases, the six-volume shoestring guides are known around the world as 'backpackers bibles'.

For the discerning short-term visitor, **Condensed** guides highlight the best a destination has to offer in a full-colour, pocket-sized format designed for quick access. They include everything from top sights and walking tours to opinionated reviews of where to eat, stay, shop and have fun.

CitySync lets travellers use their Palm™ or Visor™ hand-held computers to guide them through a city with handy tips on transport, history, cultural life, major sights, and shopping and entertainment options. It can also quickly search and sort hundreds of reviews of hotels, restaurants and attractions, and pinpoint their location on scrollable street maps. CitySync can be downloaded from **www.citysync.com**

MAPS & ATLASES

Lonely Planet's **City Maps** feature downtown and metropolitan maps, as well as transit routes and walking tours. The maps come complete with an index of streets, a listing of sights and a plastic coat for extra durability.

Road Atlases are an essential navigation tool for serious travellers. Cross-referenced with the guidebooks, they also feature distance and climate charts and a complete site index.

LONELY PLANET

ESSENTIALS

Read This First books help new travellers to hit the road with confidence. These invaluable predeparture guides give step-by-step advice on preparing for a trip, budgeting, arranging a visa, planning an itinerary and staying safe while still getting off the beaten track.

Healthy Travel pocket guides offer a regional rundown on disease hot spots and practical advice on predeparture health measures, staying well on the road and what to do in emergencies. The guides come with a user-friendly design and helpful diagrams and tables.

Lonely Planet's **Phrasebooks** cover the essential words and phrases travellers need when they're strangers in a strange land. They come in a pocket-sized format with colour tabs for quick reference, extensive vocabulary lists, easy-to-follow pronunciation keys and two-way dictionaries.

Miffed by blurry photos of the Taj Mahal? Tired of the classic 'top of the head cut off' shot? **Travel Photography: A Guide to Taking Better Pictures** will help you turn ordinary holiday snaps into striking images and give you the know-how to capture every scene, from frenetic festivals to peaceful beach sunrises.

Lonely Planet's **Travel Journal** is a lightweight but sturdy travel diary for jotting down all those on-the-road observations and significant travel moments. It comes with a handy time-zone wheel, a world map and useful travel information.

Lonely Planet's eKno is an all-in-one communication service developed especially for travellers. It offers low-cost international calls and free email and voicemail so that you can keep in touch while on the road. Check it out on **www.ekno.lonelyplanet.com**

FOOD & RESTAURANT GUIDES

Lonely Planet's **Out to Eat** guides recommend the brightest and best places to eat and drink in top international cities. These gourmet companions are arranged by neighbourhood, packed with dependable maps, garnished with scene-setting photos and served with quirky features.

For people who live to eat, drink and travel, **World Food** guides explore the culinary culture of each country. Entertaining and adventurous, each guide is packed with detail on staples and specialities, regional cuisine and local markets, as well as sumptuous recipes, comprehensive culinary dictionaries and lavish photos good enough to eat.

LONELY PLANET

OUTDOOR GUIDES

For those who believe the best way to see the world is on foot, Lonely Planet's **Walking Guides** detail everything from family strolls to difficult treks, with 'when to go and how to do it' advice supplemented by reliable maps and essential travel information.

Cycling Guides map a destination's best bike tours, long and short, in day-by-day detail. They contain all the information a cyclist needs, including advice on bike maintenance, places to eat and stay, innovative maps with detailed cues to the rides, and elevation charts.

The **Watching Wildlife** series is perfect for travellers who want authoritative information but don't want to tote a heavy field guide. Packed with advice on where, when and how to view a region's wildlife, each title features photos of over 300 species and contains engaging comments on the local flora and fauna.

With underwater colour photos throughout, **Pisces Books** explore the world's best diving and snorkelling areas. Each book contains listings of diving services and dive resorts, detailed information on depth, visibility and difficulty of dives, and a roundup of the marine life you're likely to see through your mask.

LONELY PLANET

OFF THE ROAD

Journeys, the travel literature series written by renowned travel authors, capture the spirit of a place or illuminate a culture with a journalist's attention to detail and a novelist's flair for words. These are tales to soak up while you're actually on the road or dip into as an at-home armchair indulgence.

The range of lavishly illustrated **Pictorial** books is just the ticket for both travellers and dreamers. Off-beat tales and vivid photographs bring the adventure of travel to your doorstep long before the journey begins and long after it is over.

Lonely Planet **Videos** encourage the same independent, tough-minded approach as the guidebooks. Currently airing throughout the world, this award-winning series features innovative footage and an original soundtrack.

Yes, we know, work is tough, so do a little bit of deskside dreaming with the spiral-bound Lonely Planet **Diary** or a Lonely Planet **Wall Calendar**, filled with great photos from around the world.

TRAVELLERS NETWORK

Lonely Planet Online. Lonely Planet's award-winning Web site has insider information on hundreds of destinations, from Amsterdam to Zimbabwe, complete with interactive maps and relevant links. The site also offers the latest travel news, recent reports from travellers on the road, guidebook upgrades, a travel links site, an online book-buying option and a lively travellers bulletin board. It can be viewed at **www.lonelyplanet.com** or AOL keyword: lp.

Planet Talk is a quarterly print newsletter, full of gossip, advice, anecdotes and author articles. It provides an antidote to the being-at-home blues and lets you plan and dream for the next trip. Contact the nearest Lonely Planet office for your free copy.

Comet, the free Lonely Planet newsletter, comes via email once a month. It's loaded with travel news, advice, dispatches from authors, travel competitions and letters from readers. To subscribe, click on the Comet subscription link on the front page of the Web site.

Lonely Planet Guides by Region

onely Planet is known worldwide for publishing practical, reliable and no-nonsense travel information in our guides and on our Web site. The Lonely Planet list covers just about every accessible part of the world. Currently there are 16 series: Travel guides, Shoestring guides, Condensed guides, Phrasebooks, Read This First, Healthy Travel, Walking guides, Cycling guides, Watching Wildlife guides, Pisces Diving & Snorkeling guides, City Maps, Road Atlases, Out to Eat, World Food, Journeys travel literature and Pictorials.

AFRICA Africa on a shoestring • Botswana • Cairo • Cairo City Map • Cape Town • Cape Town City Map • East Africa • Egypt • Egyptian Arabic phrasebook • Ethiopia, Eritrea & Djibouti • Ethiopian Amharic phrasebook • The Gambia & Senegal • Healthy Travel Africa • Kenya • Malawi • Morocco • Moroccan Arabic phrasebook • Mozambique • Namibia • Read This First: Africa • South Africa, Lesotho & Swaziland • Southern Africa • Southern Africa Road Atlas • Swahili phrasebook • Tanzania, Zanzibar & Pemba • Trekking in East Africa • Tunisia • Watching Wildlife East Africa • Watching Wildlife Southern Africa • West Africa • World Food Morocco • Zambia • Zimbabwe, Botswana & Namibia
Travel Literature: Mali Blues: Traveling to an African Beat • The Rainbird: A Central African Journey • Songs to an African Sunset: A Zimbabwean Story

AUSTRALIA & THE PACIFIC Aboriginal Australia & the Torres Strait Islands •Auckland • Australia • Australian phrasebook • Australia Road Atlas • Cycling Australia • Cycling New Zealand • Fiji • Fijian phrasebook • Healthy Travel Australia, NZ & the Pacific • Islands of Australia's Great Barrier Reef • Melbourne • Melbourne City Map • Micronesia • New Caledonia • New South Wales • New Zealand • Northern Territory • Outback Australia • Out to Eat – Melbourne • Out to Eat – Sydney • Papua New Guinea • Pidgin phrasebook • Queensland • Rarotonga & the Cook Islands • Samoa • Solomon Islands • South Australia • South Pacific • South Pacific phrasebook • Sydney • Sydney City Map • Sydney Condensed • Tahiti & French Polynesia • Tasmania • Tonga • Tramping in New Zealand • Vanuatu • Victoria • Walking in Australia • Watching Wildlife Australia • Western Australia
Travel Literature: Islands in the Clouds: Travels in the Highlands of New Guinea • Kiwi Tracks: A New Zealand Journey • Sean & David's Long Drive

CENTRAL AMERICA & THE CARIBBEAN Bahamas, Turks & Caicos • Baja California • Belize, Guatemala & Yucatán • Bermuda • Central America on a shoestring • Costa Rica • Costa Rica Spanish phrasebook • Cuba • Cycling Cuba • Dominican Republic & Haiti • Eastern Caribbean • Guatemala • Havana • Healthy Travel Central & South America • Jamaica • Mexico • Mexico City • Panama • Puerto Rico • Read This First: Central & South America • Virgin Islands • World Food Caribbean • World Food Mexico • Yucatán
Travel Literature: Green Dreams: Travels in Central America

EUROPE Amsterdam • Amsterdam City Map • Amsterdam Condensed • Andalucía • Athens • Austria • Baltic States phrasebook • Barcelona • Barcelona City Map • Belgium & Luxembourg • Berlin • Berlin City Map • Britain • British phrasebook • Brussels, Bruges & Antwerp • Brussels City Map • Budapest • Budapest City Map • Canary Islands • Catalunya & the Costa Brava • Central Europe • Central Europe phrasebook • Copenhagen • Corfu & the Ionians • Corsica • Crete • Crete Condensed • Croatia • Cycling Britain • Cycling France • Cyprus • Czech & Slovak Republics • Czech phrasebook • Denmark • Dublin • Dublin City Map • Dublin Condensed • Eastern Europe • Eastern Europe phrasebook • Edinburgh • Edinburgh City Map • England • Estonia, Latvia & Lithuania • Europe on a shoestring • Europe phrasebook • Finland • Florence • Florence City Map • France • Frankfurt City Map • Frankfurt Condensed • French phrasebook • Georgia, Armenia & Azerbaijan • Germany • German phrasebook • Greece • Greek Islands • Greek phrasebook • Hungary • Iceland, Greenland & the Faroe Islands • Ireland • Italian phrasebook • Italy • Kraków • Lisbon • The Loire • London • London City Map • London Condensed • Madrid • Madrid City Map • Malta • Mediterranean Europe • Milan, Turin & Genoa • Moscow • Munich • Netherlands • Normandy • Norway • Out to Eat – London • Out to Eat – Paris • Paris • Paris City Map • Paris Condensed • Poland • Polish phrasebook • Portugal • Portuguese phrasebook • Prague • Prague City Map • Provence & the Côte d'Azur • Read This First: Europe • Rhodes & the Dodecanese • Romania & Moldova • Rome • Rome City Map • Rome Condensed • Russia, Ukraine & Belarus • Russian phrasebook • Scandinavian & Baltic Europe • Scandinavian phrasebook • Scotland • Sicily • Slovenia • South-West France • Spain • Spanish phrasebook • Stockholm • St Petersburg • St Petersburg City Map • Sweden • Switzerland • Tuscany • Ukrainian phrasebook • Venice • Vienna • Wales • Walking in Britain • Walking in France • Walking in Ireland • Walking in Italy • Walking in Scotland • Walking in Spain • Walking in Switzerland • Western Europe • World Food France • World Food Greece • World Food Ireland • World Food Italy • World Food Spain **Travel Literature:** After Yugoslavia • Love and War in the Apennines • The Olive Grove: Travels in Greece • On the Shores of the Mediterranean • Round Ireland in Low Gear • A Small Place in Italy

Lonely Planet Mail Order

onely Planet products are distributed worldwide. They are also available by mail order from Lonely Planet, so if you have difficulty finding a title please write to us. North and South American residents should write to 150 Linden St, Oakland, CA 94607, USA; European and African residents should write to 10a Spring Place, London NW5 3BH, UK; and residents of other countries to Locked Bag 1, Footscray, Victoria 3011, Australia.

INDIAN SUBCONTINENT & THE INDIAN OCEAN Bangladesh • Bengali phrasebook • Bhutan • Delhi • Goa • Healthy Travel Asia & India • Hindi & Urdu phrasebook • India • India & Bangladesh City Map • Indian Himalaya • Karakoram Highway • Kathmandu City Map • Kerala • Madagascar • Maldives • Mauritius, Réunion & Seychelles • Mumbai (Bombay) • Nepal • Nepali phrasebook • North India • Pakistan • Rajasthan • Read This First: Asia & India • South India • Sri Lanka • Sri Lanka phrasebook • Tibet • Tibetan phrasebook • Trekking in the Indian Himalaya • Trekking in the Karakoram & Hindukush • Trekking in the Nepal Himalaya • World Food India **Travel Literature**: The Age of Kali: Indian Travels and Encounters • Hello Goodnight: A Life of Goa • In Rajasthan • Maverick in Madagascar • A Season in Heaven: True Tales from the Road to Kathmandu • Shopping for Buddhas • A Short Walk in the Hindu Kush • Slowly Down the Ganges

MIDDLE EAST & CENTRAL ASIA Bahrain, Kuwait & Qatar • Central Asia • Central Asia phrasebook • Dubai • Farsi (Persian) phrasebook • Hebrew phrasebook • Iran • Israel & the Palestinian Territories • Istanbul • Istanbul City Map • Istanbul to Cairo • Istanbul to Kathmandu • Jerusalem • Jerusalem City Map • Jordan • Lebanon • Middle East • Oman & the United Arab Emirates • Syria • Turkey • Turkish phrasebook • World Food Turkey • Yemen **Travel Literature**: Black on Black: Iran Revisited • Breaking Ranks: Turbulent Travels in the Promised Land • The Gates of Damascus • Kingdom of the Film Stars: Journey into Jordan

NORTH AMERICA Alaska • Boston • Boston City Map • Boston Condensed • British Columbia • California & Nevada • California Condensed • Canada • Chicago • Chicago City Map • Chicago Condensed • Florida • Georgia & the Carolinas • Great Lakes • Hawaii • Hiking in Alaska • Hiking in the USA • Honolulu & Oahu City Map • Las Vegas • Los Angeles • Los Angeles City Map • Louisiana & the Deep South • Miami • Miami City Map • Montreal • New England • New Orleans • New Orleans City Map • New York City • New York City City Map • New York City Condensed • New York, New Jersey & Pennsylvania • Oahu • Out to Eat – San Francisco • Pacific Northwest • Rocky Mountains • San Diego & Tijuana • San Francisco • San Francisco City Map • Seattle • Seattle City Map • Southwest • Texas • Toronto • USA • USA phrasebook • Vancouver • Vancouver City Map • Virginia & the Capital Region • Washington, DC • Washington, DC City Map • World Food New Orleans **Travel Literature**: Caught Inside: A Surfer's Year on the California Coast • Drive Thru America

NORTH-EAST ASIA Beijing • Beijing City Map • Cantonese phrasebook • China • Hiking in Japan • Hong Kong & Macau • Hong Kong City Map • Hong Kong Condensed • Japan • Japanese phrasebook • Korea • Korean phrasebook • Kyoto • Mandarin phrasebook • Mongolia • Mongolian phrasebook • Seoul • Shanghai • South-West China • Taiwan • Tokyo • Tokyo Condensed • World Food Hong Kong • World Food Japan **Travel Literature**: In Xanadu: A Quest • Lost Japan

SOUTH AMERICA Argentina, Uruguay & Paraguay • Bolivia • Brazil • Brazilian phrasebook • Buenos Aires • Buenos Aires City Map • Chile & Easter Island • Colombia • Ecuador & the Galapagos Islands • Healthy Travel Central & South America • Latin American Spanish phrasebook • Peru • Quechua phrasebook • Read This First: Central & South America • Rio de Janeiro • Rio de Janeiro City Map • Santiago de Chile • South America on a shoestring • Trekking in the Patagonian Andes • Venezuela **Travel Literature**: Full Circle: A South American Journey

SOUTH-EAST ASIA Bali & Lombok • Bangkok • Bangkok City Map • Burmese phrasebook • Cambodia • Cycling Vietnam, Laos & Cambodia • East Timor phrasebook • Hanoi • Healthy Travel Asia & India • Hill Tribes phrasebook • Ho Chi Minh City (Saigon) • Indonesia • Indonesian phrasebook • Indonesia's Eastern Islands • Java • Lao phrasebook • Laos • Malay phrasebook • Malaysia, Singapore & Brunei • Myanmar (Burma) • Philippines • Pilipino (Tagalog) phrasebook • Read This First: Asia & India • Singapore • Singapore City Map • South-East Asia on a shoestring • South-East Asia phrasebook • Thailand • Thailand's Islands & Beaches • Thailand, Vietnam, Laos & Cambodia Road Atlas • Thai phrasebook • Vietnam • Vietnamese phrasebook • World Food Indonesia • World Food Thailand • World Food Vietnam

ALSO AVAILABLE: Antarctica • The Arctic • The Blue Man: Tales of Travel, Love and Coffee • Brief Encounters: Stories of Love, Sex & Travel • Buddhist Stupas in Asia: The Shape of Perfection • Chasing Rickshaws • The Last Grain Race • Lonely Planet ... On the Edge: Adventurous Escapades from Around the World • Lonely Planet Unpacked • Lonely Planet Unpacked Again • Not the Only Planet: Science Fiction Travel Stories • Ports of Call: A Journey by Sea • Sacred India • Travel Photography: A Guide to Taking Better Pictures • Travel with Children • Tuvalu: Portrait of an Island Nation

LONELY PLANET

You already know that Lonely Planet produces more than this one guidebook, but you might not be aware of the other products we have on this region. Here is a selection of titles that you may want to check out as well:

Boston Map
ISBN 1 86450 175 8
US$5.99 • UK£3.99

Boston Condensed
ISBN 1 86450 326 2
US$11.99 • UK£5.99

Travel Journal
ISBN 1 86450 343 2
US$12.99 • UK£7.99

Drive Thru America
ISBN 0 86442 506 6
US$12.95 • UK£6.99

USA
ISBN 1 74104 192 9
US$27.99 • UK£15.99

Hiking in the USA
ISBN 0 86442 600 3
US$24.99 • UK£14.99

USA Phrasebook
ISBN 1 86450 182 0
US$6.99 • UK£4.50

**New York New Jersey
& Pennsylvania**
ISBN 1 86450 138 3
US$21.99 • UK£13.99

New England
ISBN 1 74059 025 2
US$19.99 • UK£12.99

New York City
ISBN 1 74059 305 7
US$16.99 • UK£10.99

Available wherever books are sold

Index

Text

Bold indicates maps.

Bold indicates maps.

Places to Stay

Places to Eat

Boxed Text

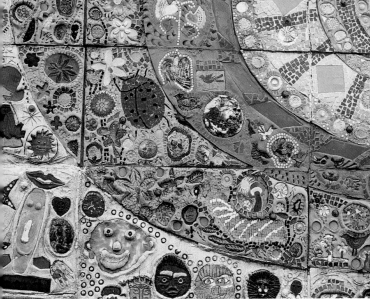

KIM GRANT

Boston Map Section

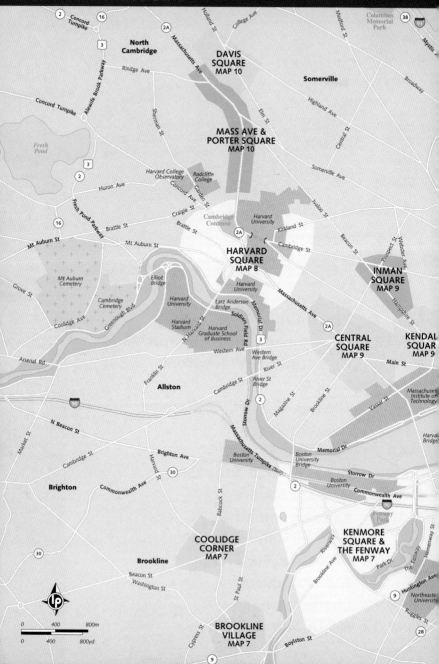

MAP 1 GREATER BOSTON

2
Concord Turnpike
16
3

North Cambridge

2A
Massachusetts Ave

Holland St
College Ave

Medford St

Columbus Memorial Park

38

Mystic

DAVIS SQUARE
MAP 10

Somerville

Broadway

Rindge Ave

Sherman St

Elm St

Highland Ave

Central St

Somerville Ave

Concord Turnpike

Alewife Brook Parkway

Fresh Pond

MASS AVE & PORTER SQUARE
MAP 10

3
2

Harvard College Observatory

Radcliffe College

Concord Ave

Garden St

Ivaloo St

Huron Ave

16

Fresh Pond Parkway

Brattle St

Craigie St

Brattle St

Cambridge Common

Harvard University

Kirkland St

Beacon St

2A

Cambridge St

Prospect St
Webster Ave

Mt Auburn St

Mt Auburn St

HARVARD SQUARE
MAP 8

Elliot Bridge

Harvard University

INMAN SQUARE
MAP 9

Grove St

Mt Auburn Cemetery

Cambridge Cemetery

Greenough Blvd

Harvard University

Harvard Stadium

Larz Anderson Bridge

Harvard University

Soldiers Field Rd

N Harvard St

Memorial Dr

Massachusetts Ave

Hampshire St

Coolidge Ave

Harvard Graduate School of Business

2A

CENTRAL SQUARE
MAP 9

KENDAL SQUAR
MAP 9

Arsenal Rd

Western Ave

Western Ave Bridge

River St

Main St

Franklin St

Cambridge St

River St Bridge

Magazine St

Brookline St

Vassar St

Massachusetts Institute of Technology

Allston

90

Storrow Dr

2

Harva Bridge

N Beacon St

Market St

Cambridge St

Brighton Ave

Harvard St

30

Massachusetts Turnpike

Boston University

Boston University Bridge

Memorial Dr

Storrow Dr

Boston University

Commonwealth Ave

Harva

Brighton

Commonwealth Ave

2

Fenway Park

COOLIDGE CORNER
MAP 7

Babcock St

KENMORE SQUARE & THE FENWAY
MAP 7

Riverway

Park Dr

The Fenway

Hemenway St

30

Brookline

Beacon St

Washington St

St Paul St

Brookline Ave

9

Huntington Ave

Northeaste University

9

Ruggles St

28

LP

0   400   800m
0   400   800yd

Cypress St

BROOKLINE VILLAGE
MAP 7

Boylston St

9

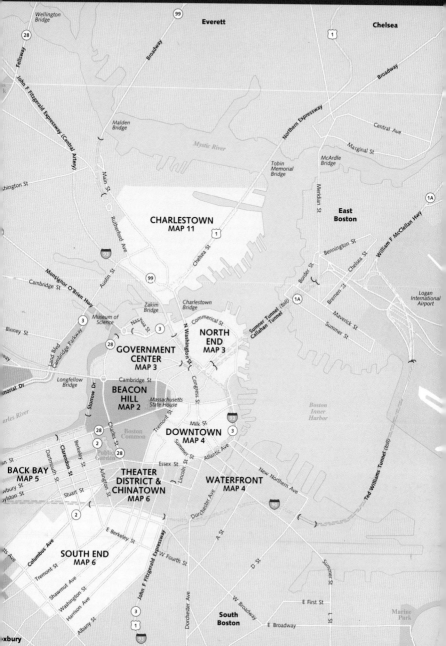

Wellington Bridge

Everett

Chelsea

28

Falsway

Broadway

John F Fitzgerald Expressway (Central Artery)

99

1

Broadway

Washington St

Malden Bridge

Mystic River

Northern Expressway

Central Ave

Marginal St

McArdle Bridge

Tobin Memorial Bridge

Meridian St

East Boston

1A

Main St

CHARLESTOWN
MAP 11

1

William F McClellan Hwy

Bennington St

Logan International Airport

Rutherford Ave

Chelsea St

Monsignor O'Brien Hwy

Cambridge St

Austin St

99

Zakim Bridge

Charlestown Bridge

Commercial St

Border St

Chelsea St

Bremen St

1A

Maverick St

Sumner St

Museum of Science

3

Nashua St

N Washington St

NORTH END
MAP 3

Sumner Tunnel (toll)
Callahan Tunnel

Binney St

Land Blvd
Cambridge Parkway

3

28

GOVERNMENT CENTER
MAP 3

Congress St

Charlestown Ave

Cambridge St

Boston Inner Harbor

Memorial Dr

Longfellow Bridge

Storrow Dr

BEACON HILL
MAP 2

Massachusetts State House

Ted Williams Tunnel (toll)

arles River

Tremont St

Milk St

3

28

2

Charles St

Boston Common

DOWNTOWN
MAP 4

Sumner St

Atlantic Ave

Back Bay St

Dartmouth St

Berkeley St

Clarendon St

Arlington St

28

Public Garden

Essex St

Lincoln St

Dorchester Ave

New Northern Ave

BACK BAY
MAP 5

Stuart St

THEATER DISTRICT & CHINATOWN
MAP 6

WATERFRONT
MAP 4

wbury St
Boylston St

2

Columbus Ave

E Berkeley St

John F Fitzgerald Expressway

W Fourth St

A St

D St

Sumner St

SOUTH END
MAP 6

Tremont St

Shawmut Ave

Washington St

Harrison Ave

Albany St

3

Dorchester Ave

W Broadway

South Boston

E First St

L St

Marine Park

1

W Broadway

E Broadway

xbury

MAP 2 BEACON HILL

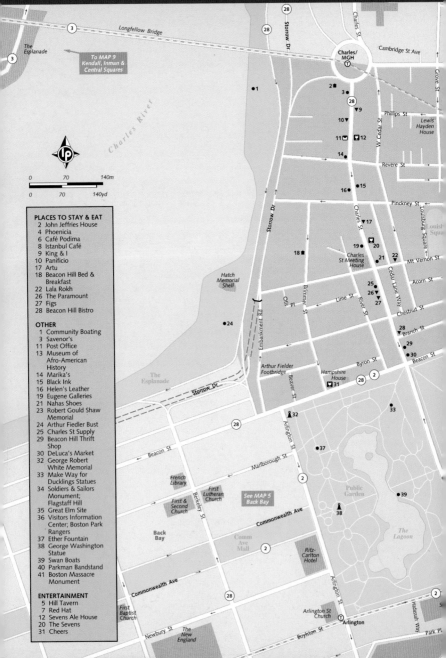

PLACES TO STAY & EAT
2 John Jeffries House
4 Phoenicia
6 Café Podima
8 Istanbul Café
9 King & I
10 Panificio
17 Artu
18 Beacon Hill Bed &
  Breakfast
22 Lala Rokh
26 The Paramount
27 Figs
28 Beacon Hill Bistro

OTHER
1 Community Boating
3 Savenor's
11 Post Office
13 Museum of
  Afro-American
  History
14 Marika's
15 Black Ink
16 Helen's Leather
19 Eugene Galleries
21 Nahas Shoes
23 Robert Gould Shaw
  Memorial
24 Arthur Fiedler Bust
25 Charles St Supply
29 Beacon Hill Thrift
  Shop
30 DeLuca's Market
32 George Robert
  White Memorial
33 Make Way for
  Ducklings Statues
34 Soldiers & Sailors
  Monument;
  Flagstaff Hill
35 Great Elm Site
36 Visitors Information
  Center; Boston Park
  Rangers
37 Ether Fountain
38 George Washington
  Statue
39 Swan Boats
40 Parkman Bandstand
41 Boston Massacre
  Monument

ENTERTAINMENT
5 Hill Tavern
7 Red Hat
12 Sevens Ale House
20 The Sevens
31 Cheers

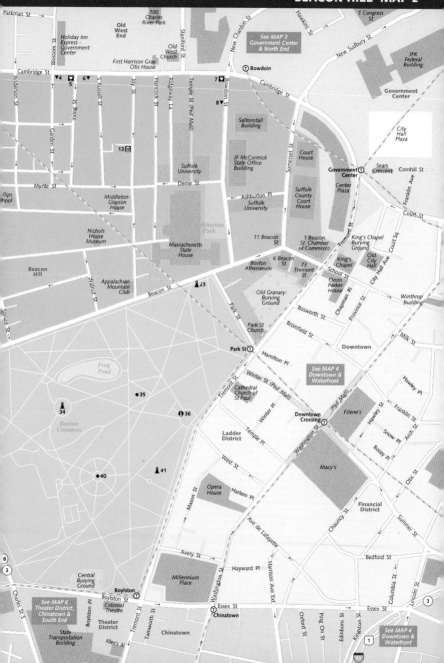

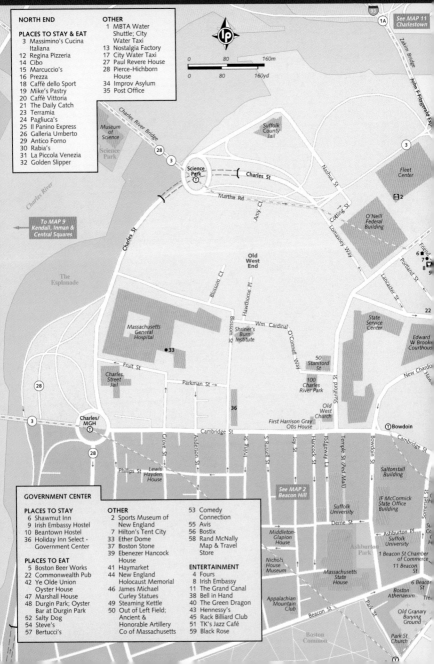

MAP 3 GOVERNMENT CENTER & NORTH END

See MAP 11
Charlestown

NORTH END

PLACES TO STAY & EAT
3 Massimino's Cucina Italiana
12 Regina Pizzeria
14 Cibo
15 Marcuccio's
16 Prezza
18 Caffè dello Sport
19 Mike's Pastry
20 Caffè Vittoria
21 The Daily Catch
23 Terramia
24 Pagliuca's
25 Il Panino Express
26 Galleria Umberto
29 Antico Forno
30 Rabia's
31 La Piccola Venezia
32 Golden Slipper

OTHER
1 MBTA Water Shuttle; City Water Taxi
13 Nostalgia Factory
17 City Water Taxi
27 Paul Revere House
28 Pierce-Hichborn House
34 Improv Asylum
35 Post Office

Museum of Science

Science Park

Charles River Bridge

28

3

Science Park

Charles St

Martha Rd

Amy Ct

Nashua St

Suffolk County Jail

3

Fleet Center

2

Cotting St

O'Neill Federal Building

Lomasney Way

Charles St

To MAP 9
Kendall, Inman &
Central Squares

Charles River

The Esplanade

Old West End

Blossom Ct

Hawthorne Pl

Blossom St

Wm Cardinal O'Connell Way

Shriner's Burn Institute

Portland St

6
7
8
9

22

Lancaster St

State Service Center

Edward W Brooke Courthouse

Massachusetts General Hospital

33

Fruit St

Charles Street Jail

Parkman St

50 Stamford St

100 Charles River Park

Staniford St

New Chardon

28

3

Charles/ MGH

28

First Harrison Gray Otis House

Old West Church

Bowdoin

Cambridge St

Cambridge St

Grove St

Anderson St

Phillips St

Lewis Hayden House

Blossom St

S Russell St

Irving St

Joy St

Hancock St

Ridgeway La

Temple St (Ped Mall)

Bowdoin St

Saltonstall Building

JF McCormick State Office Building

See MAP 2
Beacon Hill

Suffolk University

Derne St

Ashburton Pl

Suffolk University

1 Beacon St Chamber of Commerce
11 Beacon

Middleton-Glapion House

Nichols House Museum

Ashburton Park

Massachusetts State House

6 Beacon
Boston Athenaeum

GOVERNMENT CENTER

PLACES TO STAY
6 Shawmut Inn
9 Irish Embassy Hostel
10 Beantown Hostel
36 Holiday Inn Select - Government Center

PLACES TO EAT
5 Boston Beer Works
22 Commonwealth Pub
42 Ye Olde Union Oyster House
47 Marshall House
48 Durgin Park; Oyster Bar at Durgin Park
52 Salty Dog
54 Steve's
57 Bertucci's

OTHER
2 Sports Museum of New England
7 Hilton's Tent City
33 Ether Dome
37 Boston Stone
39 Ebenezer Hancock House
41 Haymarket
44 New England Holocaust Memorial
46 James Michael Curley Statues
49 Steaming Kettle
50 Out of Left Field; Ancient & Honorable Artillery Co of Massachusetts

53 Comedy Connection
55 Avis
56 Bostix
58 Rand McNally Map & Travel Store

ENTERTAINMENT
4 Fours
8 Irish Embassy
11 The Grand Canal
38 Bell in Hand
40 The Green Dragon
43 Hennessy's
45 Rack Billiard Club
51 TK's Jazz Café
59 Black Rose

Appalachian Mountain Club

Beacon St

Old Granary Burying Ground

Park St
Church

Boston Common

Park St

0   80   160m
0   80   160yd

1A

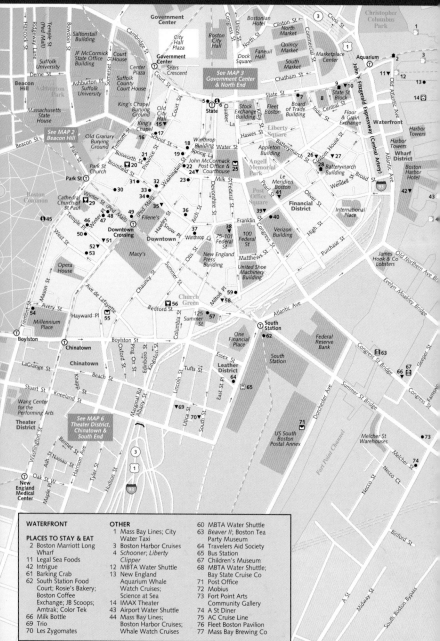

MAP 4 DOWNTOWN & WATERFRONT

WATERFRONT

PLACES TO STAY & EAT
2 Boston Marriott Long
   Wharf
11 Legal Sea Foods
42 Intrigue
61 Barking Crab
62 South Station Food
   Court; Rosie's Bakery;
   Boston Coffee
   Exchange; JB Scoops;
   Amtrak; Color Tek
66 Milk Bottle
69 Trio
70 Les Zygomates

OTHER
1 Mass Bay Lines; City
   Water Taxi
3 Boston Harbor Cruises
4 Schooner; Liberty
   Clipper
12 MBTA Water Shuttle
13 New England
   Aquarium Whale
   Watch Cruises;
   Science at Sea
14 IMAX Theater
43 Airport Water Shuttle
44 Mass Bay Lines;
   Boston Harbor Cruises;
   Whale Watch Cruises

60 MBTA Water Shuttle
63 Beaver II; Boston Tea
   Party Museum
64 Travelers Aid Society
65 Bus Station
67 Children's Museum
68 MBTA Water Shuttle;
   Bay State Cruise Co
71 Post Office
72 Mobius
73 Fort Point Arts
   Community Gallery
74 A St Diner
75 AC Cruise Line
76 Fleet Boston Pavilion
77 Mass Bay Brewing Co

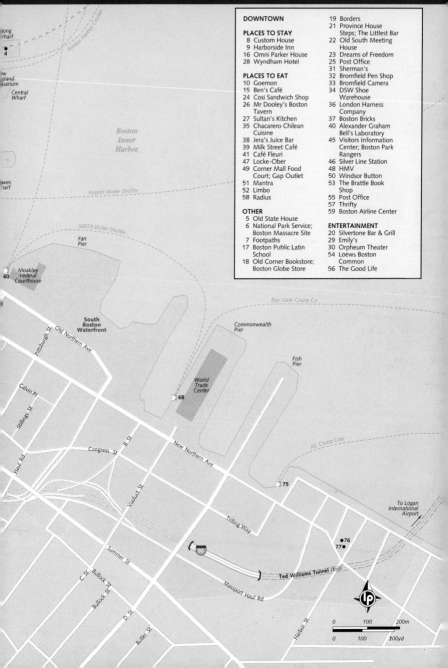

DOWNTOWN

PLACES TO STAY
8 Custom House
9 Harborside Inn
16 Omni Parker House
28 Wyndham Hotel

PLACES TO EAT
10 Goemon
15 Ben's Café
24 Cosi Sandwich Shop
26 Mr Dooley's Boston Tavern
27 Sultan's Kitchen
35 Chacarero Chilean Cuisine
38 Jera's Juice Bar
39 Milk Street Café
41 Café Fleuri
47 Locke-Ober
49 Corner Mall Food Court; Gap Outlet
51 Mantra
52 Limbo
58 Radius

OTHER
5 Old State House
6 National Park Service; Boston Massacre Site
7 Footpaths
17 Boston Public Latin School
18 Old Corner Bookstore; Boston Globe Store

19 Borders
21 Province House Steps; The Littlest Bar
22 Old South Meeting House
23 Dreams of Freedom
25 Post Office
31 Sherman's
32 Bromfield Pen Shop
33 Bromfield Camera
34 DSW Shoe Warehouse
36 London Harness Company
37 Boston Bricks
40 Alexander Graham Bell's Laboratory
45 Visitors Information Center; Boston Park Rangers
46 Silver Line Station
48 HMV
50 Windsor Button
53 The Brattle Book Shop
55 Post Office
57 Thrifty
59 Boston Airline Center

ENTERTAINMENT
20 Silverstone Bar & Grill
29 Emily's
30 Orpheum Theater
54 Loews Boston Common
56 The Good Life

MAP 5 BACK BAY

Charles
River

The
Esplanade

Storrow Dr
Storrow Dr

Beacon St

Marlborough St

Fairfield St

Commonwealth Ave

Commonwealth Ave

Back
Bay

Newbury St

Boylston St

Storrow Dr

Back St

Boston
University

Kenmore
Square

Charlesgate Overpass

Charlesgate East

Beacon St

Marlborough St

Hereford St

Gloucester St

Massachusetts Ave

Newbury St

Newbury St
Stables

Boston
Architectural
Center

Institute for
Contemporary
Art

360
Newbury St

Hynes/ICA

Ipswich St

Boylston St

Berklee
Performance
Center

Cambria St

Berklee
College
of Music

Dalton St

Hynes
Convention
Center

Prudential
Center &
Skywalk

Sheraton
Boston
Hotel

Scotia
St Cecilia
Church

Back
Bay
Hilton

Belvidere St

Prudential

See MAP 7
Kenmore Square,
The Fenway &
Brookline

Berklee
College
of Music

Hemenway St

Norway St

Edgerly Rd

St Germain St

Clearway St

Burbank St

Westland Ave

Massachusetts Ave

Christian
Science
Church

Christian
Science
Church

Reflecting
Pool

Midtown
Hotel

Huntington Ave

Cumberland St

Durham St

Southwest
Corridor
Park

Symphony Rd

Horticultural
Hall

Symphony
Hall

Gainsborough St

Symphony

St Botolph St

Blackwood St

PLACES TO STAY

2 463 Beacon St Guest
   House
4 Commonwealth
   Court Guest House
6 College Club
28 Newbury Guest House
54 Lenox Hotel
55 Copley Square Hotel

PLACES TO EAT

1 Kebab-N-Kurry
5 Geoffrey's Café & Bar
10 JP Licks
12 Trident Booksellers &
   Café
15 Sonsie
20 Emack & Bolio's
21 Casa Romero
23 Kashmir
27 Tapeo
34 Herrell's
41 Pho Pasteur
44 Torrefazione Italia
   Cafe
52 Café Jaffa
53 Legal Sea Foods;
   Enterprise
63 Parish Café & Bar
65 Terrace Food Court
66 Marche Movenpick

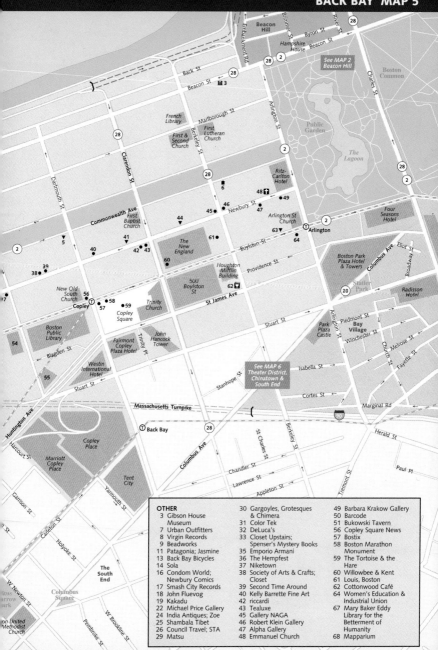

OTHER

3 Gibson House Museum
7 Urban Outfitters
9 Beadworks
11 Patagonia; Jasmine
13 Back Bay Bicycles
14 Sola
16 Condom World; Newbury Comics
17 Smash City Records
18 John Fluevog
19 Kakadu
22 Michael Price Gallery
24 India Antiques; Zoe
25 Shambala Tibet
26 Council Travel; STA
29 Matsu

30 Gargoyles, Grotesques & Chimera
31 Color Tek
32 DeLuca's
33 Closet Upstairs; Spenser's Mystery Books
35 Emporio Armani
36 The Hempfest
37 Niketown
38 Society of Arts & Crafts; Closet
39 Second Time Around
40 Kelly Barrette Fine Art
42 riccardi
43 Tealuxe
45 Gallery NAGA
46 Robert Klein Gallery
47 Alpha Gallery
48 Emmanuel Church

49 Barbara Krakow Gallery
50 Barcode
51 Bukowski Tavern
56 Copley Square News
57 Bostix
58 Boston Marathon Monument
59 The Tortoise & the Hare
60 Willowbee & Kent
61 Louis, Boston
62 Cottonwood Café
64 Women's Education & Industrial Union
67 Mary Baker Eddy Library for the Betterment of Humanity
68 Mapparium

MAP 6 THEATER DISTRICT, CHINATOWN & SOUTH END

THEATER DISTRICT & CHINATOWN

PLACES TO STAY
24 Radisson Hotel
30 Milner Hotel
31 Tremont House;
   Matrix; Roxy

PLACES TO EAT
1 The Bristol
7 Wai Wai
9 Finale Desserterie
10 Legal Sea Foods
11 City Place Food
   Court
12 Rock Bottom
13 Jacob Wirth's
14 Penang
15 Buddha's Delight
16 Pho Pasteur
17 Hu Tieu Nam Vang
18 Mix Bakery
19 Grand Chau Chow
21 Apollo Grill
22 Shabu-Zen
23 Ginza

OTHER
2 Ghosts &
   Gravestones
6 Jack's Joke Shop
8 Hertz; Budget
20 Chinatown Gate
26 Hub Ticket Agency
28 Boston Costume
32 Beacon Hill Skate

ENTERTAINMENT
3 Pravda 116
4 Big Easy
5 Envy
25 Nick's Comedy Stop;
   Venu; Chaps/Vapor
27 Aria
29 Jacques

See MAP 5
Back Bay

See MAP 7
Kenmore Square,
The Fenway
& Brookline

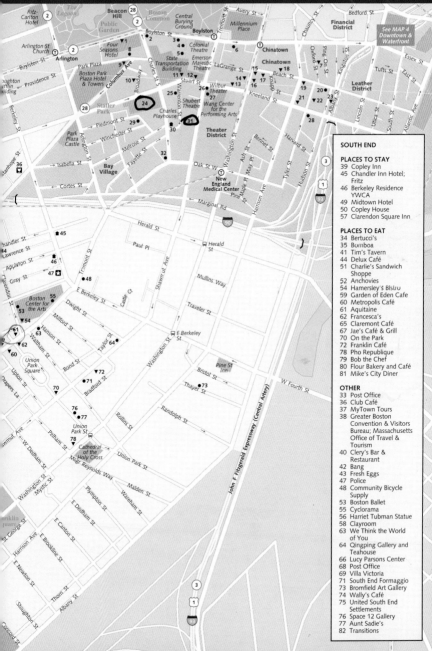

SOUTH END

PLACES TO STAY
39 Copley Inn
45 Chandler Inn Hotel; Fritz
46 Berkeley Residence YWCA
49 Midtown Hotel
50 Copley House
57 Clarendon Square Inn

PLACES TO EAT
34 Bertucci's
35 Bomboa
41 Tim's Tavern
44 Delux Café
51 Charlie's Sandwich Shoppe
52 Anchovies
54 Hamersley's Bistro
59 Garden of Eden Cafe
60 Metropolis Café
61 Aquitaine
62 Francesca's
65 Claremont Café
67 Jae's Café & Grill
70 On the Park
72 Franklin Café
78 Pho Republique
79 Bob the Chef
80 Flour Bakery and Café
81 Mike's City Diner

OTHER
33 Post Office
36 Club Café
37 MyTown Tours
38 Greater Boston Convention & Visitors Bureau; Massachusetts Office of Travel & Tourism
40 Clery's Bar & Restaurant
42 Bang
43 Fresh Eggs
47 Police
48 Community Bicycle Supply
53 Boston Ballet
55 Cyclorama
56 Harriet Tubman Statue
58 Clayroom
63 We Think the World of You
64 Qingping Gallery and Teahouse
66 Lucy Parsons Center
68 Post Office
69 Villa Victoria
71 South End Formaggio
73 Bromfield Art Gallery
74 Wally's Café
75 United South End Settlements
76 Space 12 Gallery
77 Aunt Sadie's
82 Transitions

MAP 7 KENMORE SQUARE, THE FENWAY & BROOKLINE

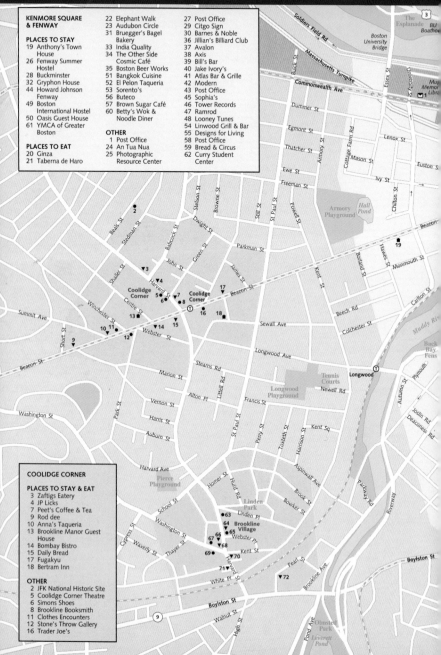

KENMORE SQUARE & FENWAY

PLACES TO STAY
- 19 Anthony's Town House
- 26 Fenway Summer Hostel
- 28 Buckminster
- 32 Gryphon House
- 44 Howard Johnson Fenway
- 49 Boston International Hostel
- 50 Oasis Guest House
- 61 YMCA of Greater Boston

PLACES TO EAT
- 20 Ginza
- 21 Taberna de Haro
- 22 Elephant Walk
- 23 Audubon Circle
- 31 Bruegger's Bagel Bakery
- 33 India Quality
- 34 The Other Side Cosmic Café
- 35 Boston Beer Works
- 51 Bangkok Cuisine
- 52 El Pelon Taqueria
- 53 Sorento's
- 56 Buteco
- 57 Brown Sugar Café
- 60 Betty's Wok & Noodle Diner

OTHER
- 1 Post Office
- 24 An Tua Nua
- 25 Photographic Resource Center
- 27 Post Office
- 29 Citgo Sign
- 30 Barnes & Noble
- 36 Jillian's Billiard Club
- 37 Avalon
- 38 Axis
- 39 Bill's Bar
- 40 Jake Ivory's
- 41 Atlas Bar & Grille
- 42 Modern
- 43 Post Office
- 45 Sophia's
- 46 Tower Records
- 47 Ramrod
- 48 Looney Tunes
- 54 Linwood Grill & Bar
- 55 Designs for Living
- 58 Post Office
- 59 Bread & Circus
- 62 Curry Student Center

COOLIDGE CORNER

PLACES TO STAY & EAT
- 3 Zaftigs Eatery
- 4 JP Licks
- 7 Peet's Coffee & Tea
- 9 Rod dee
- 10 Anna's Taqueria
- 13 Brookline Manor Guest House
- 14 Bombay Bistro
- 15 Daily Bread
- 17 Fugakyu
- 18 Bertram Inn

OTHER
- 2 JFK National Historic Site
- 5 Coolidge Corner Theatre
- 6 Simons Shoes
- 8 Brookline Booksmith
- 11 Clothes Encounters
- 12 Stone's Throw Gallery
- 16 Trader Joe's

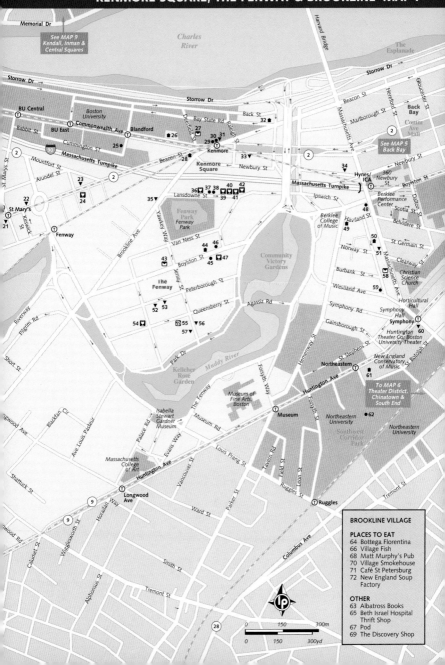

Memorial Dr

Charles
River

See MAP 9
Kendall, Inman &
Central Squares

The
Esplanade

Storrow Dr

Storrow Dr

Harvard Bridge

Storrow Dr

Beacon St

Back
Bay

BU Central

Boston
University

Storrow Dr

Bay State Rd

Back St

32

Marlborough St

Comm
Ave
Mall

Babbit St

BU East

Commonwealth Ave

Blandford

Dedford St

27

30 31

See MAP 5
Back Bay

Massachusetts Ave

26

25

Cummington St

29

Kenmore

33

Hereford St
Gloucester St

Mountfort St

Massachusetts Turnpike

Beacon St

28

Kenmore
Square

Newbury St

Hynes/
ICA

360
Newbury
St

Newbury St

Boylston St

34

Arundel St

23

Massachusetts Turnpike

Dalton St

St Mary's St

24

36

37 38

40 42

39 41

Ipswich St

Berklee
Performance
Center

Scotia St

Belvidere St

22

Lansdowne St

35

Berklee
College
of Music

Haviland St

48

St
Mary's

21

Kenwick St

Fenway

Yawkey Way

Fenway
Park
Fenway Park

Van Ness St

49

50

Norway St

51

St Germain St

Brookline Ave

44 46

45

47

Community
Victory
Gardens

Burbank St

Clearway St

58

Christian
Science
Church

43

Boylston St

Jersey St

The
Fenway

Peterborough St

Westland Ave

59

Horticultural
Hall

52 53

Queensberry St

Agassiz Rd

Symphony Rd

Symphony
Hall
SYMPHONY

Gainsborough St

54

55

56

57

Park Dr

Riverway

Pilgrim Rd

Short St

Kelleher
Rose
Garden

Muddy River

The Fenway

Forsyth Way

Hemenway St

St Stephens St

Huntington
Theater Co; Boston
University Theater

60

New England
Conservatory
of Music

Huntington Ave

61

Northeastern

St Botolph St

To MAP 6
Theater District,
Chinatown &
South End

Bladden Cir

Isabella
Stewart
Gardner
Museum

Museum of
Fine Arts,
Boston

Museum Rd

Museum

Forsyth St

Northeastern
University

62

Northeastern
University

ngwood Ave

Ave Louis Pasteur

Palace Rd

Evans Way

Massachusetts
College
of Art

Huntington Ave

Louis Prang St

Vancouver St

Tavern Rd

Field St

Leon St

Southwest
Corridor
Park

Tremont St

Shattuck St

Longwood
Ave

9

Parker St

Ward St

Ruggles St

Ruggles

ngwood Rd

9

Hoadham Dr

Wigglesworth St

Columbus Ave

Calumet St

Alphonsus St

Smith St

Tremont St

N

0   150   300m

0   150   300yd

28

MAP 8 HARVARD SQUARE

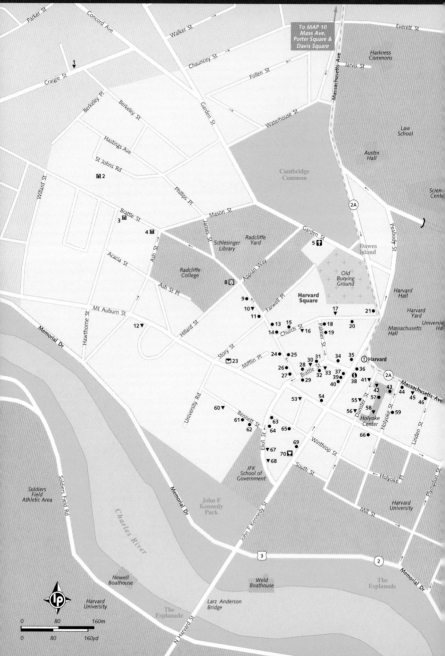

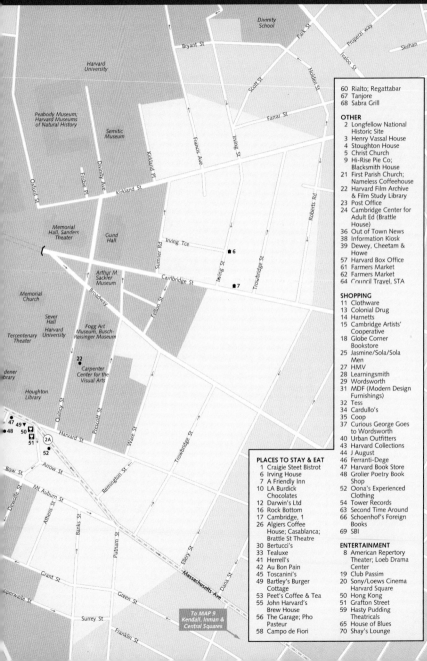

60 Rialto; Regattabar
67 Tanjore
68 Sabra Grill

OTHER
2 Longfellow National
   Historic Site
3 Henry Vassal House
4 Stoughton House
5 Christ Church
9 Hi-Rise Pie Co;
   Blacksmith House
21 First Parish Church;
   Nameless Coffeehouse
22 Harvard Film Archive
   & Film Study Library
23 Post Office
24 Cambridge Center for
   Adult Ed (Brattle
   House)
36 Out of Town News
38 Information Kiosk
39 Dewey, Cheetam &
   Howe
57 Harvard Box Office
61 Farmers Market
62 Farmers Market
64 Council Travel, STA

SHOPPING
11 Clothware
13 Colonial Drug
14 Harnetts
15 Cambridge Artists'
   Cooperative
18 Globe Corner
   Bookstore
25 Jasmine/Sola/Sola
   Men
27 HMV
28 Learningsmith
29 Wordsworth
31 MDF (Modern Design
   Furnishings)
32 Tess
34 Cardullo's
35 Coop
37 Curious George Goes
   to Wordsworth
40 Urban Outfitters
43 Harvard Collections
44 J August
46 Ferranti-Dege
47 Harvard Book Store
48 Grolier Poetry Book
   Shop
52 Oona's Experienced
   Clothing
54 Tower Records
63 Second Time Around
66 Schoenhof's Foreign
   Books
69 SBI

PLACES TO STAY & EAT
1 Craigie Steet Bistrot
6 Irving House
7 A Friendly Inn
10 LA Burdick
   Chocolates
12 Darwin's Ltd
16 Rock Bottom
17 Cambridge, 1
26 Algiers Coffee
   House; Casablanca;
   Brattle St Theatre
30 Bertucci's
33 Tealuxe
41 Herrell's
42 Au Bon Pain
45 Toscanini's
49 Bartley's Burger
   Cottage
53 Peet's Coffee & Tea
55 John Harvard's
   Brew House
56 The Garage; Pho
   Pasteur
58 Campo de Fiori

ENTERTAINMENT
8 American Repertory
   Theater; Loeb Drama
   Center
19 Club Passim
20 Sony/Loews Cinema
   Harvard Square
50 Hong Kong
51 Grafton Street
59 Hasty Pudding
   Theatricals
65 House of Blues
70 Shay's Lounge

To MAP 9
Kendall, Inman &
Central Squares

MAP 9 KENDALL, INMAN & CENTRAL SQUARES

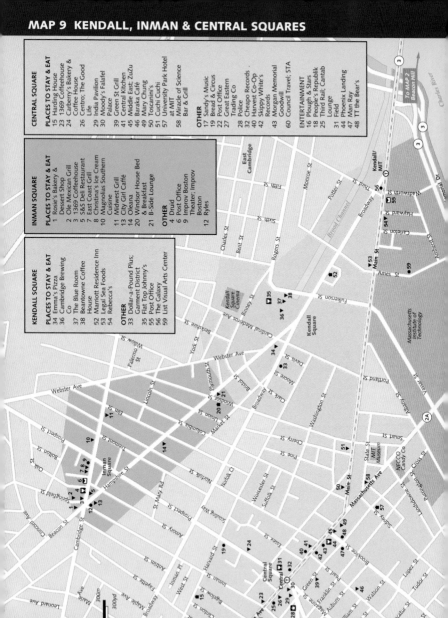

CENTRAL SQUARE

PLACES TO STAY & EAT
15 Harding House
23 1369 Coffeehouse
24 Carberry's Bakery & Coffee House
26 Centro; The Good Life
29 India Pavilion
30 Moody's Falafel Palace
39 Green St Grill
41 Central Kitchen
45 Middle East; ZuZu
46 Baraka Café
49 Mary Chung
50 Toscanini's
51 Cuchi Cuchi
57 University Park Hotel at MIT
58 Miracle of Science Bar & Grill

OTHER
17 Sandy's Music
19 Bread & Circus
22 Post Office
27 Great Eastern Trading Co
28 Police
32 Cheapo Records
40 Harvest Co-Op
42 Skippy White's Records
43 Morgan Memorial Goodwill
60 Council Travel; STA

ENTERTAINMENT
16 Plough & Stars
18 People's Republik
25 Third Rail; Cantab Lounge
31 Field
44 Phoenix Landing
47 Man Ray
48 TT the Bear's

INMAN SQUARE

PLACES TO STAY & EAT
1 Rosie's Bakery & Dessert Shop
2 Emma's Pizza
3 Ole Mexican Grill
5 1369 Coffeehouse
6 S&S Deli Restaurant
7 East Coast Grill
8 Christina's Ice Cream
10 Magnolias Southern Cuisine
11 Midwest Grill
13 City Girl Caffé
14 Oleana
20 Windsor House Bed & Breakfast
21 B-Side Lounge

OTHER
4 Druid
6 Post Office
9 Improv Boston Theater; Improv Boston
12 Ryles

KENDALL SQUARE

PLACES TO STAY & EAT
34 Emma's Pizza
36 Cambridge Brewing Co
37 The Blue Room
38 Beantowne Coffee House
52 Marriott Residence Inn
53 Legal Sea Foods
54 Rebecca's

OTHER
33 Dollar-a-Pound Plus; Garment District
35 Flat Top Johnny's
55 Post Office
56 The Galaxy
59 List Visual Arts Center

MAP 10 MASS AVE, PORTER SQUARE & DAVIS SQUARE

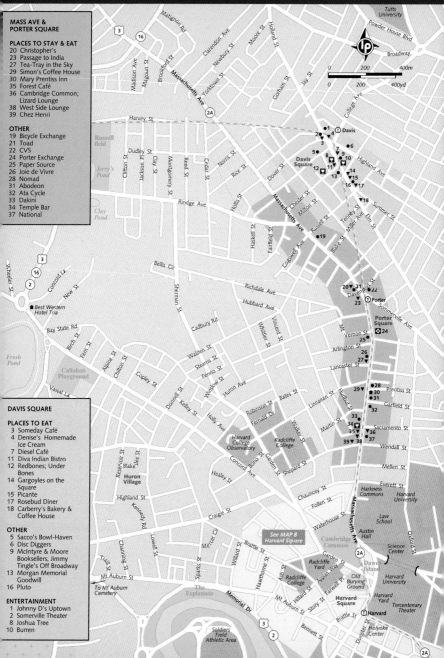

MASS AVE & PORTER SQUARE

PLACES TO STAY & EAT
20 Christopher's
23 Passage to India
27 Tea-Tray in the Sky
29 Simon's Coffee House
30 Mary Prentiss Inn
35 Forest Café
36 Cambridge Common;
   Lizard Lounge
38 West Side Lounge
39 Chez Henri

OTHER
19 Bicycle Exchange
21 Toad
22 CVS
24 Porter Exchange
25 Paper Source
26 Joie de Vivre
28 Nomad
31 Abodeon
32 Ata Cycle
33 Dakini
34 Temple Bar
37 National

DAVIS SQUARE

PLACES TO EAT
3 Someday Café
4 Denise's Homemade
   Ice Cream
7 Diesel Café
11 Diva Indian Bistro
12 Redbones; Under
   Bones
14 Gargoyles on the
   Square
15 Picante
17 Rosebud Diner
18 Carberry's Bakery &
   Coffee House

OTHER
5 Sacco's Bowl-Haven
6 Disc Diggers
9 McIntyre & Moore
   Booksellers; Jimmy
   Tingle's Off Broadway
13 Morgan Memorial
   Goodwill
16 Pluto

ENTERTAINMENT
1 Johnny D's Uptown
2 Somerville Theater
8 Joshua Tree
10 Burren

See MAP 8
Harvard Square

MAP 11 CHARLESTOWN

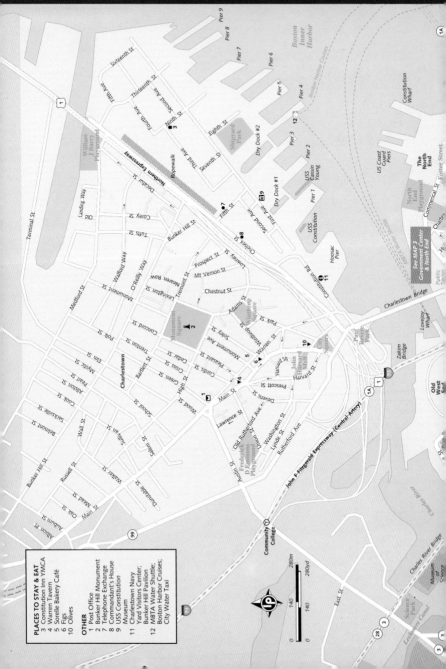

PLACES TO STAY & EAT
3 Constitution Inn YMCA
4 Warren Tavern
5 Sorelle Bakery Café
6 Figs
10 Olives

OTHER
1 Post Office
2 Bunker Hill Monument
7 Telephone Exchange
8 Commandant's House
9 USS *Constitution*
11 Charlestown Navy
   Yard Visitors Center;
   Bunker Hill Pavilion
12 MBTA Water Shuttle;
   Boston Harbor Cruises;
   City Water Taxi

MAP 12 MBTA SUBWAY MAP

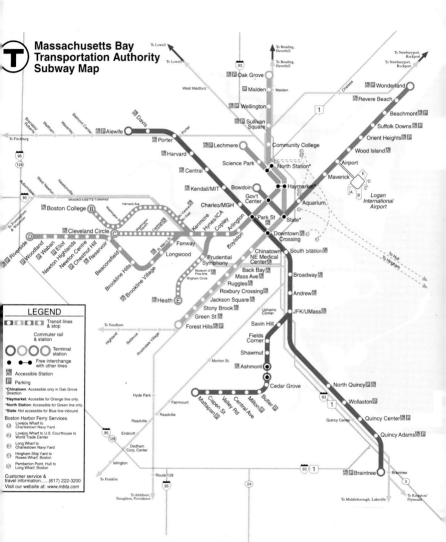

Massachusetts Bay Transportation Authority Subday Map

LEGEND

- Transit lines & stop
- Commuter rail & station
- Terminal station
- Free interchange with other lines
- Accessible Station
- Parking

*Chinatown: Accessible only in Oak Grove Direction
*Haymarket: Accessible for Orange line only.
*North Station: Accessible for Green line only.
*State: Not accessible for Blue line inbound.

Boston Harbor Ferry Services
① Lovejoy Wharf to Charlestown Navy Yard
② Lovejoy Wharf to U.S. Courthouse to World Trade Center
③ Long Wharf to Charlestown Navy Yard
④ Hingham Ship Yard to Rowes Wharf, Boston
⑤ Pemberton Point, Hull to Long Wharf, Boston

Customer service & travel information......(617) 222-3200
Visit our website at: www.mbta.com

MAP LEGEND

CITY ROUTES

Freeway	Freeway		Unsealed Road
Highway	Primary Road		One Way Street
Road	Secondary Road		Pedestrian Street
Street	Street		Stepped Street
Lane	Lane		Tunnel
	On/Off Ramp		Footbridge

HYDROGRAPHY

River, Creek	Lake
Canal	Waterfalls

REGIONAL ROUTES

Tollway, Freeway	
Primary Road	
Secondary Road	
Minor Road	

TRANSPORT ROUTES & STATIONS

Train	
Metro - T Station	
Tramway	
Cable Car, Chairlift	

BOUNDARIES

International	
State	
Disputed	
Fortified Wall	

Walking Trail	
Walking Tour	
Path	
Pier or Jetty	

AREA FEATURES

Building		Market		Beach	Campus
Park, Gardens		Sports Ground		Cemetery	Plaza

ROUTE SHEILDS

Interstate Freeway	US Highway	State Highway

POPULATION SYMBOLS

○ CAPITAL National Capital	● CITY City	● Village Village
◉ CAPITAL State Capital	● Town Town	Urban Area

MAP SYMBOLS

Place to Stay	▼ Place to Eat, Café	● Point of Interest
✕ Airport	Ferry	Shopping Centre
Bank	Hospital	Stately Home
Bar, Club	Information	Swimming Pool
Bus Station	Internet Café	Telephone
Cathedral	Monument	Theatre
Church, Monastery	Museum, Gallery	Tram Stop
Cinema	Parking Area	Transport
Embassy	Post Office	Zoo

Note: not all symbols displayed above appear in this book

LONELY PLANET OFFICES

Australia
Locked Bag 1, Footscray, Victoria 3011
☎ 03 8379 8000 fax 03 8379 8111
email: talk2us@lonelyplanet.com.au

USA
150 Linden St, Oakland, CA 94607
☎ 510 893 8555 TOLL FREE: 800 275 8555
fax 510 893 8572
email: info@lonelyplanet.com

UK
10a Spring Place, London NW5 3BH
☎ 020 7428 4800 fax 020 7428 4828
email: go@lonelyplanet.co.uk

France
1 rue du Dahomey, 75011 Paris
☎ 01 55 25 33 00 fax 01 55 25 33 01
email: bip@lonelyplanet.fr
www.lonelyplanet.fr

World Wide Web: www.lonelyplanet.com *or* AOL keyword: lp
Lonely Planet Images: www.lonelyplanetimages.com